Warfare in the
Age of Bonaparte

WARFARE IN THE
AGE OF BONAPARTE

Michael Glover

PEN & SWORD MILITARY CLASSICS

First published in Great Britain in 1980 by Cassell Ltd
Published in 2003, in this format, by
PEN & SWORD MILITARY CLASSICS
an imprint of
Pen & Sword Books Limited
47 Church Street
Barnsley
S. Yorkshire
S70 2AS

ISBN 0 85052 993 X

A CIP record for this book is
available from the British Library

Printed in England by
CPI UK

FRONTISPIECE: The battle of
Borodino, 1812

OPPOSITE FOREWORD: The
capture and destruction of
four Spanish frigates, 1804

The Conditions of War on Land

THE EIGHTEENTH CENTURY is often referred to as a period of 'limited wars'. This suggests that the slow pace of the armies, the infrequency of battles, and the extreme rarity of clear-cut decisions were the deliberate choice of the governments and commanders concerned. While eighteenth-century generals were more careful of lives than their successors have been, the apparent limits placed on warfare were fundamentally the result of the extreme difficulties experienced in trying to conduct anything but restricted campaigns. It was only possible to fight a battle if the generals on both sides wished to do so, or if one of them made a serious miscalculation.

Moving an army was an extremely cumbersome business. 24 kilometres a day was a good average march for any army and that of Frederick the Great, widely considered to be the finest in Europe, believed 20 kilometres a day to be a sensible day's journey. Metalled roads were few, and away from them it was difficult for even field artillery to keep up with this steady pace by the infantry.

Even at 20 or 24 kilometres a day the supply problem was almost insoluble. Every soldier was entitled to a ration of 600–1,000 grams of bread a day. In the Austrian army, probably the best fed in the days of Maria Theresa, the ration was one 1 kilogram loaf (weighing 800 grams when baked) and each soldier carried four days' supply in his haversack while a similar supply was carried in the regimental transport. Thus a corps of 40,000 men would require eighty-four four-horse waggons (each carrying $1\frac{1}{2}$ tonnes) for the immediate reserve of bread and at least as many again to keep the regimental reserves supplied from the depots. The ration of wine, spirits, or beer called for more transport, and complicated problems with the supply of casks, but the meat supply posed no transport demands as it moved on its own hooves. Live beef or mutton is not, however, susceptible to military discipline (nor were its civilian drovers) and since it lived by grazing at the roadside, it was difficult to keep the supply moving at even 20 kilometres a day and it inevitably caused traffic blockages. The inadequacies of its diet reduced its weight (to say nothing of its taste) and thus more beasts were required to supply the ration.

Any army depended on horses for the transport of its supplies, for

communications, for reconnaissance, for the movement of its artillery, and for some fighting functions. Horses required a much greater bulk of rations than men. In the British army each horse was entitled to 9 kilograms of forage daily so that a strong squadron of cavalry, 112 horses, needed a tonne of forage daily. A six-gun battery of field artillery had six horses to each gun with its limber, eighteen four-horse ammunition waggons, four two-horse waggons, and eighteen riding horses for officers and NCOs, a total of 134 horses with a forage demand of $1\frac{1}{4}$ tonnes daily. The requirement for a troop of horse artillery, where all the gun-numbers rode, was almost 2 tonnes daily. Nor should it be forgotten that the horses drawing the supply waggons also had to be fed, so that one $1\frac{1}{2}$ tonnes supply waggon in every forty-two was required each day to feed the horses for the other waggons.

This lumbering supply train had no cross-country capability and, particularly in the Low Countries and north Italy, the roads on which it had to travel were blocked at intervals by substantial fortresses which would have to be overcome by the time-consuming but essential rituals of siegecraft.

Even before the first shot was fired the army was shrinking steadily. Battle casualties represented only a small proportion of any army's losses. The Hapsburg Empire in the Seven Years' War lost 32,622 men in battle and 93,404 in hospital. In less than six years' campaigning in the Peninsula (1808–14) the British army had 8,889 men killed or mortally wounded in battle while 24,930 men died from disease. Soldiers lost from any cause were hard and expensive to replace since all were, in theory, volunteers and, so uncomfortable was the soldier's life that only the most desperate could be induced to enlist. The Prussian army was the only western army which, before 1792, had some measure of conscription. But even there a high proportion of the private soldiers were foreigners who had been bribed (or occasionally shanghai'd) into the ranks. Between 1763 and 1786, one officer in three of those who reached the rank of general was foreign born. Until 1773 all orders in the Danish army were given in German since that was the language most widely understood and in pre-revolutionary France one third of the infantry, forty-six battalions, was composed of foreigners – Flemish, German, Swiss, Scots, or Irish. All soldiers, home-bred 'volunteers' or foreign mercenaries, represented a substantial investment in their recruitment and training. Their lives were not to be risked unnecessarily, if only for economic reasons. It was only conscription which gave generals a licence to waste lives.

When battle was eventually joined it was extremely difficult to obtain a clear-cut result. All the weapons employed were grossly inaccurate and it was always hard to bring them to bear. One officer who fought in the Peninsula remarked that both sides 'were so badly armed that I wonder we killed each other at all, but the distances were very short at times'. The musket, the principal weapon of all armies, was a weapon of astonishing inefficiency. It was accurate only to 75 metres and had a rate of fire of two, or possibly three, rounds a minute. In dry weather it had a misfire rate of 2:13 and it was unlikely to fire at all in wet weather.

PREVIOUS PAGE: Action from the battle of Leipzig, 1813

ABOVE: In all armies, supply waggons were hired or requisitioned from the local farmers and were usually overloaded with baggage and the wives of soldiers as is shown in this etching of 1802

The ineffectiveness of the musket greatly impressed Frederick the Great, who believed that:

Battles are won by fire superiority. Infantry firing more rapidly will undoubtedly defeat infantry firing more slowly.

In consequence he forbade his men to aim, insisting that they merely pointed their muskets from the hip and, by constant training, succeeded in achieving a rate of fire of nine rounds in two minutes. Other armies did not take the dogma so far but all adhered to the principle that musketry could only be effective if as much of it as possible could be brought to bear. They thus deployed their men in a long thin line so that as many muskets as possible could be brought to bear on the enemy. The number of ranks in the line was a matter of continuing controversy. One school of thought contended that unless there was a third rank the line would lack strength. The third rank:

serves to fill up the vacancies made in action in the other two; without it the battalions would soon be in single rank.

Their opponents maintained that, since the third rank could not fire

with safety, they were useless. Marshal Gouvion St Cyr went so far as to assert that a quarter of all action casualties were caused by the rear rank firing into the front two. In the seventeen-nineties every drill book in Europe called for three ranks.

While fighting in line permitted the maximum of fire-power to be brought to bear, it imposed its own problems. A brigade of four battalions at full strength would occupy almost 800 metres when deployed three deep. To manoeuvre such a line, even over unobstructed ground, required a very high standard of foot drill, which could only be achieved by long-term professionals. And although Frederick the Great was said to have manoeuvred with a line 10 kilometres long, it was a formation to be avoided as often as possible. All major movements were thus made in columns of march which were deployed into line as close as possible outside the effective range of the enemy's weapons. To do this required daylight and, with the prevailing procedures for deployment, by the time that both sides had gone through this complicated business there was little of the day left in which to fight to a finish, and no chance of surprise.

Many efforts were made during the eighteenth century to break out of this tactical strait-jacket. The Austrians introduced light infantry, mostly Croats, whose task was to harass the line during its measured, stately deployment and advance, to draw its volleys and to attack its flanks and rear. In France a school arose which advocated omitting to deploy and relying on the momentum of fast-moving columns to drive through the enemy's line. As early as 1727 Jean de Folard asserted, 'The only road to victory [lies] in shock and sudden attacks'. He proposed to divide the army into columns linked by a screen of light infantry and these columns would puncture the enemy front and roll it up:

The true force of a corps lies in its weight, or in the depth of its files, in their union, in their compactness, and in that of its ranks at bayonet point. That weight ensures that the flanks are as secure, or almost as secure, as its front . . . In war the weight of the files is all-important since it augments the power and speed of the shock.

De Folard's ideas were put into practice by Marshal de Saxe who had convinced himself that muskets and artillery were more noisy than dangerous and that the bayonet was the most effective weapon.

In October 1746, Saxe attacked an over-extended 'Pragmatic' army at Raucoux (or Roucoux or Rocoux). Eight battalions of British, Hanoverians, and Hessians were defending the villages of Raucoux, Liers, and Varoux when, according to Sir John Ligonier who commanded them:

Our battalions were attacked by fifty battalions, en colonne *by brigades, and as soon as two brigades were repulsed at each village, a third ran in without firing a shot and we were at last obliged to give up Varoux and Rocoux.*

This limited and expensive success was sufficient to earn, for columns of attack, the approval of French mid-century drillbooks. But for the next

The early days of the revolutionary wars were a time of desperate improvisations for France. Many of the newly-raised troops had to do without uniforms and wore their ordinary working clothes as is shown in these contemporary prints (ABOVE AND LEFT). The new mass armies created an insatiable demand for arms at a time when the manufacture of muskets was little more than a cottage industry (BELOW)

dangerous only to those who stood in its direct path and even the 12-pounder ball was only 11 centimetres in diameter. A 9-pounder field gun, which had an effective range (calculated to the point where the shot first pitched) of 1,300 metres, could fire nine rounds a minute but threw out such clouds of white smoke that only two rounds of aimed fire were practicable. In addition to round shot, two other types of projectile were available. One was canister or case-shot, a tin container filled with balls, weighing either 100 or 240 grams in the British models. When fired the container disintegrated and the balls formed a lethal spray from the muzzle. This was a most effective form of discharge but unfortunately had only a short range, only the 12-pounders being dangerous beyond 270 metres. The other was 'common shell', a hollow ball with a small bursting charge which, in the somewhat unlikely event of the fuse being accurate, would scatter fragments before or after landing. In all armies at least one piece in a six-gun battery was a howitzer used mainly for throwing shells to a range, for field howitzers, of about 1,230 metres. These rather ineffective missiles provided the only chance which gunners had of harming an enemy behind the crest of a ridge or a stone wall; since round and canister shot had a flat trajectory.

The tactical employment of artillery had not kept abreast of its increased mobility and range during the eighteenth century. The larger field guns were used almost wholly defensively and the offensive use of artillery was confined to the use of small pieces, 4-pounders or smaller, which were manhandled forward in the intervals between infantry units. Such 'battalion guns' made only a small contribution to the infantry's fire-power and were widely considered as being more trouble than they were worth. During the last years of the *ancien régime* some French gunners were advocating a bolder handling of guns in the attack, with mobile batteries being thrust forward to soften the enemy's line before the infantry attacked. The leader of the movement was the Chevalier du Teil, whose brother commanded the artillery school at Auxonne when Bonaparte was a pupil. His teachings bore fruit sooner than might have been expected since, in the early republican armies, the artillery was sometimes the only arm on which dependence could be placed and the bold handling of guns became essential.

Despite the increased mobility of both infantry and artillery, two problems remained intractable. Communications depended on the rate at which a horse could travel. Over long distances in a friendly countryside a courier could cover 100 kilometres a day with relays of horses. Over shorter stretches a well-mounted ADC could ride 20 kilometres an hour or 6 kilometres in 18 minutes. This was the maximum speed for the transmission of any orders.

There was no satisfactory answer to the supply problem before the coming of the railways but Guibert attempted to provide one. Searching for a quick decision in war, something hitherto unattainable, he recommended that armies should strike 'into the interior of states, even to their capitals'. To do so it would be necessary to by-pass 'those pretended barriers', the fortresses, and thus abandon the road-bound supply train. Thus, once inside an enemy country the army must live at the expense of that land. 'It is astonishing,' he said, 'how much a good

military administration can extract from the resources of a country'.

Once again the young French Republic adopted Guibert's idea because they could not afford to do otherwise. It therefore became the custom for French armies to live at the expense of their enemies. It is clear that Guibert did not foresee the enmity that such plundering would arouse in the occupied territory, nor did he anticipate the size of the new armies. Although an advocate of universal military service, he did not approve of large armies and believed that no field force should exceed 60,000 men. Before French expansion was finally checked, Napoleon Bonaparte was to employ an army ten times that size.

Shortly before the French revolution the Austrians successfully used their enemy's supply difficulties to bring a superior enemy operation to a halt. In the War of Bavarian Succession (1778) the Prussians attempted to invade Bohemia, but were frustrated by small detachments which held each of the passes through the encircling mountains. Working on interior lines and with an excellent supply service (which employed 21,388 drivers and 37,797 draught animals) the Austrians fed well while the Prussians were reduced to grubbing what they could from the fields and eventually had to withdraw. The Potato War, as the disgruntled Prussian soldiery termed it, was a military non-event but it had significant results. The Austrian High Command decided that no enemy could make headway against them if they blocked every possible avenue of approach. This was a defensible theory in mountainous country but in featureless areas, such as the Netherlands, where they were to fight the French in 1792–4, the only result of this 'cordon system' was to divide their army into many small parties at the mercy of any substantial body which was sent against them. Worse still, they decided that the cordon system was equally applicable to offensive operations and tried to make advances on wide fronts in unconnected columns. The cordon system was a recipe for the dispersal of strength.

CHAPTER ONE

Improvisation versus Inertia

IN 1792 THE GOVERNMENT OF revolutionary France, although it was still carried on in the name of Louis XVI, declared war on Austria, Prussia, and Sardinia for no better reason than its urgent need to keep the population's attention focussed on events outside their own frontiers. On 27 April three columns, 15,000 men in all, crossed the border into the Austrian Netherlands in the belief that 30,000 Belgians were anxious to join the French army. Hardly any of the Frenchmen involved were regular soldiers but it was hoped that the hastily-raised volunteers who took part would make up for their lack of training by their revolutionary fervour. Two of the columns returned to France without firing a shot (although one came back at a brisk double to cries of *Nous sommes trahis*), the third came under fire as they crossed the frontier and fled for Lille, pausing only long enough to murder their general.

In June, 20,000 men under the veteran Marshal Luckner made another attempt and reached Menin (Menen) and Courtrai (Kortrijk) only to retreat, though in good order when General Beaulieu, an Austrian general whose subsequent conduct in Italy hardly shows him to have been a dynamic commander, gathered some troops to oppose them. The only interest in this brief foray lies in the two staff officers who assisted Luckner. One was Alexandre Berthier who, as the Marshal Prince of Neufchatel and Wagram, was to be Napoleon's chief of staff (*major général*); the other was François Jarry who had already organized the *Kriegs Akademie* in Berlin and who was later to be the first commandant of the senior department of Britain's Royal Military College, the precursor of the Staff College.

Meanwhile France was struggling desperately to recreate her army. Opinions differ as to how many regular troops had survived the disbandments and desertions which accompanied the revolution but it can scarcely have been more than 100,000 and may have been as few as 65,000 and even these were seriously short of experienced officers. The Assembly therefore called for 101,000 volunteers who would serve in their own units and elect their own officers, though these could only be men with army or militia experience. These first volunteers had, for the most part, some military experience, as many of them came from the disbanded Household Troops or the abolished militia. In April 1792

the first batch of conscripts had been called up, but few of them took part in the fighting in that year. There was also a severe shortage of arms. Only 158,233 muskets were in store and the annual production amounted to 42,000. The abortive invasions of Belgium had resulted in many muskets being lost and many of the new levies had to be content with pikes, which did at least give them some security against cavalry. Among other expedients used to arm the new units, substantial orders for muskets were placed in Birmingham.

France was fortunate that her enemies were slow in reacting, the more so since her troops were split into a multiplicity of armies, each covering a fraction of one of her several frontiers. This gave her a complicated command structure, further confused by personal animosities and incompetent direction from the centre. It was not until 19 August that 55,000 Prussians, with 16,000 Austrians in distant support, crossed into France at Longwy. Their commander, Ferdinand of Brunswick, a hero of the Seven Years' War, disapproved of his orders, which were to march on Paris, and advanced with a deliberation which bordered on lethargy. He announced that it was impracticable to advance beyond the Meuse and was only drawn further forward by the unsolicited surrender of the fortress of Verdun.

On 20 September, Ferdinand found himself opposed by a French

PREVIOUS PAGE: Kellermann's staff at the cannonade of Valmy, 1792. The troops engaged are French regulars in white coats; the reserves by the windmill are newly-raised forces in blue

BELOW: Dumouriez urging his troops forward at the battle of Jemappes. Two of the soldiers in front of him are grenadiers recognizable by their tall caps; since grenades could not be thrown in cocked hats

force drawn up near Valmy. There were nearly 60,000 of them, partly regulars from the *Armée du Rhin* under Kellermann, partly volunteers from the *Armée du Nord* under Dumouriez. The regulars put up an impressive front and they were superbly supported by their gunners. When the Prussian army had suffered 184 casualties from artillery fire, Ferdinand declared the French position impregnable and set out to evacuate France. He was not pursued and took even longer in retreating to Longwy than he had spent in advancing from that place.

There had been panic in Paris when Ferdinand entered France but the 'victory' at Valmy changed the mood to frenzied elation. The royal family were imprisoned, a republic proclaimed, and 'all nations wishing to regain their freedom' were offered fraternity and aid. Savoy and Nice (then Sardinian territory) were occupied, French columns surged up to the Rhine, and Dumouriez attacked the Austrian Netherlands.

On 2 November 1792, with 40,000 men, of whom only 10,000 were untrained, he attacked 14,000 Austrians at Jemappes and beat them, his troops attacking some in line, some in column, according to their competence at drill. The Austrians evacuated Belgium and regrouped in Luxemburg.

Encouraged by this success, the French celebrated by executing their King and declaring war on Holland, Britain, and Spain. Dumouriez, with his eyes fixed on the wealth of Amsterdam, badly needed to shore up the tottering finances of the infant republic, invaded Holland only to be held up on the formidable obstacle of the Hollandsch Diep by a scratch force which included a brigade of British Guards. While he was pondering how to overcome this opposition, an Austrian army of 40,000 under the Prince of Coburg-Saalfeld crashed into his open right flank. Dumouriez fell back and, between Brussels and Liège, concentrated about 45,000 men. With these he attacked the Austrians at Neerwinden on 18 March 1793. Attacking in eight heavy columns, he was repeatedly repulsed by the steady Austrian line. An Austrian counterattack broke the French army which fled, evacuating the whole of Belgium. Dumouriez declared himself a supporter of constitutional monarchy and went over to the Austrians.

Dumouriez' defection caused a crisis in the French army, its morale already shattered by its defeat at Neerwinden. It was, however, noted by the future Marshal Macdonald that deserters flocking to the rear were singing patriotic songs. The blame was placed firmly on the generals and henceforward every commander in the field had, at his elbow, a political 'commissar' to query his decisions and report his lightest word to a highly suspicious Committee of Public Safety in Paris. While the *Représentants en Mission* did much to restore the morale and keep alive the patriotic fervour of the soldiers, their influence on the generals was baleful. If a commander ignored his *Représentant's* advice, no matter how impractical or ill-informed it might be, and then suffered a reverse, he was likely to be removed or, as became increasingly usual, executed.

THREATENED ON ALL FRONTS

The summer of 1793 was a critical time for France. Almost the whole of Europe had formed a coalition against her, a large allied army was

23

building up in Belgium and a Spanish army actually spilled over the Pyrenees and established itself in Roussillon. To make matters worse, a decree of 23 February calling for 300,000 conscripts caused a revolt in western France and, later in the summer, Toulon, the base of the Mediterranean fleet, handed itself over to the Royal Navy. Fortunately this coalition seemed more dangerous than it actually was. Russia sent no more than expressions of support and most of Prussia's strength was devoted to occupying parts of Poland. The Spaniards proved wholly unable to support their army in France and the Dutch were bitterly divided amongst themselves. The British were determined to prosecute the war but, apart from their overwhelmingly powerful fleet, had few forces with which to do so. Most of their pitifully small army was devoted to capturing French islands in the West Indies and they could find the men neither to support the revolt in La Vendée, which gradually collapsed under the weight of troops sent against it, or to retain Toulon, which was recaptured by the republic in December thanks largely to the acting commander of the French artillery, Captain (later Major) Napoleone Buonaparte.

The threat to France from the Netherlands was a long time in developing. The allied army there, though it contained British, Dutch, Hanoverian, Hessian, and other German troops, was mainly an Austrian force and the high command was wholly Austrian. No state had a better organized supply train than the Hapsburg Empire and no Austrian general would contemplate moving even a short distance without his waggons. It was unfortunate that no part of the world was more heavily sewn with fortresses than the Franco-Netherlands frontier and, since the supply train had to move through the towns which were fortified, the

24

time was filled with the intricate mysteries of siegecraft, while fortress after fortress was subdued. Nor was this process hastened when, doubtless because the Hapsburg army was the most bureaucratized in the world, a siege train needed at Valenciennes was despatched from Vienna while that needed at Mainz was sent from the Netherlands. A great gap was torn in the French defences when Condé, Valenciennes, and Le Quesnoy were all taken by the allies and for a moment it seemed as if the Austrians might steel themselves for an advance on Paris. At that stage, the British government decided to withdraw their contingent (which included many Germans) to prosecute the siege of Dunkirk, a project which ended in defeat at Hondschoote (8 September) and almost in disaster. Six weeks later the Austrians, who had decided to fill in the time by laying siege to Maubeuge, were narrowly defeated at Wattignies by General Jourdan who had a three to two superiority. Both French generals were almost immediately recalled, Jourdan being retired on a small pension while Houchard, the victor of Hondschoote, was executed.

France, 1792–5, showing the main scenes of action

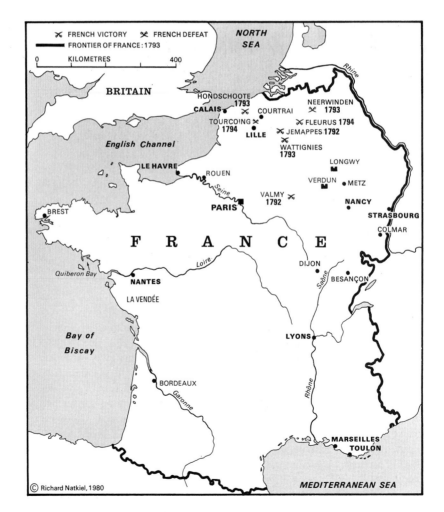

Lazarre Carnot
(1753–1823), the
organizer of victory

THE TURNING POINT

1794 was to be the turning point in the war. The French army, while
still an uncertain weapon, had regained much of its confidence with the
victories at Hondschoote and Wattignies. A start had been made in
welding together the remains of the regulars with the newly raised units
and a blue uniform common to both was introduced, the regulars having
hitherto worn white. The worst of the arms shortage was over and, above
all, the French army was now extremely large thanks to conscription,
there being 732,000 men under arms by April 1794.

One of the greatest of the new French assets was Lazarre Carnot, an
engineer officer who became head of the Committee of Public Safety. He
had a flair for organization and administration and, although a poor
tactician (his advice as *Représentant* to Jourdan at Wattignies had prolonged the battle into a second day and caused many needless casualties),

he had a sound grasp of strategy. He insisted that French troops should be used *en masse* and not frittered away in cordons or penny packets. He was prepared to take risks that no Austrian general would contemplate and he was determined to win the war in the Netherlands as soon as possible:

We must finish matters this year. To begin again next year would mean that we must die of hunger and exhaustion.

He saw that the enormous size of the French army gave the chance of overwhelming the allies even if the cost in casualties was high.

On the other side, circumstances were less favourable. A strong party in Vienna was in favour of abandoning the Netherlands in favour of joining Russia and Prussia in the less costly pursuit of filching parts of Poland. Nevertheless the Emperor Francis went to Belgium to take nominal command of the army and there was talk of a breakthrough into France.

The year started badly for France. The Austrians started, as was their habit, with besieging another fortress, on this occasion Landrécies. All French attempts to relieve the place were beaten off. Their most spectacular repulse occurred on 26 April when General Chappuis attacked along the Cambrai–Le Cateau road with 30,000 men. This brought him against the sector of the allied covering force commanded by the Duke of York who, near the village of Beaumont, held the French in front with his artillery and infantry while he detached to his right the Austrian General Otto with six Austrian and thirteen British squadrons. The manoeuvre succeeded perfectly and the allied cavalry fell on the exposed French flank, achieving total surprise, taking forty guns and causing 7,000 casualties. It is noticeable that the six Austrian squadrons were commanded by Colonel Karl Schwartzenberg who, nineteen years later, was to command 335,000 allied troops at the battle of Leipzig.

At the action at Beaumont (which the French call Troisvilles), General Chappuis was among the prisoners and on him was found the French plan for the opening of the campaign. Intent on deciding the fate of the Netherlands in a single campaign, Carnot had ordered Pichegru, who had succeeded to the command of the *Armée du Nord* after the execution of his two predecessors, to swing up the 70,000 men of his left wing so as to cut the British communications with Ostend and to threaten Brussels.

This advance started in a most promising fashion since the bulk of the troops on the allied right, more than 20,000 men under Count François Sebastian de Clerfayt, a sixty-year-old Belgian in the Hapsburg service, had been ordered south to assist in the siege of Landrécies. Pichegru's wheel, therefore was able to drive a deep salient from its base at Lille and on 26 April reached Courtrai which was held by only 150 invalids. However, the orders captured at Beaumont gave Clerfayt time to countermarch and, trying to save Menin, he reached Mouscron. There he was fiercely attacked on 29 April and, since he had failed to protect his flanks and had stationed his reserves 10 kilometres to his rear, he was driven away in some disorder, losing twenty-three guns and 2,000 men.

Menin surrendered on the following day but most of the garrison, consisting of Hanoverians and *emigré* Frenchmen, fought their way out to the allied lines.

Clerfayt was not discouraged and when, on 3 May, the Duke of York arrived at Tournai with 24,000 men from Landrécies, he suggested that their two corps should attempt to pinch out the 24,000 Frenchmen who he estimated to be in their salient east of Courtrai. The Duke, despite doubts about Clerfayt's fixity of purpose, agreed to the attempt which was due to begin on 6 May. Clerfayt therefore passed his troops to the north bank of the Lys, only to write to the Duke, 'that it was impossible for him to proceed, as he thought himself too weak'. This angered the Duke who sent their correspondence to the Austrian Emperor, who responded with a peremptory order for Clerfayt to advance.

Nevertheless, it was the French who made the first move when, on 10 May, three of their columns attacked the Duke of York's corps around Tournai. To the north of the city the Hanoverians were driven back from Dottignies and Coyghem but managed to cling on to Espierres, a vital point since it was there that communications were maintained with Clerfayt. The most serious attack fell on the British troops astride the Lille–Tournai road. The Duke tried to repeat the tactics that had been so successful at Beaumont and threw the British cavalry on the French left but, for the first time since the revolution, the French infantry formed squares and beat off the attack. Nevertheless they started to retreat and, harassed by the fire of 3-pounder battalion guns, changed their formation into columns, which could march faster than squares. Near Willems they were charged again by the cavalry and, before they could reform squares, an officer of the Scots Greys broke into one column, opening the way for his men. Seeing one column broken the cavalry rode down two more battalions. According to one British dragoon:

Quarter was implored in vain. A more cold-blooded butchery was never perpetrated, since the execution lasted nearly half an hour.

In fact the massacre seems to have been somewhat less ruthless since, apart from 13 guns, 400 French prisoners were taken. The total French loss can scarcely have been less than 1,000. The British cavalry, and two Austrian squadrons who charged with them, lost 113 men and 230 horses killed and wounded.

On the following day Clerfayt, obedient to his orders, advanced against Courtrai on the north bank of the Lys. He surprised the French outposts and could have stormed into the town immediately. Instead he made a long pause during which a substantial French force was collected and, in a leisurely fashion, formed into line in front of Courtrai. In this formation they advanced to attack their attacker and there followed an indecisive action in which Clerfayt lost almost 1,500 men. The French fell back to the shelter of the town, allowing Clerfayt to claim a victory but he retreated 19 kilometres to Thielt (Tielt) on the following day.

Meanwhile Landrécies had surrendered on 30 April and it was intended to move a large corps from there to deal with the situation

around Tournai. Unfortunately a French advance towards Mons caused the Emperor to halt his move northward and York was induced, despite his doubts about Clerfayt's resolution, to propose that the idea for a joint attack on the salient should be revived. Clerfayt agreed and, having picked up reinforcements including a British brigade from Ostend, marched south-west from Thielt on 15 May. Next day his advance guard had reached the Ypres–Menin road west of the latter town when he was halted by a message from the Emperor. The threat to Mons having been summarily dealt with, Francis made up his mind to bring 29,000 men north. As the Duke wrote to his father:

To my great surprize I was awakened in the middle of the night [14–15 May] with the intelligence of his arrival and that his army would be at St. Armand in the morning. I had before determined to attack in spite of the great risk which I must have run, but with this information I delayed my march until I had seen the Emperor, who immediately desired me to put off my march until his army arrived.

The scene was now set for a battle which could decide the fate of the Netherlands. Apart from the garrison of Lille, the French had about 80,000 men available, a slight numerical advantage over the 74,000 allies now against them. The French, however, were deployed in a long narrow corridor from Lille to Courtrai and they had no knowledge of 29,000 allied reinforcements. There was every chance that the allies could cut the French army in two, isolating some 50,000 men in the north who would be forced to surrender. All that was required was a sound plan on which the allies could work.

CHAPTER TWO

Tourcoing, 17-18 May 1794

T HE ORIGINAL PLAN for the coming operation, put forward first by Clerfayt and then by the Duke of York, had envisaged the isolation of the French force between the Lys and the Scheldt. The orders which emerged from the Emperor's headquarters late on 16 May had a grander but vaguer aim:

The intention of this attack is to act upon the enemy's communications between Lille and Menin and Courtrai, to defeat the armies he has advanced upon the Lys and to drive him out of Flanders.

In the current mode of Austrian strategy the orders called for many columns moving on a wide front. In all there were to be six attacking forces, one on the north bank of the Lys and five on the south.

Clerfayt, whose strength was now 19,600, was to move to Werwicq on the river, masking Menin on his left, and force a crossing. From there he would advance on Linselles where he would link up with the allied troops coming from the south. To meet him 25,000 allied troops in three columns were to seize and hold the low L-shaped ridge marked by the villages of Lannoy, Mouveaux, and Mouscron. Thus 45,000 allies were to undertake the original plan of cutting off 50,000 Frenchmen and the remaining 29,000 allies were to be left for more ambitious targets. Instead of throwing their weight into the fight to cripple the *Armée du Nord*, they were to undertake the reduction of Lille. 19,000 Austrians under the Emperor's brother, the Archduke Charles, were to cross the Marque stream at Pont-à-Marque and advance against the French camps at Flers and Bouvines while the remaining 10,000 under Kinsky were to cover the Archduke's right by going to the Marque at Pont Tressin. There they would wait until the other columns had forced the French defending the line of the stream to withdraw. As a gesture to communications between the two attacks, Kinsky was told to detach a token force, one battalion and two squadrons, to keep in touch with the striking force attacking Lannoy.

It is hard to understand the thinking behind these orders. If the intention was to trap the French in the salient, the obvious course would have been to cover Tournai, now the allied base, with a small corps, say

Kinsky's 10,000 men, by holding the line of the Marque, an inconsiderable stream but, from its marshy banks, one very difficult to cross except at the bridges. This would have left the Archduke's 19,000 free to strengthen the striking force on the ridge so that it could scarcely have failed. Instead the Emperor, or rather his favourite military adviser, Major General Karl von Mack, had decided that the objectives should be diversified to include the siege of yet another fortress. As the Duke of York was told in confidence on 16 May:

the whole plan of attack is altered and should this attack succeed it is the Emperor's intention to besiege Lisle [sic] with one hundred and eight battalions and one hundred and twenty squadrons . . . The intention of besieging Lisle is known to no one except General Mack, not even any one of the Austrian ministers.

In considering the inadequacies of these orders it is only fair to observe that their author, who was to play an even more disastrous part in the war eleven years later, was far from well. A British officer, later to become a distinguished cavalry general, wrote of him at this time:

He has extremely bad health proceeding from violent pains in the head. In consequence he wears a black caul on his head which is sewn round the bottom with stiff black hair, which gives him an extraordinary appearance. He lays on his bed during the whole day and with pencil writes all his instructions to the army, and when any action takes place he is lifted from his bed to his horse. Withal it is very odd that he is so fond of females that one constantly attends him.

It may have been Mack's ill-health which made him utterly misjudge the timing of his plan.

Issued during the evening of 16 May the orders called for the advance to start at dawn on the following day yet the head of the Archduke's column was still at St Amand which was 24 kilometres, a full day's march, from their start line at Pont-à-Marque. In the event the advance guard set out from St Armand at 10.30 pm on 16 May, reaching Orchies at dawn. They fought their way across the stream at Pont-à-Marque during the afternoon, some eight hours behind their orders. Kinsky meanwhile had brought his men forward from Froidmont to the eastern ends of the bridges, broken by the French, at Tressin and Bouvines.

At the other extremity of the attack things moved even more slowly. Clerfayt's orders had to travel more than 80 kilometres by way of Desselghem to reach him in his position on the Ypres–Menin road. They can scarcely have reached him until shortly before dawn and failed to stir him to any display of energy. It was mid-afternoon before his leading troops had covered the 5 kilometres to the Lys at Werwicq, at which stage it was realized that the bridging-train had been left in the rear. Darkness had fallen before it reached the front and it was 1 am on 18 May before two squadrons and two battalions of Württembergers reached the south bank. No attempt was made to pass the rest of the corps across until daylight came.

With the two wings hanging back, serious fighting on 17 May was

PREVIOUS PAGE: A captured Austrian colour being brought to General Souham during the battle of Tourcoing

32

Austrian officers in bivouac before the battle of Tourcoing. From left to right: Jäger, infantryman, and staff officer

confined to the three columns detailed to seize the L-shaped ridge. These were, from north to south, 4,000 Hanoverians under General Bussche with orders to take Mouscron, 10,000 Austrians and Hessians, commanded by General Otto whose objective was Tourcoing, and 10,750 British, Austrians, and Hessians under the Duke of York. Their task was to take Mouveaux while securing the left flank of the whole striking force by holding Lannoy and Roubaix.

On the right Bussche's division, already too weak for its task, was further reduced by being ordered to detach a third of its strength to form a screen to the north. Nevertheless, with only 2,700 men, Bussche succeeded in taking Mouscron from its sleepy garrison. An immediate counterattack from Compére's powerful brigade re-established the French position and drove the Hanoverians back to Dottignies, barely 3 kilometres from their start line.

Both Otto and the Duke of York delayed their advance until 7 am, when a morning mist, which would have made the close country ahead of them extremely dangerous, cleared. Then Otto's men took Leers without difficulty and, by mid-afternoon, were in Wattrelos. There they paused before pushing on the final 6 kilometres to Tourcoing which, like Roubaix, was no more than a small market town. On the left, York's column, six British, five Austrian, and two Hessian battalions with six British and four Austrian squadrons, moved parallel with them. The first village they came to, Lannoy, was carried easily, the French evacuating it 'after a cannonade which, on their part, seemed to be intended as a signal communication rather than as a resisting fire'. Five kilometres further on, Roubaix was more firmly defended, but after a bombardment the Duke sent the Guards Brigade to attack it while the cavalry turned it on the left. The French resisted stoutly until they saw the light

33

dragoons moving on their rear. Then they fell back.

It was now after 5 pm and, although cavalry patrols were sent to search for them, there was no sign of Kinsky's men on the left, nor could anything be seen or heard of the Archduke's attack. Nothing could be heard from Clerfayt to the north. From his right, the Duke of York heard that Mouscron had been won and lost and that Otto was no further forward than Wattrelos. He therefore decided to halt for the night. The country ahead, intersected by woods, orchards, hedges, walls, and farm buildings, was ideal for ambushes and he was unwilling to press forward in isolation. Moreover, his column was being eroded. The Duke had had to leave his Hessian battalions as a garrison for Lannoy and at least as many men would have to be left in Roubaix. He was redeploying his men in defensive positions for the night when a staff officer rode up from Tournai with orders from the Emperor. The Duke of York and Otto were to push on to their final objectives so as to be certain of meeting Clerfayt. The Duke 'represented the state of affairs but the orders were positive.'

With no option but to continue his advance, York reluctantly gave orders for the attack on Mouveaux. The advance was to be led by the six flank companies of the Guards Brigade with the First (later Grenadier) Guards in support. The Seventh and Fifteenth Light Dragoons would simultaneously move round the north of the village. According to a young officer of the Fifteenth, the advance was made:

Joseph Souham
(1760–1837)

through a very close country. On arriving in front of Mouveaux it was found to be very strongly entrenched and palisaded. About fifteen hundred men defended it with several pieces of cannon. The British cannon opened a practicable entrance, the Guards stormed while the cavalry were ordered to proceed at a gallop round the work and get in the rear and cut off the flying enemy. When we moved the Guards had not got into the place. The enemy were still firing their cannon charged with grape down the road lined with an avenue of trees, and had set on fire a house at the roadside. By the scorching flames of this we were obliged to pass, as a deep ditch and fences rendered it impossible for us to break off the road until we got close to the walls. The rattling of the shot through the trees, the burning house, the huzzas of the infantry and the roar and smoke of the guns, with all the confusion of the assault, was a sublime spectacle. The French kept their ground manfully until they saw us, in spite of their fire, wheeling round the very edge of their entrenchments, when they deserted them and fled. We took three guns and a number of prisoners on the other side of the town.

The light dragoons pursued the fugitives for more than 3 kilometres, crossed the Lille–Menin road and beat up a French camp at Bondues.

The capture of Mouveaux meant that York had now wholly fulfilled his orders but that his force was greatly over-extended. The Guards Brigade held Mouveaux, the five Austrian battalions were in Roubaix, and the Hessians in Lannoy. His second British brigade, three battalions under Henry Fox, he posted south of Roubaix to block the road from Lille, the most probable route for a French counterattack against his flank. With 10,000 men spread over more than 7 kilometres he felt vulnerable. He heard that Otto was now in Tourcoing but he could find

no sign of support on his left. To minimize the risks, he decided to leave only the light companies in Mouveaux and to pull back the two battalions of Guards to Roubaix. Orders for this change had been issued when another positive order arrived from the Emperor. Mouveaux was to be held in strength.

This order, like the Emperor's last, stemmed from the belief at Austrian headquarters that everything would be as it was intended to be. In fact there was a gap of 8 kilometres between York's left flank at Lannoy and Kinsky's nearest post at Pont-à-Tressin. Beyond Kinsky the Archduke's advanced guard had got as far as the area Lesquin—Bouvines where it had taken up positions for the night. Nothing had been heard from Clerfayt who, as has been seen, was waiting near Werwicq for the arrival of his pontoons. With Bussche's column driven back to Dottignies, York and Otto with 20,000 men were holding a long narrow salient threatened on three sides by some 40,000 Frenchmen.

17 May had been even worse for the French than it had been for the allies. Since they had been planning to strike at Clerfayt on the north bank of the Lys they had left only a covering force on the line Mouveaux—Mouscron and were taken utterly by surprise. To make matters worse, Pichegru was absent from his headquarters visiting the extreme right wing of the *Armée du Nord.* The situation around Tourcoing became in consequence the responsibility of the senior divisional commander, Joseph Souham.

INITIATIVE VERSUS INDECISION
Souham, who was twenty-seven, had been a trooper in the royal cuirassiers before the revolution. At Tourcoing he showed himself to be a bold and decisive commander but his career was a disappointment and he was still *général de division* in 1814. He realized that, unless the situation could be resolved on 18 May, the French forces in the salient, which were not as large as the allies had estimated, would be lost. Under his own command, north of the allied salient, he had his own division of 20,000 men and the 10,000 men of Vandamme's brigade from Moreau's division. South of the salient were 15,000 men of Bonnaud's division (which under Chappuis had been so heavily defeated at Beaumont three weeks earlier) and the large garrison of Lille. Together these could produce a field force of 23,000. He ordered Bonnaud to leave only small detachments to delay the Archduke and to use his main force to strike at the Duke of York's left flank at 3 am on 18 May. He intended to lead his own division against Mouveaux, Tourcoing, and Wattrelos at the same time, leaving only Vandamme to hold Clerfayt.

Meanwhile the Duke of York continued to be worried about his exposed position and sent another request to be allowed to bring the bulk of the Guards Brigade back from Mouveaux. Permission was refused but he was given a confident assurance that Kinsky and the Archduke would be moving up on his left from dawn onwards and that Kinsky would take over responsibility for Lannoy by noon. Orders to ensure that this happened had been despatched from Tournai at 1 am and repeated two hours later but when the ADC arrived at the Archduke's headquarters at 4 am, he was told that the prince was asleep and

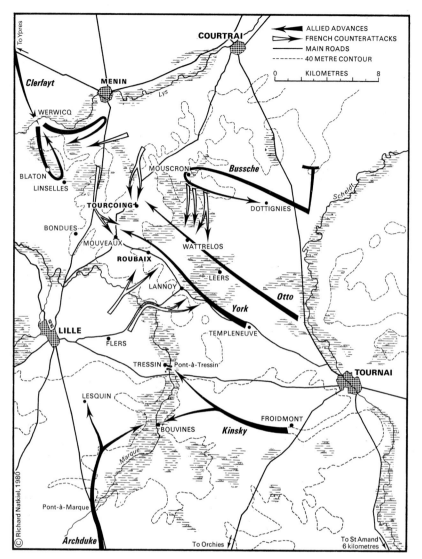

ALLIED ADVANCES
FRENCH COUNTERATTACKS
MAIN ROADS
40 METRE CONTOUR

0   KILOMETRES   8

COURTRAI

To Ypres

Clerfayt

MENIN

Lys

WERWICQ

BLATON
LINSELLES

MOUSCRON

Bussche

Scheldt

TOURCOING

DOTTIGNIES

BONDUES

MOUVEAUX

WATTRELOS

ROUBAIX

LEERS

LANNOY

Otto

LILLE

York

FLERS

TEMPLENEUVE

TRESSIN   Pont-à-Tressin

TOURNAI

LESQUIN

BOUVINES

Kinsky

FROIDMONT

Marque

© Richard Natkiel, 1980

Pont-à-Marque

Archduke

To Orchies

To St Amand
6 kilometres

The battle of Tourcoing,
17–18 May

must not be woken. This was not wholly true. The Archduke was the best Austrian commander in all these long wars but he had one serious disablement – he was an epileptic and was suffering an attack during the night 17–18 May. Unforgivably his staff neglected to implement the new orders until Charles had recovered. It was mid-morning before a single man started to march and by that time there was nothing to do but retire on Tournai. Kinsky's behaviour was less explicable. When his orders arrived during the night he merely replied 'Kinsky knows what he has to do' and failed to move a man.

At 4 am on 18 May the Duke of York, who was at Roubaix, heard musketry from the north as two French brigades attacked Otto's advance guard under Montfrault, at Tourcoing. Soon one of Montfrault's staff arrived at Roubaix to ask for help and was given two

Austrian battalions, on the distinct understanding that they should be returned if Tourcoing had been evacuated before they arrived. The village had already been taken by the French but the two battalions never rejoined York. Meanwhile two more French brigades had attacked Wattrelos and, after a sharp resistance, the two Hessian battalions which formed the garrison retreated on Leers.

It was not until 6 am that York's division came under attack but when it came the assault was heavy and multi-thrusted. Souham's right wing struck at Mouveaux from the north-west and Bonnaud sent 18,000 men in two brigades across the Marque, one marching on Roubaix and one between there and Lannoy. The Guards under Ralph Abercromby at Mouveaux, and Fox's brigade on the slope west of Roubaix, had no difficulty in holding their ground, but with only three Austrian battalions in Roubaix the situation between there and Lannoy was soon serious and became desperate when one Austrian battalion broke and fled.

The Duke therefore sent his Adjutant General to Mouveaux with orders to bring the Guards back to Roubaix but, before the orders could be implemented, the French cut the road at Le Fresnoy between the two villages, and York, riding forward to co-ordinate the retreat, found himself unable to advance. Further Frenchmen barred his way to Fox's brigade so, cut off from all his troops, he decided to ride to Wattrelos in the hope that Otto could lend him some battalions. Accompanied by two aides and an Austrian liaison officer, he was within 45 metres of the village when he was greeted by a French volley which unhorsed the Austrian. As the Duke turned his horse for Lannoy, a 6-pounder opened on them and soon they were pursued by French dragoons. Fortunately York, conspicuous from the star of the Order of the Garter on his chest, was better mounted than the French, but his horse refused to attempt the boggy Espierres brook and he had to wade across. Eventually a horse was found for him on the far bank but by that time he could only ride to Leers where he joined General Otto.

While the Duke was being hunted across country, Clerfayt at last showed some signs of activity. His infantry drove 5 kilometres south of the river and took the villages of Blaton and Linselles while two squadrons of the British Eighth Light Dragoons, which were under his command, made a spectacular, if over-enthusiastic charge which took them to Halluin on the outskirts of Menin. This success, though costly, encouraged the Austrian infantry to push on up to the Menin–Lille road. For a moment it seemed that a significant breakthrough might be made from the north where the Austrian had a two to one superiority over Vandamme's brigade. Unfortunately, as the Duke of York had written to his father the King:

No man on earth has more personal courage than General Clerfayt, but unfortunately his lack of resolution and decision is beyond all description.

Just when everything seemed to be going well, two French *chasseur* battalions which had lost their way on the previous day reached the scene of action and Vandamme flung them into a counterattack. Clerfayt

lost his nerve and called in his troops, forming them into a tight, secure bridgehead based on the low heights westward from Bousbeque. There they remained until the end of the day.

Meanwhile the two British brigades had been left leaderless and it was as well that Fox and the 'Little Brigade' stood immovably west of Roubaix and gave Ralph Abercromby with the Guards time to retire, covered by the British and Austrian cavalry, on Roubaix. According to the Adjutant General:

We began our retreat with great order and regularity, but an unfortunate circumstance, which would require a great deal of time to detail to you, soon introduced confusion amongst us, from which we never really recovered. We rallied the Guards once indeed, and they formed very readily, but the [Austrian] hussars at that instant running full up the hill, fairly broke through us, and from that moment I gave up the idea of saving our artillery. Had the enemy possessed either courage or conduct, I believe we should not have saved ourselves.

CRISIS AT ROUBAIX

The crisis came at Roubaix where the three battalions of Austrians in garrison had, apart from some Jäger companies, vanished – 'we never saw an Austrian but by twos and threes running away' – but the western end of the village was held by a dismounted squadron of Sixteenth Light Dragoons. The difficulty started at the eastern end of the village where the single long street, which went straight on towards Wattrelos, turned immediately to the right for Lannoy:

Hedges lined each side of the straight road; ditches, very deep – one indeed a rivulet – flanked the other.

The French were in position across the Wattrelos road and had a cannon firing straight down the village street. To make the confusion complete the hired civilians who drove the guns decided that they had had enough. They cut the traces and rode off on the horses, leaving a chaos of guns, limbers, and ammunition waggons around the road junction at the east of the village.

By climbing through the houses and gardens, the Guards were eventually extricated but the light dragoons of the rearguard had to run the gauntlet of the road junction:

The cry of Charge to the right! *ran down the column and, at the same moment, we were all at full speed. The enemy redoubled his efforts, and struck at us with bayonets fixed at the end of his muskets as we wheeled round the dreaded and dreadful corner, already choked with fallen men and horses. My little mare received a bayonet wound in the crest of her neck. Two balls lodged in my cloak-case and another carried away part of my sash. Our surgeon and his horse were killed close by my side, and above a dozen fell at that spot. We still urged on* ventre à terre, *pursued by bullets.*

The evacuation of Roubaix was not however, the end of the Guards' troubles for, although the Hessians were still bravely holding on to

Lannoy they were surrounded by 9,000 French. Abercromby had to make a circuit around both Lannoy and its attackers, sustaining 'a heavy fire'. Fortunately the diversion thus caused enabled the Hessians to break out and rejoin the Duke of York at Leers. The Guards fell back to their starting point at Templeneuve.

The hardest time was had by Fox's brigade on the slopes above the Marque, who had to hold their position until the Guards had passed Roubaix. When it was their turn to retire they set off south-east along the slope aiming for Lannoy. Approaching the village they found their way blocked by a French battery firing from behind cover. For a time it seemed that they must surrender but a French *emigré* serving in the ranks of the Fourteenth Foot stepped forward and, claiming to know the countryside intimately, volunteered to lead the brigade through the woods to Leers. They were fired on most of the way but eventually reached safety, triumphantly dragging one of their battalion guns with them. They had suffered 534 casualties out of the 1,120 all ranks with whom they had started the battle.

Tourcoing cost the allied armies only 3,000 casualties, 930 of them coming from the British army which also lost nineteen guns, seven of them 12-pounders, out of the twenty-eight which they had taken into action. It was not a very serious defeat, especially compared to the loss suffered by the French less than a week later when, led by Pichegru, they hurled themselves at the allied positions near Tournai in what one French officer described as 'a butchery without plan, success or result', and suffered 6,000 casualties. Nevertheless, it marked the end of the allied hopes of retaining the Netherlands and of invading France. The debacle gave the anti-Netherlands party in Vienna the excuse they needed for breaking off the war in that country and concentrating their efforts in Poland and Italy. It also sowed dissension between Britain and Austria the two main partners in the allied army. Many of the British believed that they had been deliberately betrayed and pointed to the columns of the Archduke, Kinsky, and Clerfayt, all predominantly Austrian, which had scarcely been engaged while the bulk of the fighting had fallen on the British, Hanoverians, and the Hessians who were in British pay. This view, although supported by so eminent an authority as Sir John Fortescue, is most unlikely to be true.

The real reason for the defeat was what the Duke of York described as the 'exceedingly pernicious as well as dangerous' tactical system practised by the Austrian generals. Their plan had been produced by Mack scribbling pencil notes in his bed. Souham had countered it by instant decision, by the acceptance of great risks but risks almost certain to be cancelled out by the lumbering method in which Austrians took their troops into battle. It was the difference between those who treated war as an academic exercise and those who saw their opportunities and seized them. The initiative shown by Souham was the kind of spirit which was to give the French army another twelve years of almost uninterrupted victory.

CHAPTER THREE

The Emergence of Bonaparte

THE BLOW WHICH THE TOURCOING FIASCO struck at the Austrian will to continue the war in the Netherlands was reinforced on 26 June when Coburg, in a belated and ill-co-ordinated attempt to relieve Charleroi, was defeated at Fleurus by the re-employed Jourdan, whose forces handsomely outnumbered him. Thereafter the Hapsburg armies fell back to the German bank of the Rhine, leaving Belgium and Holland to the protection of an inadequate force of British and Dutch with their German auxiliaries. The Dutch had entered the war disunited and every French victory increased the number of Dutchmen who believed their country's wisest course would be to join the winning side. Their troops became increasingly unreliable and, without them, the British and Hanoverians had not the strength to stand on any line against the numbers which Pichegru could send against them. Their retreat became increasingly disorderly and in mid-April 1795 the 15,000 survivors (of whom only 6,000 were fit to fight) were embarked at Bremen. By that time Prussia had made her peace with France, Holland was a French satellite, and Belgium *'une partie intégrante et inséparable de la République Française'*. When Spain abandoned the war in July the great coalition was reduced to Austria, Sardinia, Britain, Portugal, and Naples, of which only the first two had troops within reach of the enemy in Europe.

France was in no position to take advantage of the disarray among her enemies. The lifting of the immediate threat from the Netherlands and the containment of her internal strife led to a revulsion against the determined but bloodstained government which had wrenched her through her crisis. On 27 July 1794 (9th Thermidor II) Robespierre was driven from power and followed his many victims, guilty and innocent, to the guillotine. France entered a five-year period of uncertain, incompetent, and corrupt governments punctuated by *coups d'état* and even the rich loot from Holland was insufficient to stave off the financial crisis which the revolution had inherited from the Bourbons. Royalist discontent continued to simmer although a large-scale landing of *emigré* troops, armed, financed, and transported by Britain, ended in chaos and massacre at Quiberon Bay in July 1795. In that year two French armies tried to penetrate beyond the Rhine but were sharply defeated by the

41

Austrians. The war on land was deadlocked.

This lull in the war was invaluable for the consolidation of the French army. The makeshift army which had overrun the Low Countries had done so largely thanks to the mistakes of its adversaries and the overwhelming numbers it was able to put in the field. Despite the administrative talent of Carnot the clothing, arming, and paying of this horde presented insoluble difficulties in a country which was, for all practical purposes, bankrupt. These problems were eventually alleviated, though never solved, by conquering territories from which resources could be drawn but, before conquests could be undertaken, the army must be reorganized so that it was fit for offensive operations. France was fortunate that Carnot survived the downfall of his colleague Robespierre and continued in the governing clique until 1797.

ABOVE: General Jourdan defeating the Austrians at Fleurus, 1794; the first time that an observation balloon was used in battle

MANPOWER AND CONSCRIPTION

The least of his difficulties was manpower. The Constitution of Year I (24 June 1793) had laid down that:

All Frenchmen shall be soldiers; all shall be trained to arms.

As a result the army became three quarters of a million strong during 1794 although desertion, largely caused by lack of pay, was running at an abysmally high rate and conscription became increasingly unpopular. This was reflected in the Constitution of Year III (22 August 1795) which laid down that:

The army shall be recruited by voluntary enlistment.

a pious hope that was never fulfilled.

Carnot's greatest assistance to the army was the *Amalgame* of 1793 by which the regulars, the volunteers, and the conscripts were fused. The 213 surviving regular battalions were combined with 426 newer units to form 213 *demi-brigades* each of three battalions, one regular and two of newly-raised men. The term *demi-brigade* was coined to supersede regiment, which was considered to have Bourbon overtones, although it was retained in the cavalry. A further *Amalgame* reduced the number of *demi-brigades* to 110 of infantry of the line and 30 of light infantry, each having a strength of 3,208. By that date the distinction between regulars and others had to all intents disappeared.

No *Amalgame* was necessary in the cavalry since there were few new horsed units and those worthy to survive were merely added to the roll of regular regiments, the number of cavalry units rising from 62 (1789) to 84 (1798), most of the increase being in light regiments.

In artillery fewer changes needed to be made as that arm had been least affected by the revolution, largely because fewer of the officers were drawn from the *noblesse.* However, horse artillery was introduced into the French army, as it was in the British, in 1792, and in the following year twelve battalions of sappers were added to the establishment, the previous engineer establishment having consisted, as in Britain, entirely of officers.

PREVIOUS PAGE: General Bonaparte watching the *Armée d'Italie* march into Milan, May 1796

All arms suffered a shortage of officers since of the 9,578 regular officers on the establishment in 1789, some 5,500 had left the service by 1794 for one reason or another. In the early, desperate days many promotions were made from the ranks, some of which led to further promotion and great distinction but, despite the great play made with the idea that any soldier could gain a commission and rise to the top of his profession, the vast majority of officers continued to come from the middle and upper classes, although, thanks to the conscription, many of them would serve a short period in the ranks before gaining their commission. The reason for this was simple, and common to all the armies of Europe. Very few of those in the ranks could read and write and even a revolutionary army has little use for an illiterate officer. Another of Carnot's achievements was the abolition, in 1795, of that sacred cow of all revolutionary armies, the election of officers.

COMMUNICATION AND INNOVATION

Some progress was made with the communications available to the forces when in 1794 chains of telegraph stations, using a form of semaphore, were established between Paris and the frontiers and ports. These were the invention of Claude Chappe, a physician who based his system on preliminary work done by Guillaume Amontons, another physician, a century earlier. It is interesting that while in France telegraphs were pioneered by medical men, in Britain the pioneers were clergymen. The chain of signal stations which connected the Admiralty to the ports was designed by the Rev Lord George Murray, later Bishop of St Davids, while the British army's telegraph service was the creation of the Rev John Gamble who was Chaplain General. Nor was this the only contribution of the Church of England to Britain's defence. The Very Rev Richard Watson, Bishop of Llandaff, who was successively Regius Professor of Divinity and of Chemistry at Cambridge, devised a method of manufacturing gunpowder which enabled 1 kilogram of powder to be used where 2 kilograms would earlier have been needed. In the great tradition of English amateurism Watson admitted that when applying for the professorship of chemistry he knew nothing of the subject but was anxious to learn.

Another French innovation in warfare was the observation balloon. In April 1794 they formed a balloon company using silk spheres filled with hydrogen and at least one balloon was used in action at the battle of Fleurus. The drawback was that each balloon took two days to fill and, after Bonaparte's balloon equipment was captured by the Royal Navy on the way to Egypt in 1798, the idea was allowed to sink into disuse.

It is impossible to generalize on the tactics used by the French army during these wars. The *Ordonnance* of 1791, with its prescription of three-deep line as the normal formation for attack except in certain cases (see p. 16), remained in force until after Waterloo but Carnot's exhortation always to manoeuvre *en masse* remained equally valid. In fact the formation in which any unit attacked became a matter for the commander on the spot who was guided by the nature of the ground, the state of training of his troops and, probably the most important factor, his own preference in the matter based on his experience of what had succeeded

LEFT: A *Représentant en Mission* haranguing French troops

BELOW: General Jourdan (1762–1833)

in previous attacks. Some generals habitually attacked in line, some in column, and some preferred *l'ordre mixte*, a compromise whereby one battalion (or brigade or *demi-brigade*) in line was flanked on each side by another in column. This was a formation much used immediately after the *Amalgame* of 1793 since, in each *demi-brigade* the regular battalion had the training to manoeuvre in line while the less experienced sister battalions formed the flanking columns. Great stress was laid also on the use of light infantry both from the regiments so designated and from the *voltigeur* company which formed part of each line battalion. The function of light infantry in the attack was to form a screen to protect the advance of the main body. A hostile line was particularly susceptible to the galling attacks of skirmishers and it had no effective reply since volley firing was ineffective against men in loose order and partial counter-attacks disordered the line just at the time when it required to be at its most firm to receive an assault. The eventual answer was to be more and better light infantry who could neutralise the attacks of the *voltigeurs*, but in the first decade of the wars no European army could field light infantry which, in quality or quantity, could compete with the French.

What can be asserted is that the French army in the revolutionary period was very much more flexible than any of their opponents who were still tied to the formal and precise manoeuvres of the earlier parts of the century. The French wasted far less time in forming column from line and line from column and could, on occasions, form line from skirmishing order to complete an attack. Thus French assaults were liable to fall on their opponents while they were still checking the dressing of their line.

Nor was it only in tactics that the French had the advantage of speed. Their supply trains were much smaller and thus less likely to delay the march of the fighting troops. Guibert's dictum, culled from Cato, that 'War must supply war', that an army should live at the expense of the countryside it overran, was only partially the reason for this slender waggon train. Once the early crises of the war were over, the governments reverted to the pre-revolutionary practice of providing the armies with food through contractors. The contractors, however, even when they were honest, had great difficulty in finding sufficient capital

44

ABOVE: General Moreau
(1763–1813)

to finance their operations and their task was made no easier by a high and increasing rate of inflation and a high level of corruption prevalent among government officials under the Directory. The army was thus forced to live from the country and requisition and more personal forms of looting became the accepted way of feeding the soldiers since no other method existed.

BONAPARTE AND THE *Armée d'Italie*

When the Directory emerged from the disorders of 13th Vendemaire IV (5 October 1795) as the effective government of France the country as a whole would gladly have seen their leaders make peace with the remaining allies on the basis of *uti possidetis* (i.e., retaining possession of acquisitions already made) but the army insisted on continuing the war, if only to have the chance of collecting its back pay, and the Directory was anxious for a victory to establish its prestige and to divert attention from the cost of living, of which the index, taking 1790 as 100, passed the 5,000 mark in November 1795. Carnot, still at the head of war plans, envisaged a three-pronged attack on Austria with the main offensives being entrusted to the armies facing the Rhine, *Sambre et Meuse* (Jourdan) and *Rhin et Moselle* (Moreau). The *Armée d'Italie* was allotted a subordinate role and its command was given to General Bonaparte (as he had recently re-spelled his name) who was five months short of his twenty-seventh birthday. On the face of it, this was a political appointment. Apart from his distinguished contribution to the attack on Toulon in 1793, Bonaparte, though a regular artillery officer, had seen little active service. On the other hand it was his 'whiff of grapeshot' that had settled matters on 13th Vendemaire and he had subsequently added to the obligations which the Directors owed him by marrying the discarded mistress of the most influential of them. He had also spent some months studying the problems of campaigning in Italy as a member of Carnot's embryo general staff, the *Bureau Topographique*. Napoleon took with him to his new command of the *Armée d'Italie*, a most experienced staff officer, Alexandre Berthier, and three intelligent ADCs, Colonel Joachim Murat, Major Androche Junot, and Captain August Frédéric de Marmont.

Reaching his headquarters at Nice in the last days of March, Bonaparte was faced with an ill-found force. On paper the *Armée d'Italie* was 63,000 strong but, due to sickness, wounds, and widespread desertion, only 37,000 were *présent sous armes*. They were months in arrears with their pay, their rations were issued irregularly, many men lacked boots, and at least 1,000 of the infantry were without muskets. Disaffection was widespread and some units were in open mutiny. There were plenty of guns available but there were only draught horses to move sixty field pieces and a few mountain guns. Transport was almost non-existent. The army's position, on the southern slopes of the Ligurian Alps, with its right secured on neutral Genoa and its left to the north of Nice, was an infertile region while lack of money and the incompetence of the contractors meant that little food could be brought from France. Bonaparte was faced with the choice of taking the army back into France or breaking out into the rich plains of Lombardy. Since

45

the first course was politically unthinkable, he resolved on the second and spent two weeks in making such preparations as were possible. In doing so his decisiveness greatly impressed his three divisional commanders – Sérurier, aged 53, Augereau, 38, and Massena, 37, who had been suspicious of being placed under the orders of an inexperienced stripling. He also endeared himself to his soldiers by bringing them an issue of pay and by promising them the plunder of 'Rich provinces, opulent towns'.

SARDINIA AND LOMBARDY

Opposing him was an Austro-Sardinian army of 56,000 men under the 72-year-old Beaulieu. These were deployed with two corps in the front line and a reserve based on Alessandria in the rear. This reserve moved on 11 April towards Voltri on the French extreme right on a false report that Bonaparte was moving on Genoa.

Seizing his opportunity Bonaparte, who had not intended to attack until 15 April, ordered an immediate attack up the Col de Cadibone where the inner flanks of the two allied corps met. On 12 April, 9,000 French drove 6,000 Austrians out of Montenotte by an enveloping attack and the enemy line was breached. The Austrian left counterattacked fiercely and was held only with difficulty, but as soon as the French grip on the crest of the mountains was firm, Bonaparte turned his main strength westward and drove Colli, with a predominately Sardinian corps, back from defence line to defence line. On 22 April Sérurier led a storming column into the town of Mondovi, thereby forcing an entrance into the Piedmontese plain and on the following evening Colli asked for an armistice. Five days later Sardinia made peace, granting France the right to march troops across her territory and releasing for service elsewhere the 20,000 men of the *Armée des Alpes*, who had been guarding the Franco-Sardinian frontier in Savoy.

Meanwhile Beaulieu, who claimed he had only 16,000 men left under command, was arranging his army for the defence of Lombardy. He relied on the formidable obstacle of the river Po and thought to secure his left by resting it on neutral Parma. In doing so he underestimated the ruthlessness of the new style of warfare. Bonaparte unhesitatingly violated this neutrality by sending his men across the river at Piacenza, pausing only to mulct the Grand Duke of Parma of £80,000 and twenty fine paintings. With their defence line turned and useless, the Austrians retreated as fast as they could to Venetian territory and took up a strong position between Lake Garda and the almost impregnable fortress of Mantua. Bonaparte followed for some of the way but, having driven in the Austrian rearguard at the spectacular but pointless battle of Lodi (10 May) turned aside to enter Milan in triumph. He was greeted as a liberator but the enthusiasm quickly turned to revulsion and revolt when £800,000 was extorted from the city, which was extensively plundered. It was a foretaste of many triumphs and as many revulsions that were to lie ahead.

After a week's rest at Milan, the French army continued their eastward drive and with little trouble beat the Austrians out of their new positions but Mantua, protected by lagoons, marshes, and endemic

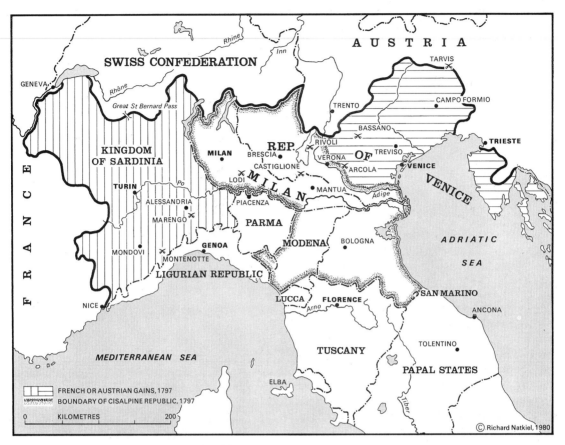

The north Italian theatre of war

fever, was not to be reduced by the field guns of the *Armée d'Italie.* Bonaparte invested the place, sent for siege guns and established an outpost line on the Adige. Then he set off on a fund raising expedition in central Italy before the inevitable Austrian counterstroke developed.

In April and May 1796 Bonaparte established himself as the first general in Europe. Faced with a superior army, he had defeated Sardinia and driven Austria out of all her Italian possessions except the beleaguered fortress of Mantua. It was essentially a general's victory. The Austrian soldiers, and on occasions the Sardinians, had fought at least as well as the French but the Austrian command had been outclassed and outpaced. From the moment that Bonaparte seized the junction point at Montenotte, Beaulieu and his subordinates had irreversibly lost the initiative and were reduced to reacting as best they could to the French moves. They did not come within sight of succeeding. Tied to their slow-moving supply train, while the French had no transport except sixty underfed mules, the Austrians could not cope with the flexibility displayed by their opponents.

The only consolation to be found in Vienna was that the two French thrusts across the Rhine were hanging fire and it was possible for them to switch troops from Germany to Italy so that the situation could be retrieved.

47

CHAPTER FOUR

Castiglione, 5 August 1796

A FTER HIS DISASTROUS PERFORMANCE in Piedmont and Lombardy, Beaulieu was replaced by another septuagenarian, Marshal Sigismond von Würmser, who in his youth had gained a reputation as a dashing leader of advance guards. He brought with him 25,000 men from Germany but his first task was to restore the morale of the remains of Beaulieu's army. In Trento he found 400 officers who had abandoned their men and were idling away their time in the town. The countryside around was full of stragglers and a steady stream of Croats was making its way eastward. The Croats were one of the main sources of strength of the Hapsburg army. These fine natural fighters had originally been raised as auxiliaries to guard the southern frontiers of the Empire against the Turks but they had rendered magnificent service as irregular light infantry against Frederick the Great. When not engaged in battle their habits of looting and rapine had made them as much a menace to their friends as to their enemies and, after the Seven Years' War, steps had been taken to convert them into regular troops, a process that had not been wholly successful. Beaulieu's setback had sickened many of them of military discipline.

The Croats were only one of the nationalities which went to make up the Emperor's army. Seven languages – German, Czech, French, Flemish, Italian, Magyar, and Croat – were officially recognized and several dialects were also used. To add to this linguistic confusion, a very tight bureaucratic control was exercised from Vienna. Each company of infantry had to maintain seventy-two separate files and was required to render two weekly, ten monthly, and two quarterly returns, as well as a consolidated half yearly return. It was scarcely surprising that the company clerk was paid more than the sergeant-major.

Despite these disadvantages it was a far from negligible force. The infantry of the line, especially those from Bohemia, were very staunch and the Hungarians, Tyrolese, and Croats made excellent light infantry. The artillery was good in training and material and the cavalry was the model for Europe. The supply system was very good at delivering the rations although its very size made it an obstruction to fast movement. To set against these virtues, the staff work was precise rather than inspired and most of the generals were too old to cope with the new style

of fluid warfare. Nor had the training of the troops kept abreast of new French techniques. In June 1796 a British liaison officer was horrified to see three battalions drawn up in three-deep line on top of a dyke being shot at from the cover of bushes on the far side of the Adige river. Occasionally the Austrians would fire a ceremonial volley at their invisible tormentors:

By stepping back six or eight yards and lying down on the reverse slope of the dyke, not a shot from the enemy could have told, whereas a loss of nearly 150 men killed and wounded was the consequence of this stupid bravado . . . It is to be observed that the Adige was at this time perfectly unfordable.

Würmser's first task was clear-cut – to relieve Mantua and its garrison of 12,000 men and he had a field force of 48,000 with which to undertake it. He was well informed of the strength of the *Armée d'Italie*, about 44,000, many of them scattered in small garrisons, and knew how dispersed the divisions were. Sérurier's division, reinforced to 10,000 men, was undertaking the siege of Mantua and had the reserve of cavalry, 3,000 strong, close at hand. Although one of the fortified bridgeheads across the lagoon had been taken as early as 3 June, little progress had been made in reducing the city and both garrison and besiegers were losing many sick from malaria. The main part of the covering army was on the Adige. The divisions of Augereau and Despinoy (8,000 men together) held the river line from Bardia to near Verona, and Massena held the line from there to the east shore of Lake Garda with 7,600 men, with orders to keep his main strength at Bussolengo, west of Verona. The long line from the west shore of the lake to Lake Iseo, north-west of Brescia, was watched by Sauret's weak division of 3,800 and, westward again, 3,000 men held Bergamo. Towards the end of July Bonaparte had his tactical headquarters at Montechiaro while Berthier and most of the staff were at Brescia. Thus the covering force was dispersed over a front of more than 130 kilometres.

THE AUSTRIAN PLAN
Two plans were put before Würmser. One came from Colonel Zach, who had been Beaulieu's chief staff officer, and recommended that the great bulk of the army, 40,000 men, should march down the shortest road to Mantua on the east of Garda while the remaining 8,000 men would make demonstrations through the passes on either flank, threatening Brescia and Bassano. The second scheme came from Würmer's own chief of staff, Colonel Duka, a wholehearted believer in the cordon system even on the offensive. He proposed to divide the army into three columns and to attack on a wide front. To the east 7,000 men would go down the Val de Sugano aiming for Verona by way of Bassano and Vicenza. On the western flank 16,000 men under Quasdanovitch would move to the west of the lake and take Brescia before turning to their left to meet the main body which would come down to the east of Garda. This central column would itself be divided into two. The bulk of the infantry under General Melas would move over the high ground

PREVIOUS PAGE: Bonaparte paying tribute to the wounded at Castiglione – an early example of his personality cult

BELOW: Marshal Würmser (1724–1797)

between the lake and the upper Adige valley while the artillery, cavalry, and an escort of infantry would come down the road which followed the valley on the east side of the river. Most unfortunately Würmser chose the second plan since, if he had marched 40,000 men directly to Mantua it would have been impossible for Bonaparte to collect his scattered divisions to oppose him.

Bad as Duka's plan was it achieved considerable early success. At dawn on 29 July, Melas drove Massena's left brigade from the strong La Corona spur on the southern massif of Monte Baldo, which commanded the Adige valley. Simultaneously Quasdanovitch caught Sauret unprepared and seized Salo although Brigadier Guieu with 600 men managed to hold out in a cluster of strongly-built houses backing on to the lake. Soon afterwards 8,000 Austrians entered Brescia, capturing the four companies who formed the garrison and many sick including Joachim Murat. Although they had been aware that an attack was imminent, the French were taken completely by surprise while they were still widely dispersed. Their loss on that day was 1,500 men and 12 guns.

THE FRENCH PLAN

This was a crisis for Bonaparte and, according to his report to the Directory (written eight days later when the decisive battle had been won), he reacted instantly and boldly:

In this difficult situation, with our line broken by a powerful army which would be heartened by its successes, I felt that I must adopt a wide-ranging strategy (plan vaste). By coming down from the Tyrol both by Brescia and by the Adige, the enemy had put me in a central position; if my army was not strong enough to stand against both enemy divisions, it could deal with each of them separately and I was between them. By making a rapid retreat I could surround the enemy at Brescia and make them prisoners or rout them. Then I could return to the Mincio, attack Würmser and drive him back to the Tyrol. To achieve this the siege of Mantua would have to be raised within twenty four hours, although it was on the point of succeeding, and the forty guns already in battery against it would have to be abandoned. If this plan was to succeed we must retire immediately over the Mincio before the two enemy divisions could unite. Fortunately fortune smiled on this scheme.

This version of an heroic and immediate decision has passed into Napoleonic legend as a brilliant stroke. The reality, as told in Bonaparte's own letters, is rather different. The *plan vaste* was the third scheme which he tried to implement and he was only saved from disaster by the fumbling hesitations of his opponent. There may, indeed, be more truth than is generally conceded in Augereau's claim that it was largely or wholly due to his own stiffening that Bonaparte did not order a retreat towards Milan.

Far from deciding on an immediate retreat across the Mincio (*repasser sur-le-champ le Mincio*), his first orders, based on an over-sanguine report from Massena that La Corona could be retaken, were for a concentration of the troops from the lower Adige on the east bank of the Mincio, ready for an advance up the east side of Lake Garda. For this

purpose tactical headquarters were moved from Montechiara, where it would have been excellently placed to direct the manoeuvre to 'surround the enemy at Brescia', first to Castelnovo (30 July) and then to Rover-bella (31 July), both on the east bank of the Mincio. Far from raising the siege of Mantua 'within twenty-four hours', Bonaparte's first orders to Sérurier were to press on with the attack on the remaining *tête-de-pont*, a useless operation if the siege was to be raised.

When it became clear that Würmser could not be held before he debouched into the plain, new orders were issued to take up a defensive position against Würmser which would follow the Mincio as far south as Goito and then swing east on the line of the marshy Molinella stream. Under cover of this Sérurier was to move the siege guns south to the Po where they were to be embarked on twenty-four boats kept ready at Borgoforte.

On 31 July, forty-eight hours after the Austrian attack, the decision was taken to raise the siege during the following night. Any guns that could not be got away to Borgoforte were to be buried and the ammunition was to be thrown into the marsh. The consequence of this delay was that rather than forty guns, which Bonaparte reported as having been lost, 179 fell into Austrian hands.

ATTACK AND COUNTERATTACK

Meanwhile Augereau, reinforced by half of Sérurier's siege corps, was marching his men westward through the night. On 1 August he galloped into Brescia, from which most of the Austrians had been withdrawn, at the head of his cavalry, as befitted an ex-trooper of both the royal French and Russian armies. His infantry followed at their best pace. To the north of him Massena's division left the line of the Mincio and marched towards Lonato to support Sauret and Despinoy who advanced to drive back Quasdanovitch and recapture Salo and Gavardo. The *plan vaste* was, at last, being implemented and the only troops left to face Würmser's central column was the garrison of Peschiera, the fortress guarding the point where the Mincio flows out of the lake, which amounted to 500 infantry and 150 gunners, with a chain of cavalry posts on the Mincio. Behind them, at Castiglione della Stiviere, General Valette with 1,500 men guarded the rear of the troops attacking Quasdanovitch and away to the south Sérurier with his remaining 5,000 men stood at Ponte de Marcaria, guarding the communications with Cremona and Milan.

1 August was a good day, with Brescia and Salo being regained, but on the next day Bonaparte wrote 'Fortune seems to be against us'. On both fronts things went wrong. Sauret was driven out of Salo by a counterattack and Valette lost his nerve and, although his orders were to defend Castiglione at all costs, he retired with half his men, announcing that the remainder were prisoners. In fact they had not been attacked and made their way back to the Chiese whereupon Bonaparte dismissed their pusillanimous general from his command at the head of his troops.

Meanwhile, Würmser was dithering. He had reached Castelnovo on 31 July, sleeping in the house which Bonaparte had occupied on the previous night. Next day he had moved to Valeggio on the Mincio,

sending a strong brigade to blockade Peschiera, and reports reached him that the siege of Mantua had been raised. To confirm this he despatched a small force to reconnoitre Roverbella, where Sérurier had had his headquarters. That town was empty but the commander had no orders to move further south and the task of making contact with Mantua fell to Colonel Baron Vincent, an ADC to the Emperor, who was attached to the army as an observer, and to Colonel Thomas Graham, the British liaison officer. Having spoken to the governor and discovered that the state of Mantua's garrison was not as desperate as had been anticipated, they returned quickly to Valeggio as:

Colonel Thomas Graham, later General Lord Lynedoch (1748–1843)

it seemed to be of the utmost importance that, after issuing orders for the immediate supply of Mantua, not a moment should be lost in sending across the Mincio the greatest possible force which the marshal had it in his power to collect in order to give assistance to the corps of Quasdanovitch which there was too much reason to apprehend had been forced to retire into the mountains. Instead, however, of these decided steps being taken, the headquarters remained all next day at Valeggio and, on the following day, they were transferred to Goito, thus making one day's march in a contrary direction.

The two days thus wasted gave Bonaparte his chance to deal with Quasdanovitch and on 3 August he launched his attack. Sending Augereau's hard-marching division back to reoccupy Castiglione, the other three divisions struck north from the Chiese river. On the left Sauret's division, led by Giueu's brigade, aimed for Salo while Massena's division, supported by Despinoy, advanced on Lonato.

Quasdanovitch's men, though greatly outnumbered, fought well and ambushed Massena's advance guard as it approached Lonato, capturing its commander, General Pijou. The situation was restored by Bonaparte himself who formed two *demi-brigades* in close battalion columns (*en colonne serrée de batallion*) and led them at the centre of the Austrian line. The enemy tried the classic countermeasure of swinging forward their wings so as to fire into the flanks of the column but Massena sent forward skirmishers against both Austrian wings and succeeded in delaying them long enough for Bonaparte's column to break in to their line, whereupon the 15me *Dragons* charged through the gap, recapturing Pijou and three French guns. When the Austrians scattered Bonaparte launched his escort squadron of *Guides* with orders to head them off from Lonato. Led by Androche Junot, the *Guides* charged a regiment of Uhlans (Junot receiving six sabre wounds) but achieved their purpose of heading the fugitive infantry north towards Salo, which fell to Giueu that day. By nightfall Massena held both Lonato and Desenzado, on the lake side, and several Austrian brigades were wandering round the countryside seeking a way of escape.

The action at Lonato is interesting as being one of the few occasions on which Bonaparte took personal command of a small body of infantry. Despite his expressed preference for the *ordre mixte* in the attack, he formed the 18me and 32me *demi-brigades* into battalion columns for this attack. Had the Austrians secured their front with sufficient skirmishers to hold back Massena's *tirailleurs*, the advance of their wings would have

led to the French columns being shot to pieces from three sides.

While Bonaparte was supervising the fighting at Lonato, Augereau was heavily engaged near Castiglione for it was on that day, 3 August, that Würmser finally decided to move westward to join Quasdanovitch. As the troops started their march Colonel Zach rode ahead to mark out a camp near Castiglione which, as a result of Valette's defection, had been reported as unoccupied.

What followed is somewhat obscure. French accounts say that an Austrian battalion succeeded in capturing the castle of Castiglione, which stands high above the houses on the steep hills which separate the plain from Lake Garda, and were only ejected after a sharp struggle. The Austrian version is that Zach, with a small mounted escort, narrowly escaped capture when he found Augereau's leading troops in the town. What is certain is that Augereau secured Castiglione, halted Würmser's advance and ensured that the two Austrian columns could not unite. There was fighting throughout the day and Augereau's men were increasingly outnumbered as the main Austrian strength came up but they held on grimly and even made some advance. Würmser seems to have used little energy and less skill in directing the battle for, according to Graham, the fighting was confined to 'a kind of ravine' where a stream cut into the hills and:

The contest was kept up during the day by a fire of musketry across this gap without either party attempting to force, either by direct attack or by a circuitous route on the flanks, the position held by the other . . . Towards dusk the firing ceased without any advantage having been gained by either side.

During the day the Austrians lost 1,500 men while the French admitted to 150 killed and 500 wounded.

This unexpected check destroyed such determination as Würmser still had. He sent an officer riding off that evening with orders to Quasdanovitch that he should bring his corps round the head of Lake Garda to join the main body on the west bank of the Mincio. He anticipated, rather optimistically, that this manoeuvre would be completed in four days and intended that his own troops would remain meanwhile in the 'accidental position' which they occupied after the fighting of 3 August. It was not an ideal place to withstand a French attack. The right was strong enough, being secured on the sharp hills on the village of Solferino (where, 63 years later, Bonaparte's nephew was to defeat another Austrian army) but the centre and left of the Austrian line received no help from the ground and inclined slightly forward. The whole front was nearly 4 kilometres long and somewhat in front of the left was a small height, Monte Medolano, on which was established a battery of a dozen guns, mostly 12-pounders. Here also, with more courage than acumen, Würmser established his command post. He had 25,000 men in hand.

On this front, 4 August passed quietly, 'scarce a musket shot was exchanged between the advanced sentries'. There was a flurry of excitement at Lonato where Bonaparte had gone to despatch Sauret's division in pursuit of Quasdanovitch up the western side of the lake, while

ordering every other available man to concentrate at Castiglione. A flag of truce was sent into the town demanding its surrender since, it was said, it was surrounded on all sides. Bonaparte had only 1,200 men with him but, guessing that the Austrians were cut off and trying desperately to escape, decided to bluff:

I therefore had the messenger brought to me and his blindfold removed. I told him that if his general hoped to capture the Commander in Chief of the Armée de l'Italie, *he had only to advance to attempt it, but that he should realise that as I was in Lonato, it was obvious that my army would be with me.*

Within a few minutes 4,000 men and two guns were surrendered to him.

Having extracted himself from this imbroglio, he moved his head-quarters to Castenedolo, midway between Brescia and the Chiese river and set about getting his men in position to crush Würmser on the following morning. Massena's division was already on the move to take over the left, northern, end of Augereau's line facing the Austrians and an improvised brigade of grenadiers was formed as a reserve behind the

The battle of Castiglione

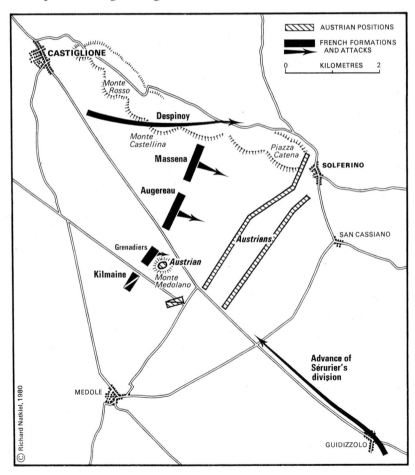

extreme right. Two *demi-brigades* from Despinoy's division north of
Lonato were told to join the army by forced march, in the hope that they
would arrive by dawn on 5 August, and Sérurier was ordered to march
north from Marcaria so as to threaten the Austrian rear. (See note at end
of chapter.) Bonaparte's plan was that Massena and Augereau should
hold the whitecoats in front until Sérurier pressed in on their rear and
Despinoy's detachment turned their right on the hills beyond Solferino.

According to Thomas Graham, the French started at daybreak on 5
August to make a 'vigorous attack at every point of our line'. On the
other hand Bonaparte, a less reliable witness, wrote:

*At 6 am nothing had happened. I then ordered a move to the rear by the whole
army in order to draw the enemy after us. This movement had some of the effect
which I hoped.*

What actually happened was that the two French divisions attacked the
Austrian line but did not press matters and were ordered back in the
hope that the Austrians would follow them. It is most improbable that
this did happen, despite French accounts of the Austrian right swinging
forward, for it was totally contrary to Würmser's plan to advance until
Quasdanovitch had joined him and Graham makes no reference to an
Austrian counterattack. The truth is probably that as the French pulled
back they were pursued by some *Jäger* companies for a short distance.

The only serious fighting taking place at this time was around
Monte Medolano where Marmont, now a colonel, brought forward
eighteen guns to neutralize the fire of the battery on the hillock which
would otherwise have enfiladed the French infantry as they advanced.
Round the foot of the little height there was an exchange of charges and
countercharges between the Austrian cavalry and those of the French
under Kilmaine. Several of the Austrian attacks were led by Würmser in
person, conspicuous from the fact that he was always closely followed by
a footman in yellow livery.

At this stage the Austrians had every hope of holding their ground
but, towards the end of the morning, news arrived of a large body of
French approaching from Guidizzolo in their rear. This could only be
Sérurier's division of whose whereabouts Würmser's staff had no idea
'except the conjecture that [it] had been sent to the lower Adige'. It says
little for the Austrian light cavalry that they had failed to locate a body
of 5,000 men who had been stationary for several days only 30
kilometres from their flank and had for twenty-four hours been marching towards them.

For some time Würmser had been under pressure from Colonel Zach
to wheel back his exposed left flank but his only reaction to the news of a
large French force approaching his rear was to send two squadrons of
hussars to check if the news was true. It was not until the hussars
brought back prisoners from Sérurier's division (commanded on that
day by Fiorella) that he would agree to:

throw back the infantry that extended across the plain and, by placing them en
potence *on the ridge, show a front to this new enemy and subsequently to give an
opportunity of withdrawing with the least disorder possible to Valeggio.*

A view from the French side of the battle of Castiglione; the tower in the centre marks the village of Solferino

It was an admission of defeat and the manoeuvre itself proved disastrous. It was impossible to withdraw the guns from Monte Medolano but as soon as their fire stopped the French cavalry swept round the now open flank and reached the village of San Cassiano. Nor could the Austrian infantry carry out their realignment:

This hazardous movement in the heat of an action required a greater degree of discipline and steadiness than these battalions were capable of exhibiting. Instead of each battalion marching each in succession by the left on its proper point of alignment, the movement was made by all the battalions at once, and the heads of these different columns, pressing in on each other, became a confused mass which never allowed of the intended disposition taking place.

57

General Augereau
(1757–1816) later
Marshal Duke of
Castiglione

Seeing the confusion that the Austrian infantry was falling into,
Bonaparte told Massena and Augereau to advance and simultaneously
threw in Despinoy's two *demi-brigades*, just arrived breathless from their
forced march, against Solferino. The Austrians there did not stand. They
could see the confusion on their left and 'considering it to be the signal
to retreat, began to break from the position which they had so long
defended'.

As Graham reported:

*A scene of confusion and rout ensued which must have been attended with the
almost total destruction of the whole army had the enemy profited by their
advantage. They contented themselves, however, with harassing the rear by small
parties of cavalry and light infantry.*

The fact was that the French army was exhausted by the constant
marches and countermarches of the past eight days. Even Bonaparte

admitted that they were 'worn out with fatigue'. At one stage Augereau's division had marched 80 kilometres in 36 hours, fighting an action at the end of it and Massena wrote to his father that he had had less than four hours sleep in eight days. They halted on the ground they had won and let their opponents straggle away to Valeggio. The day had cost the Austrians 3,000 men and 18 guns, making their loss over the eight days some 8,000 men, 70 guns, and most of their transport. Bonaparte reported the overall French loss as 2,000 killed or wounded and 1,300 prisoners.

The French had succeeded in driving the Austrians back across the Mincio but Bonaparte had failed to destroy Würmser's army as he had hoped to do. That he had been able to achieve so much was due less to his own actions than to the hesitations of his opponent who, on 1 and 2 August, had the campaign in his hands but failed to advance until it was too late.

There is some evidence that on 31 July Bonaparte's confidence in himself and his army faltered and he certainly contemplated retreating to the Oglio near Cremona. As it was, the desperate risk of fighting on two fronts and relying on the timidity of his opponent paid off, thanks to the remarkable marching power of the French infantry. No other army in Europe could have managed to switch its strength from one side to the other with such speed and determination.

Even if Augereau did exaggerate when he claimed to have given his commander-in-chief the will to continue the fight, Bonaparte never forgot the debt he owed to the general. Whatever complaints he received about Augereau's *bêtises* on and off the battlefield or about his unbridled looting, he would always reply 'Ah! Remember what he did for us at Castiglione!' and Castiglione was the title he gave him when, in 1808, he created him a duke.

FOOTNOTE

One of the mysteries about the campaign of Castiglione is the order printed in the *Correspondance de Napoleon 1er* (Vol. i. no. 830) to General Sérurier on 4 August, the day before the battle. This tells him to march with all his troops to Pontevico and take up the most suitable position available. Pontevico is on the river Oglio and on the road from Cremona to Brescia and is thus south-west of the intended battlefield at Castiglione, a position from which Sérurier's division could not possibly affect the fighting on the following day. It would, conversely, be an ideal position to cover the retreat of the French army on Cremona and Milan.

The *Correspondance* is not without its copying errors (and includes at least one forgery) but the *Service Historique* of the French army was kind enough to check the contemporary copy in their archives and to confirm that the place name in that is also Pontevici.

There is no evidence to suggest that Sérurier disobeyed his orders and marched on the Austrian rear on his own initiative so that the possible explanations must be either that a mistake was made in the contemporary copy or that Bonaparte anticipated a retreat when he sent this order (which must have been after midday since it was sent from Castenedolo), and later sent another order to march north on the Austrian rear and that this second order has not survived.

CHAPTER FIVE

The Alpine Barrier

LACK OF COURAGE was not among Marshal Würmser's defects and early in September he made another attack to raise the siege of Mantua, using the Brenta pass. This effort was frustrated by Bonaparte at Bassano (8 September) and ended with Würmser himself and many of his men being forced to join the garrison of the besieged city. Again the Austrians found more troops and another elderly marshal, Joseph Alvinsky von Berberek, to command them. His first foray towards Mantua was narrowly held at Arcola (15–17 November) and his second at Rivoli (14 January 1797). By this time Mantua was in desperate straits and it eventually surrendered on 2 February.

After a pause to reorganize the *Armée d'Italie*, Bonaparte led it north to strike at Vienna. Coupled with pressure from the *Armée du Rhin* which had reached the Danube, the presence of Massena's division at Bruck, within 160 kilometres of their capital, induced the Austrians to seek peace. In the treaty of Campo-Formio, a treaty largely dictated by Bonaparte despite his instructions from the Directory, Belgium was ceded to France, Lombardy relinquished to become a French puppet state, and the territory of the neutral republic of Venice became an Austrian province.

With the land war ended for the time being, the Directory had to contemplate seriously the possibility of invading England and it was natural that they should appoint the triumphantly successful General Bonaparte to command the *Armée d'Angleterre*. Having examined the resources available, he came to the conclusion that the French navy was not capable at that time of ensuring the safety of the Channel crossing without which the invasion would be 'the most daring and difficult task ever undertaken'. He recommended instead that 'We could undertake an eastern expedition to threaten England's trade with the Indies.'

On 19 May 1798 Bonaparte sailed from Toulon with a powerful squadron and a flock of troop transports. On 1 July, having evaded the Royal Navy and seized Malta, the *Armée d'Orient*, 40,000 strong, landed near Alexandria. They captured the city on the following day and, having defeated the Mameluke army in the shadow of the Pyramids, occupied Cairo on 24 July. Their aim was to make the Mediterranean a French lake, to halt the lucrative British trade with the Levant and to

threaten the British predominance in India. Despite the early successes the expedition was a total failure. On 1 August Nelson found the French fleet unprepared and destroyed it at the battle of the Nile thus severing all but the most tenuous links with France. Turkey, to whom the nominal suzerainty over Egypt belonged, massed her armies in Palestine to recover her province. Bonaparte struck across the desert, defeated the forward Turkish troops but was brought to a halt by the fortress of Acre where the garrison was inspired by the presence of Colonel Phélipeaux, a former classmate of Bonaparte but now a British officer, and Captain Sir Sidney Smith RN with his Royal Marines. Balked at Acre, Bonaparte was forced back to Egypt where he defeated a Turkish seaborne invasion but was faced by the mounting demoralisation of his army, due to their isolation and the abortive foray into Palestine. Such news as trickled through from Paris was uniformly depressing and, on 23 August 1799, Bonaparte with a handful of picked officers – Berthier, Murat, Lannes, Marmont, Bessières, and a few others – abandoned the *Armée de l'Orient* and sailed away in the ex-Venetian frigate *Muiron* (40 guns).

They reached France on 9 October to find the country in a desperate situation. The victory at the Nile had called into being a second great European coalition, only the Prussians abstaining, and even allying those perpetual enemies the Russians and the Turks. All Bonaparte's Italian conquests had been lost and France was only saved from an irresistible invasion by the inability of the Russians and the Austrians to co-operate and by the massive determination of Massena's defence of Switzerland. The Directory was wholly unable to cope with either the military or the economic situation and it was finally brought down by the last of the endemic *coups d'état* on 9–10 November. The *coup* of 18 Brumaire VII established Bonaparte as First Consul and *de facto* supreme ruler of France.

The Consulate received popular support because it seemed to offer stable government and peace. Bonaparte recognized that an exhausted France needed peace and made genuine efforts to obtain it provided that it could be peace on his own terms, leaving Belgium, Piedmont, and Genoa as parts of France with Holland and Switzerland as French satellites. Since Austria and Britain would not accept these terms, the Consulate could only obtain peace by waging victorious war and the First Consul immediately set about improving the army. The engineering services were purged and improved, the artillery were at last provided with drivers who were soldiers rather than hired civilians, and the Consular Guard was reorganized on the basis of two battalions of grenadiers, a company of *chasseurs à pied*, a squadron of *grenadiers à cheval*, another of *chasseurs à cheval*, and a company of artillery of which one detachment (*escouade*) were horse gunners. Bearing in mind that the Guard was eventually to take the field 47,283 strong, it is interesting to observe that at this time, Bonaparte was definite in laying down that its strength should not exceed 2,100. Great care was taken of the morale of the soldiers. It was even suggested that the main buildings of Versailles should be taken over as an extension of *Les Invalides* for the care of disabled soldiers. The troops still in Egypt were not forgotten and the Ministry of the Interior was instructed to 'assemble a troupe of actors

PREVIOUS PAGE: A later and somewhat idealized impression of Bonaparte at the battle of Rivoli

(*comédiens*) to go to Egypt. It would be a good idea if some *danseuses* were included'. To raise morale generally Rouget de Lisle, composer of the *Marseillaise*, was commissioned to write 'A hymn embodying sentiments that would be suitable for every circumstance of war and to spread the idea that peace comes from victory'.

Meanwhile the military situation was bleak. In Italy the French were confined to a strip of coast from Nice to Genoa and a miserable army of 28,000 fit men, without pay or regular rations, was facing an Austrian force of nearly 100,000. Beyond the Rhine 120,000 more Austrians were massing in the Black Forest ready, it seemed, to invade eastern France. There were further royalist outbreaks in the west and British raids were expected on the north coast. In December 1799 Bonaparte was writing to his commander in St Malo that:

According to all reports reaching the Consuls, the English are intending to seize grain from the départements *in revolt in order to feed London where there is a shortage.*

The only consolations were that the Russians seemed to be withdrawing from the coalition in disgust and that the Austrians appeared to have decided that Switzerland was neutral territory. Not only had they decided not to attempt to advance through the country but they had guarded its frontiers with only the lightest forces.

Bonaparte thus had a central position with the chance of striking either east or south. To the north he amalgamated all the existing forces into one *Armée du Rhin* which was 120,000 strong and commanded by Moreau. The *Armée d'Italie* was confided to the indomitable Massena who, by bringing with him some pay and a few reinforcements, was able to convert it into a small but effective fighting force of 36,000 men. Between these two armies an *Armée de Réserve* was to be raised around Dijon from where it could strike either across the Rhine or over the Alps. Although its ultimate destination was left open it was always intended to move through Switzerland. On 9 January 1800 orders were given for the re-establishment of the arsenal at Auxonne, between Dijon and the Swiss border, which was to be responsible for the production of mountain warfare equipment. Arrangements were also made for sledges to be constructed at Grenoble.

The first scheme for the *Armée de Réserve* was sent confidentially to Berthier, for the time being Minister for War, on 25 January. It envisaged three *grands corps* each 18–20,000 strong and commanded by a *lieutenant général en chef* with a brigadier-general as chief of staff. Each *grand corps* was to consist of two infantry divisions, each of two brigades. There would also be two light cavalry regiments and sixteen guns, twelve field and four horse artillery, under a senior artillery officer. Administration would be in the hands of an *Ordonnateur* and three Commissaries.

In previous campaigns *ad hoc* groupings of divisions had been made for specific operations but here, for the first time, were deliberately planned corps of all arms with their own administrative structure, each being in fact a self-contained army in miniature. These corps

organizations were to give at the higher level the flexibility that the better devised deployment drills gave at regimental level. The combination of self-contained formations and easily deployable troops was to make the French army all but unbeatable until their opponents adopted similar techniques.

Although the *Armée de Réserve* was planned with great care, it was difficult to find men to fill its ranks. The reinforcements for the *Armées du Rhin et d'Italie* and the need to raise an *Armée de l'Ouest* to pacify La Vendée stretched France's manpower resources to the utmost. The first troops allocated to Dijon were the depot battalions of units stranded in Egypt and the remains of regiments which had been wrecked in Italy in 1799 (*demi-brigades ruinées*) which were made up to strength with conscripts. The greatest service was done by General Brune who, with a mixture of enterprise, mobility, and wisely applied clemency, took the heart out of the rebellion and thus was able to release the equivalent of a whole corps from the *Armée de l'Ouest*.

The existence of the *Armée de Réserve* was made public in a Consular decree in early March but great care was taken to let the outside world think that it was an improvised force intended only to make a last ditch defence against apprehended invasion. Veterans were summoned back to the colours and it was made known that not only those who had evaded the conscription (*réfractaires*) but even deserters 'who wish to show that it was not cowardice that guided them', would be accepted for service. These measures had the effect of making the Austrians discount the army's existence and not only the Austrians were deceived. The First Consul had to write to Moreau explaining that the '*Armée de Réserve ne sera pas sur le papier*'. Perhaps some of the belief in the unreality of the army was due to the command being given to Berthier who, with his many virtues, was no field commander. The reason for his appointment was that the Consular constitution forbade any of the Consuls to command an army in person and a titular commander was required.

THE ALPINE CAMPAIGN
Bonaparte intended that the campaign should be opened in mid-April by the *Armée du Rhin*. Moreau's orders, issued on 22 March were:

to drive the Austrian forces opposed to you into Bavaria so as to interupt his communications with Milan by Lake Constance and the Grisons [East Switzer-land]

He was then to send 30,000 of his best troops to cross the St Gothard and Simplon passes to join the *Armée de Réserve* in Lombardy. Meanwhile Massena was to keep the enemy in play around Genoa:

The Austrians, according to their custom, will make a three-pronged attack. Evade two of these and fall upon the third with your whole force.

Unfortunately the Austrians attacked first and so by 18 April Massena with 12,000 men was penned up in Genoa with 60,000 Austrians under Baron Melas in front and the British Mediterranean fleet behind him.

Supplies in the city were short and only a thin screen of French troops, covered the southern frontiers. Since the *Armée de Réserve* was not ready to move everything hinged on how long Massena could hold on in Genoa.

There was a flurry of activity in Paris and an ADC was sent, riding *à franc étrier* to Châlons-sur-Marne to despatch 6,000 muskets and six field forges to Dijon while another had to escort a million francs and 45,000 kilograms of lead to the same destination. Yet another messenger set off carrying two urgently-needed bullet moulds. Meanwhile orders went to Berthier to move all available troops to Geneva and from there to ship all the guns and supplies up the Lake of Geneva to Villeneuve. As soon as they had arrived the army was to cross the Alps by either the Great St Bernard or the Simplon. The nervous army commander was reassured that:

Whatever happens in Italy the Austrian army is involved at Genoa and Savona and is in no position to hold the mountain passes. It is too dispersed to be able to resist the 40,000 men whom you can collect.

Despite all the urgency it was 13 May before the advance guard, two divisions under Lannes, could leave the head of Lake Geneva. The administrative arrangements had been made with scrupulous care. While all mounted men were to take eight days' rations on their horses, Lannes was instructed that, as far as the infantry were concerned:

You will move to St Maurice on 13th May where you will draw biscuit for four days, 13th–16th May. On 15th you will be at the foot of the pass and on passing through St Pierre you will draw biscuit for three more days, 17th–19th May.

Thus every man was to receive seven days' biscuit which should see him through to Aosta while detachments of beef cattle would accompany the army on the hoof. Beyond Aosta it should be possible to start living off the country but 2,000 mules had been accumulated to ferry forward supplies, each mule having a load of 200 rations of biscuit so that, according to Bonaparte's estimate (which matched almost exactly that which Wellington made in Spain ten years later) '50,000 men require 2,000 mules for eight days'.

Moving the artillery over the snow-covered passes presented the most difficult problem. The gun carriages were dismantled and carried in sections by the infantry, but the barrels were a different proposition, the barrel of an 8-pounder weighing 580 kilograms. It had been hoped to move them on rollers but these proved uncontrollable on ice and Marmont, commanding the artillery, had them replaced with:

fir trees which were hollowed out to act as a sheath for the barrel. The underside of the trunk was flattened and the front rounded so that it would run smoothly. A curved lever, stuck in the muzzle, was held by a gunner, who steered the conveyance and stopped it turning over.

Lannes kept to his timetable exactly and at dawn on 16 May his troops,

refreshed by wine and cheese provided by the monks of the Hospice of St Bernard, started down the southern slope, driving in the Austrian outposts and reached Aosta where they were joined by another division which had crossed the Little St Bernard pass. On 17 May they chased 1,500 Austrians out of Châtillon but on the following day the advance was halted by the little fortress of Bard which blocked the Dora Beltea valley at a narrow section. An attempt to storm the place was repulsed with heavy loss and for a time it seemed that the whole campaign would founder on the stubborn resistance of the Austrian Colonel Bernkopf with 400 men and 17 guns. A track over the mountains was found by which infantry and cavalry could by-pass Bard but there was no chance

ABOVE: The French army approaching the Hospice of St Bernard

OPPOSITE: Bonaparte crossing the Alps

66

The *Armée de Réserve* starting on the descent into Italy

of guns using the track and it was not until the night of 24–25 May that two 4-pounders and a waggon were smuggled past the fort, their wheels muffled in straw and men replacing horses in the shafts. Two 8-pounders and two howitzers followed on the next night.

Meanwhile, across the Rhine, Moreau had gone reluctantly forward and on 4 May had won a victory at Stockach, near the northern end of Lake Constance. Instead of detaching 30,000 good troops to move south into Italy, he had merely sent 20,000 assorted men under Moncey to march over the St Gothard. Only 11,000 of them ever reached Italy. To the south-west, Melas had driven back the screen on the French frontier and had taken Savona and Nice. Massena in Genoa was nearing the end of his endurance. He had 3,000 men in hospital and the civilians were dying of starvation at a rate of 400 a day. He calculated that his supplies would be exhausted by 30 May.

Despite the desperate situation in Genoa, Bonaparte did not march directly to relieve it. Instead he turned east and moved on Milan. Apart from the political significance of capturing the city, there were three reasons for this move. It put the French squarely across the Austrian communications; it put him in touch with Moncey's corps from the *Armée du Rhin* and a reserve supply route over the St Gothard; it enabled him to seize more guns from the arsenal in Milan since Fort Bard continued to block the St Bernard route until 1 June.

The French entered Milan on 2 June and on that day Melas at last awoke to the danger in his rear and gave orders for the siege of Genoa to be raised so that the besieging corps could march against 'the army from Germany'. Also on that day Massena opened negotiations for a surrender and, unwilling to lose the prize he had sought so long, Melas postponed his withdrawal for two days when the 9,000 survivors of the garrison began to be repatriated to France.

Bonaparte learned of Massena's surrender from some captured Austrian mail which reached him in Milan on 8 June. He learned also that Melas intended to concentrate his army on Alessandria and this led him to think that the Austrian would either move on Turin and try to escape on the north bank of the Po or would move on Genoa where, supplied by the Royal Navy, he could hold out indefinitely. Neither of these courses would give the Consulate the spectacular victory that it needed to consolidate its position and lead to peace and it became an obsession with Bonaparte that Melas must be headed off from either or both of these moves. In attempting to do so he almost fumbled the chance of the great battle that he was anxious to fight.

Melas, as it happened, had not considered either of these plans. His first intention had been to defeat the *Armée de Réserve* while it was astride the Po but this scheme became impracticable when Lannes, leading Bonaparte's advance guard westward, roundly beat an Austrian delaying force of almost twice his own strength at Montebello, near Casteggio, on 9 June. Melas in consequence decided that his only chance lay in concentrating a sufficiently powerful force at Alessandria to enable him to smash a way through to Lombardy, in effect to engage in exactly the same kind of head-on collision that Bonaparte wanted.

Simultaneously Bonaparte was dividing his forces so as to bar every road by which Melas might escape. The *Armée de Réserve*, including Moncey's column and a small force which had joined from the *Armée d'Italie*, had 53,000 men in Italy. Of these 15,000, including the garrison of Milan, faced east from Piacenza to Lake Maggiore, 4,500 were on the north bank of the upper Po, and 1,000 more were near Milan awaiting orders. Bonaparte had a striking force of 32,000 with which he marched on Alessandria. They reached the Scrivia river near Tortona on 12 June and there they were joined by some guns, released from the Bard bottleneck, which made the army's strength in artillery up to 41 pieces. By this time Melas had succeeded in collecting nearly 31,000 men, apart from the garrison of 3,000, in Alessandria.

CHAPTER SIX

Marengo,
14 June 1800

ON THE AFTERNOON OF 13 JUNE the French advance guard, Gardanne's augmented division (5,300 infantry, 685 cavalry, and 2 guns) drove the Austrian covering force, 4,000 strong, back towards Alessandria. By 6 pm the Austrians were back to the village of Marengo, only 4 kilometres from the place where the Bormida river protects the eastern approach to Alessandria. Gardanne decided to attack the village in strength and his opponent General O'Reilly, one of the many officers of Irish descent in the Hapsburg service, decided not to stand against him as he had in his rear the Fontanove stream, a drainage ditch with steep banks and a marshy bottom. The French therefore followed their opponents until they came under fire from the fourteen guns which Melas had established in a *tête de pont* on the east bank of the Bormida.

Gardanne, a mediocre general, then considered his work done and settled down with his outposts between the river, on the left, and the Alessandria–Marengo road on his right. He reported, falsely, that he had driven O'Reilly across the Bormida. He also gave Bonaparte to understand that he had destroyed the bridge across that river. Marmont, now a general, realized that both bridge and *tête-de-pont* were still intact and brought forward eight guns in an attempt to overcome the fire of the Austrian battery. He was unsuccessful and went back to Gardanne, whom he found sitting in a ditch, to propose that the infantry should storm the fortification. When Gardanne refused, Marmont started to ride back 11 kilometres to Bonaparte's headquarters. Being overtaken by a heavy storm and the road being abominable, he decided to spend the night in a wayside farmhouse and was not able to report to the First Consul until the morning.

Bonaparte was still convinced that Melas would either make for Genoa or try to break north, crossing the Po at Valenza. To guard against the first move he had, at noon, ordered Desaix with Boudet's division (5,316 men) to march south-west through Rivalta so as to cut the Alessandria–Genoa road at Serravilla. During the evening a story from an Austrian deserter was brought in to the effect that Melas had made a detachment to Acqui, 32 kilometres to his right rear. This story was true and reinforced Bonaparte's conviction that Melas was intending to move to a flank. In fact the Austrian detachment consisted of only

a single squadron of dragoons, 115 men, but Bonaparte ordered Lapoype to take his division (3,462 strong) towards Valenza. Further confirmation of Bonaparte's delusion came with Gardanne's report that O'Reilly was on the west bank of the Bormida behind a broken bridge. The destruction of the bridge was also, according to Bonaparte, reported by his ADC, Lauriston, though that officer always denied that he made such a report.

Convinced that he had nothing to fear from a frontal attack, Bonaparte went to bed 10 kilometres behind Marengo with his army widely dispersed. Gardanne's 5,900 men were at and in front of Marengo with Chambarlhac's division (3,400) in close support. These two divisions with two cavalry regiments and 6 or 8 guns were supervised by General Victor and there was no reinforcement nearer than General Lannes with Wattrin's division (5,000) and 12 guns (5 of them Austrian pieces captured at Montebello), bivouacked 7 kilometres behind Marengo near San Giuliano Vecchio. In succession behind them were the main body of the cavalry (2,500), Monnier's division (3,600 with 2 guns) and, close to headquarters, the Consular Guard (1,000 infantry, 250 cavalry, and 8 guns).

Meanwhile Melas in Alessandria had allowed himself to be haunted by the fear that he would be crushed between the *Armée d'Italie* and the *Armée de Réserve*. He believed that the former force had pushed 12,000 men forward towards Savona and Voltri and that it would soon be reinforced by Massena with the former garrison of Genoa so as to make the total corps in his rear, according to his calculations, 22,000. In fact there were scarcely 11,000 men in all facing him on the west and the

PREVIOUS PAGE: Desaix dying as he leads the attack of Boudet's division against the Austrian column at Marengo

BELOW: The battle of Marengo

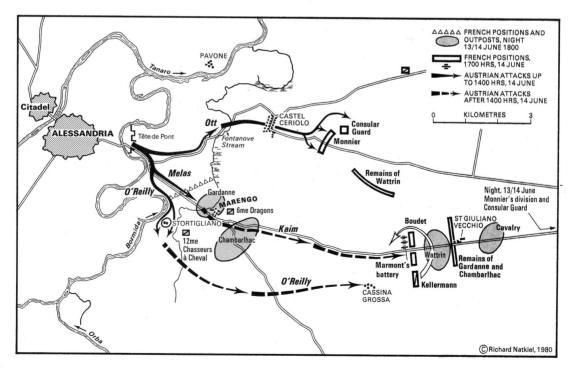

garrison of Genoa was in no state to undertake any exertions. Believing however that he was threatened by 22,000 men to the west and 35,000 to the east, Melas decided that:

So situated and with the destiny of Italy at stake, our only course was to attack the enemy with the aim of cutting our way through to the Hereditary Lands [Milan and Mantua] on the south bank of the Po, thus bringing help to the threatened fortresses of Mantua, Legnano and Verona while covering the west Tyrol [Trentino].

He gave orders to launch an attack to the east at dawn on 14 June. He divided his field force, 23,000 infantry, 7,600 cavalry and 100 guns, into three unequal columns.

The main column of 20,238 men, including 37 squadrons of cavalry, was to attack straight down the road through Marengo and San Giuliano making for Tortona and Piacenza. Its right would be covered by O'Reilly with only 3,000 men. On the left Lieutenant-General Ott with 7,500 men, including only 4 squadrons, was to move on Sale but Melas anticipated that it would find the French holding Castel Ceriola. If Ott could not force his way through at this point he was to fall back towards the Bormida, drawing the French after him. He would then detach some of the powerful cavalry force from the centre column to the left and cut the French off.

To make the debouchment from the fortress as quick as possible, the Austrian engineers had put up a pontoon bridge within the *tête de pont* but, although there were now two bridges across the Bormida, there was only one gate to that earthwork and none of the columns could emerge until O'Reilly, whose detachment had spent the night on the east bank, had driven in Gardanne's outposts. This done, the leading division of the centre column, 6 battalions and 9 squadrons under Lieutenant-General Haddick, marched out and, covered by the fire of 16 guns, formed three-deep line with each flank resting on the Bormida.

This covering bombardment was clearly heard at French headquarters at Toro de Garofoli, $12\frac{1}{2}$ kilometres to the east, where Bonaparte had just confirmed the order for Lapoype's division to march on Valenza. Even when, at about 9.30 am, a message from Victor told him that the enemy were massing for a major attack he refused to believe it, asserting that it could only be a diversion to conceal the flank march that he expected. It took Marmont's report to convince him of the truth:

The First Consul, astonished by the news, said that an Austrian attack seemed impossible and added 'General Gardanne told me that he had reached the river and destroyed the bridge'. I replied, 'General Gardanne made a false report. Last night I was closer to the tête de pont *than he ever went. It is neither taken nor blockaded by our posts and the enemy has been able to debouch from it in his own time.'*

OVERLEAF: The French army at the end of its retreat near San Giuliano. In the distance can be seen Alessandria, showing how far they had fallen back

Realizing the danger at last, orders were sent for all the available troops – the divisions of Wattrin and Monnier, the cavalry, and the Consular

Guard – to march westward while ADC's were sent to recall Desaix and Lapoype. Until they arrived there would be only 22,000 French against 31,000 Austrians.

THE AUSTRIANS ATTACK

Fortunately for the French the enemy were making slow progress. Melas' detailed orders called for extreme deliberation. He had ordered the centre column to form in four lines, the first consisting of Haddick's division and the second of Kaim's (7 battalions) also in line. Behind them would come the 1,800 horsemen of Elsnitz' cavalry division and in rear, marching in column, Morzin's 11 battalions of grenadiers. With only one narrow gateway from which they could emerge, the deployment of this column was certain to be slow and it was made much slower when, at 9 am a message arrived from the squadron of dragoons detached to Acqui reporting that they were being attacked by 'a heavy column of cavalry followed by infantry'. Since there were no substantial French forces near Acqui on that morning, it can only be supposed that the squadron leader had met a patrol probing forward from the *Armée d'Italie* and had magnified it in his imagination into a force of all arms.

False though this information was, it confirmed Melas' worst fears of being crushed between two French armies and he reacted by ordering Nimptsch's cavalry brigade, half his cavalry division, to march immediately on Acqui. The confusion caused by turning six strong squadrons in the confined space inside the *tête de pont*, already packed with infantry and guns waiting to get forward, greatly delayed the deployment while Ott's left-hand column had to wait on the west bank of the Bormida until the cavalry had filed back across the bridges.

Impatient of the delay, Haddick sent his division against Marengo without waiting for the whole column to be formed. His six battalions made a brave show in their white coats, advancing in line with their bands playing and their colours flying. They were halted at the Fontanove ditch, deep, marshy, and edged with a dense thicket while Gardanne's division on the other side poured volleys into the Austrians as they struggled to cross. A few men gained the far side only to be shot down and Haddick, recognizing that his task was impossible, ordered a retreat. Hardly had he done so than he was mortally wounded before he could consult Kaim who, as soon as Haddick's men had passed through his own division, threw his own seven battalions at the obstacle only to be repulsed in the same way. It was now recognized that the Fontanove could not be crossed without footbridges and the only pioneers available were with the grenadier division in the rear.

While the bridges were being brought forward, Melas ordered some cavalry to search for a crossing place on the right and to charge in on the flank of the defenders. Three squadrons of the Emperor's Dragoons did succeed in getting across at a point where the horses could pass in single file but, while they were still forming to charge, they were charged in their turn by French cavalry and driven over the steep banks into the stream, an experience few of them survived.

On the right O'Reilly's men were held up by the farmhouse of Stortigliano, in the narrow gap between the Bormida and the Fon-

tanove. Held by 400 men of the 44me and 101re *demi-brigades* the garrison was weakened when the hundred men of the 101re decided that their proper place was with their own unit. The remainder, although they were surrounded and suffered 194 casualties, held out until evening, although they could not entirely block the Austrian advance against the French left.

When eventually Ott extricated his left-hand column from the bridgehead he moved fast and effectively. He crossed the Fontanove without opposition and reached Castel Ceriolo, brushing away a few light infantry from Wattrin's division which Lannes had succeeded in throwing into the village. Seeing that there was no French force coming from Sale, he decided to ignore his orders and swing to his right in support of the deadlocked centre column. By this time Wattrin's main body was approaching and managed to reach Castel Ceriolo but Ott counterattacked them with such violence that they reeled back and Bonaparte was forced to send the infantry of the Consular Guard to support them.

The Guard, 1,000 strong, came up on Wattrin's right in close columns at deploying distance covered, at sixty paces, by a screen of skirmishers. Ott sent the Lobkowitz dragoons against them but the Guard unlimbered four light guns, opened with grape and forced the cavalry to turn, whereupon two hussar regiments charged and broke them only to be repulsed in their turn by two battalions of the Spleny regiment. Supported by a battalion of Fröhlich's regiment, the Spleny continued their advance until they came close to the Guard when an evenly balanced exchange of fire took place at close range with neither side gaining any advantage. The situation was resolved when four squadrons from the centre column charged on to the Guard from the rear, taking their guns and forcing them back. With Monnier's division still not effectively in action, the French right was now in a desperate state and, almost simultaneously, Marengo fell.

The village was in the charge of Rivaud, one of Chambarlhac's brigadiers, who had two battalions (1/ and 2/43me) in the houses and two more in support:

At 1 o'clock I went to the help of the village with the 3rd battalions of both the 43me and the 96me and pushed my left forward against the enemy. I was immediately charged by 3,000 grenadiers. We halted their attack with well sustained platoon fire so that they retreated. Fresh troops came at us again but we stopped this attack also and tried to advance but we were halted after ten paces by a deep ditch [Fontanove] and there followed an exchange of volleys, lasting a long quarter of an hour, at point blank range. Men fell like hail on both sides. Half my line were down and every mounted man in the brigade was killed or wounded. I received a grapeshot in the thigh.

This gallant defence could not last. Some men of the Archduke Joseph's regiment managed to secure a foothold on the east bank of the Fontanove and, supported by a shower of grape, the pioneers managed to put footbridges across. Five grenadier battalions poured across and struck at the remnants of Victor's men. With Ott pressing in from the

Trooper, 5^e *Cuirassiers*
(Prussian Campaign 1806)

Napoleon's cavalry

The main strength of Napoleon's heavy cavalry, the type used for shock action, lay in his fourteen regiments of cuirassiers (LEFT), so called because their predecessors had worn the *cuirasse*, a coat of heavy leather. They wore steel helmets to protect their heads and, about 1809, all were issued with steel body armour which gave some protection against musketry.

Light cavalry, used principally for reconnaissance and outpost work, consisted of *chasseurs-à-cheval* and hussars (BELOW RIGHT). The duties of the two types were identical but hussars were dressed in an imaginary imitation of Hungarian shepherd clothing. The *kolbak* (busby) was worn by

other ranks only in the *élite* squadron; in other squadrons the troopers wore an infantry-style shako.

Napoleon was no more successful than other generals in persuading his dragoons (BELOW LEFT) to act as mounted infantry. The fact that they wore the Grecian-style helmet with a flowing horsehair tail, a headgear wholly unsuitable for dismounted fighting, demonstrates that French dragoons had won their fight to be considered as medium-heavy cavalry. Dragoons and hussars carried carbines in addition to their sabres but cuirassiers had no firearms except horse-pistols

Trooper, Centre Company
4ᵉ *Dragons* (Peninsular
Campaign *c.* 1811)

Trooper, Elite Company
1ᵉ *Hussards* (Russian
Campaign 1807)

north and O'Reilly squeezing men past Stortigliano, the French must either retreat or be surrounded. The infantry of the centre and left gave way in some disorder, shielded by Kellermann's cavalry. They were halted 7 kilometres in the rear, in front of San Giuliano and formed astride the road with Kellermann's dragoons on their left and Champeaux's hussars on their right linking them, tenuously, with Lannes and the remains of Wattrin's division, who, facing almost due south, tried in their turn to keep in touch with the Consular Guard and Monnier's belated division which was striving to hold its ground near Castel Ceriolo.

Had Ott's column been made stronger in the first instance he could now have intervened decisively and rolled up the French right but, after a morning's hard fighting the remnants of his 7,500 men were not strong enough to drive in the Consular Guard, Monnier's fresh men and a brigade of *chasseurs à cheval*. Melas sent him no reinforcements but concentrated his attention on regrouping his own column for a final attack on the new French position.

THE TURN OF THE FRENCH

In the respite given by this Austrian pause, the French had their first piece of good luck since the battle began. At mid-afternoon Desaix, who had ridden ahead of his troops, arrived at Bonaparte's command post. Although his orders had told him to march to Serraville, 30 kilometres by road from San Guiliano, his move had been obstructed by the high level of the river Scrivia and at 9 am on 14 June they had only reached Rivalta where they heard the opening Austrian cannonade. Although Desaix did not, as is sometimes related, march to the sound of the guns, he halted his column and waited for further orders. These arrived before noon and he had only a 13 kilometre march to the battlefield.

Bonaparte, smiling, greeted him with, 'Well, General, here's a fine muddle', to which he replied, 'Ah, well, I have got here. My troops are fresh and, if necessary, we'll go and get ourselves killed.' Then, almost without reference to the First Consul, he set about making arrangements for the arrival of Boudet's division. He turned to Marmont and asked for artillery support. 'Before we make an attack we must have a brisk bombardment. We shall fail without it. That, General, is how battles are lost.'

Marmont replied that there were five guns still capable of firing with the troops at San Giuliano and that with five more which were just being brought up from the rear and the eight guns arriving with Boudet he would have eighteen in all. These he proposed to establish as a battery with the left-hand gun on the right of the San Giuliano road. Desaix replied 'That's the way, *mon cher Marmont*. Let us have guns and more guns and let us ensure that we make the best use of them.'

As his troops came up Boudet deployed them astride the road. To the south were the three battalions of 9me *Légère* with two battalions in line and the third in column on the open flank. The remainder of the division, Guénard's brigade consisting of the 30me and 59me *Ligne* (each of three battalions), went to the north of the road also formed in line with a column on its outer flank. In fact, before Guénard's brigade had

A romanticized print of the death of Desaix – in fact he died instantaneously

finished forming, Desaix, who was much worried by the unsteadiness among Victor's men, sent the 9me *Légère* forward hoping both to protect and put new heart into the men who had fought throughout the morning. In this he was successful and several of Victor's battalions reformed but the Austrian case-shot tore great gaps in the ranks of the light infantry and Desaix ordered them back to the general line. Hardly had he done so when Bonaparte ordered the whole line forward and Desaix put himself at the head of 9me and led them against two battalions of Hungarian grenadiers.

The advance went badly. On the left, Desaix was shot through the heart and fell from his horse uttering none of the last words which history has attributed to him. Simultaneously, the 9me *Légère* was attacked in flank by Austrian cavalry. Guénard's brigade came up against the three battalions of the Regiment of Wallis who proved formidable opponents. As Boudet reported:

The enemy's resistance was terrible. It was useless to try to drive them back with musketry. Only charges with the bayonet could move them.

Marmont recalled how:

when they passed my battery I gave the order to limber up and follow them but, despite my orders, the gunners went on firing through the gaps between the battalions and I could only get them advancing one gun at a time from the right. When I reached the left of the line I found three pieces, two 8-pounders and a howitzer, served by men of the Consular Guard. I got them to move only with threats and, hardly were the horses hooked in when I saw to the half left the 30me demi-brigade flying in disorder. I ordered the three pieces back into action and had them loaded with grape but waited before firing. Fifty paces beyond the 36me there appeared through the smoke a column which I took to be French but soon realised to be Austrian. We had time to get four rounds of grape off at them from each of our three guns when Kellermann with 400 horse, the remains of his brigade, charged across my guns and into the left flank of the enemy.

François Etienne Kellermann, son of the victor of Valmy, had under command the 2me and 20me *Cavalerie*, some of 6me *Dragons* and a few rallied horsemen from other units. His orders were to support Desaix but the charge was entirely his own conception, as was his move round the rear of Boudet's division so as to fall on the inner flank of the Austrians. Wallis' regiment was already fighting a bitter battle against six battalions of Guénard's brigade when a flood of heavy French cavalry plunged down on their left. A large body of Austrian cavalry on that side made no move to help them and Kellermann's charge broke their spirit. The whole column, three battalions of Wallis' and two of grenadiers, the remains of 3,000 men, laid down their arms and surrendered.

Melas had already left his army. He had been slightly wounded and two horses had been shot under him. It was too much for his seventy-one years. As soon as he had seen the French flying in confusion from Marengo he had handed command of the pursuit over to Kaim and retired to Alessandria. When Kellermann's charge broke the main

column of attack, the Austrian morale gave way. Kaim tried to impro-
vise a rearguard to cover the retreat but it melted away and the Austrian
cavalry proved a broken reed. The cavalry of the Consular Guard
pursued and Eugène de Beauharnais, then a captain in the *Chasseurs à
cheval*, described the last act of the battle:

A painting from 1902 of
the Consular Guard in
pursuit of the flying
Austrians

*Although the ground was not in our favour as we had to cross two deep ditches, we
charged a column of cavalry, which far outnumbered us, while they were
deploying. We drove them down to the bridge over the Bormida, using our sabres
all the way. The* mêlée *lasted for ten minutes and I was lucky to suffer nothing
worse than two sabre cuts on my shabraque.*

Ott's undefeated column from the left had to make a halt before crossing
back into Alessandria while panic-stricken fugitives from the centre

82

column fought with each other to get into the gateway of the *tête de pont*. They were in no danger. The French were too exhausted to do more than reoccupy their line of that morning.

Next morning Melas, totally dispirited, signed a convention agreeing to evacuate the whole of western Italy and to withdraw his army behind the Mincio. An armistice to last until peace was concluded between France and Austria was also agreed. The Austrians had lost 9,402 men (including 2,921 prisoners), a third of the men actually engaged (excluding Nimptsch's brigade of cavalry), together with 12 guns and a howitzer.

The French losses are much harder to assess. In his first report, Berthier, still technically commanding the *Armée de Réserve*, reported 600 dead, 1,500 wounded, and 900 prisoners, a total of 3,000 which he later increased to 3,900. This is a gross underestimate. The reported losses of Wattrin (2,100), Monnier (800), and the cavalry (800) alone amount to more than Berthier's first total and it is known that 121 fell in the infantry of the Guard and 645 in four out of the six battalions of Rivaud's brigade. To these must be added the casualties in the rest of Chambarlhac's division and in the whole of the divisions of Gardanne and Boudet, both of which suffered heavily. The whole of the French loss can therefore scarcely be less than 7,000 and was probably more.

Nevertheless, Bonaparte had got the victory he needed. He had restored French supremacy in Italy and brought peace in sight. His own share in the victory is more dubious. As happened so often, his strategy was brilliant but his tactics mediocre. The crossing of the Alps, thus placing himself astride Melas' communications, was superb. But once the great stroke had been made, he began to fumble. He deluded himself that Melas would do anything but what he actually did, thus depriving himself of the help of Lapoype's division and he would have lost Desaix also had the water in the Scrivia river been normal. On the day of the battle he refused to believe that he was seriously threatened and did not set out for the scene of the fighting until it had been in progress for two hours. His handling of the battle was, in fact, little better than that of Melas, and the victory was contrived by Desaix and Kellermann. The former, having died, received a modest share of praise, the latter scarcely any. The First Consul's dissatisfaction with his own performance is best demonstrated by the two revised versions of the history of the battle which he caused to be compiled by the *Dépot de la Guerre* in 1803 and 1805. Even these did not sufficiently demonstrate his skill and he was still trying to produce an acceptable version at St Helena.

Consolidation and Exploitation

THE CONVENTION OF ALESSANDRIA did not lead to peace between France and Austria as quickly as either Bonaparte or Melas expected. Vienna was not to be so easily persuaded to surrender. But after Moreau, with the *Armée du Rhin*, had defeated the Austrians at Höchstadt (19 June) and at Hohenlinden (3 December) while the reconstituted *Armée de Réserve* now under Macdonald forced its way over the Splügen pass and reached Bolzano, a further armistice was agreed leading to the Treaty of Lunéville (9 February 1801). This in effect repeated the terms agreed at Campo Formio four years earlier. The moderation of the terms imposed on Austria reflected the Consulate's need for peace. Eight months later, by which time Britain had captured Malta and forced the surrender of the French in Egypt, the preliminaries of peace were signed between Britain and France, the definitive Peace of Amiens following on 25 March 1802.

On neither side of the Channel was this peace expected to last. But its end, on 16 May 1803, came as a surprise to Bonaparte, now Consul for life, who had hoped for more time to reorganize his realm (for already he treated it as a kingdom) and his army. In particular the renewed war interrupted a thorough reform of the French artillery undertaken by Marmont which, in the event, was destined never to be completed.

There was no fighting on the continent of Europe and, with his eyes fixed on the invasion of England, Bonaparte, or as he was declared on 18 May 1804, the Emperor Napoleon, was able for the first time to organize his army in comparative tranquillity. One of his troubles in the earlier wars had been a shortage of regimental officers. The legacy of the revolution had been that half the officers had been promoted from the ranks and since many of these were barely, if at all, literate, they were unsuitable for promotion. During the short peace great steps had been made to achieve a reconciliation with all but the most extreme royalists, with a result that 40,000 *emigrés* returned to France and provided a valuable source of educated officers. Largely for their benefit the *École Spéciale Militaire* for training officers for the infantry and cavalry had been founded at Fontainebleau in 1802 (moving to St Cyr in 1808). Officers for the artillery and engineers came from the *École Polytechnique* formed soon after the revolution.

An officer of the *Chasseurs à cheval* charging in full dress

The French cavalry had not, with exceptions such as Kellermann's charge at Marengo, shown itself in a good light during the revolutionary wars. Its training and organization were taken firmly in hand. The light horses – *Chasseurs à cheval* and hussars – became excellent at manning the outpost lines, covering the flanks and rear of marching columns, and pursuing a beaten enemy, but they too often failed in their reconnaissance role. The heavy cavalry – Cuirassiers and *carabiniers* – became a splendid body of troops kept principally for shock action, to destroy enemy mounted troops and to exploit gaps torn in the enemy's infantry formations. These became the most formidable body of mounted men in Europe but the intermediate form of cavalry, the dragoons, were frequently a disappointment. Napoleon attempted to force them to fulfil their proper role as mounted infantry and, like almost every other commander before or since, he failed. For the invasion of England a body of 5,000 dragoons was deprived of their horses, for whom there would be no sea transport, in the belief that they could be mounted after landing. In the subsequent Ulm campaign these were the only French troops to suffer defeat, being trounced by the Archduke Ferdinand while they acted as infantry. The survivors were remounted on captured Austrian

French light cavalry charging at the battle of Höchstadt

86

horses and ridden over by a single regiment of Russian hussars at Burkersdorf in February 1807.

By 1805 the French cavalry, except the dragoons, were the equal of any cavalry in Europe. Their horsemastership was seldom good but, acting under a number of excellent cavalry generals, of whom Murat and Grouchy were the most outstanding, they were more than a match for anything that could be sent to oppose them. Their chief virtue lay in their ability to manoeuvre in large bodies and it is probable that Austrian, Prussian, and Russian generals would have echoed Wellington's verdict that:

Although I consider one [British] squadron a match for two French squadrons, I should not like to have seen four British squadrons opposed to four French; and as the numbers increased, I was more unwilling to risk our cavalry without having a great superiority of numbers.

In the infantry the term *demi-brigade* was abandoned in favour of regiment (though the royalist territorial titles were not resumed) and, although the process was not complete when fighting broke out again, the regiments were reconstituted from a basis of three battalions of nine companies, to four battalions each consisting of one grenadier, one light infantry (*voltigeur*), and four battalion (*fusilier*) companies with a depot unit of four companies. The establishment (seldom attained) of each company was 140 of all ranks, giving the regiment a fighting strength (apart from staff and band) of 3,300. In August 1805 the infantry consisted of 113 regiments of which 26 were designated light infantry (*Légère*). In fact, the distinction between *Ligne* and *Légère* was becoming blurred and was soon to amount to little more than slight differences in uniform and in nomenclature, such as the substitution of *Carabinier* companies in *Légère* regiments for Grenadiers. Nor, as in other armies, were the light infantry regarded as *élite* troops. The 9me *Légère*, which so distinguished itself at Marengo, was converted into a regiment of the line as a mark of appreciation.

In artillery the trend was towards larger pieces used in large numbers. The 4-pounder battalion guns had been withdrawn from the infantry, a step Napoleon was soon to regret, and the 4-pounder itself was soon to be discarded as too light. Even the 6-pounder was passing from favour and the artillery of the *Armée d'Angleterre* included only fifty-two 6-pounders compared to a total of 146 of the 8-pounders. Besides these there were no fewer than fifty-eight 12-pounders, a size of piece which in the past had seldom been used as a field gun except in a near-static role. The 12-pounder had an effective range of just over $1\frac{1}{2}$ kilometres with round shot and about 550 metres with canister but its rate of fire was slow, one round a minute, and even with the twelve horses of its gun-team was difficult to move on wet ground, scarcely surprising since barrel and carriage together weighed almost 2 tonnes.

On 13 August 1805 Napoleon, speaking of the *Armée d'Angleterre*, declared that 'There is no better army in Europe than the one I have today'. He was, for once, speaking the literal truth. For two years it had been settled in permanent camps along the Channel coast and had had

87

time to train. The corps, each commanded by a Marshal of the Empire, were now permanent and well-established formations with experienced staff officers and constituent divisions which knew each other and were used to working together. There were seven of them, varying in size between Soult's IV Corps with four infantry divisions and a total strength of 40,000 men, to Augereau's VII Corps with two divisions, 14,000, the only one of the seven which did not have a light cavalry division (more properly a brigade of four regiments). Behind them stood the Reserve Cavalry, 22,000 men, under Marshal Murat, which included twelve regiments of cuirassiers and two of carabiniers. As an ultimate reserve was the Imperial Guard, 7,000 strong under Marshal Bessières, a corps in miniature consisting of picked men of all arms, the cream skimmed off the rest of the army and forming a body of troops which, as a whole, had no equal in the world. At the end of August 1805 this remarkable force, consisting of 193,000 men, was given the name the *Grande Armée.*

The new threat to France

It needed to be a great army for in 1805 France was again assailed by a European coalition. England was joined first by Russia and then by Austria and, under the inspiration of Czar Alexander, a vast strategic plan was evolved to attack on a front with its right on the Baltic and its left at Naples. The allies had hoped to have Prussia with them but King Frederick, true to his depressing character, allowed his neutrality to be bought by Napoleon's offer of Hanover. Undeterred by this and without waiting for Russian support, Austria plunged in alone. The principle of seniority was so deeply entrenched in the Hapsburg service that the commanders-in-chief were, for the most part, in their seventies and, as has been seen, past their best. The alternative was to put a member of the imperial family in command but, although the Archduke Charles was a fine general, his brothers were barely competent. Moreover Charles was not on good terms with his brother the Emperor and in 1805 was relegated to the secondary theatre of Italy while the command of the main army was entrusted to the Archduke Ferdinand. He was, however, given as chief of staff, Karl von Mack, a stripling of 53. Mack, moreover, had the complete confidence of the Emperor Francis and could overrule his nominal chief without having to refer to Vienna.

Mack was much changed since he had evolved the complicated orders which led to the battle of Tourcoing, with its multiplicity of disconnected columns. Pondering on the Austrian lack of success in the Netherlands he had adopted the maxim that 'In war the object is to beat the enemy and not merely to avoid being beaten'. This he interpreted as meaning that the army should go bald-headed against the French. He had put this dogma into action in 1798 when he had been on loan as commander-in-chief of the Neapolitan army. He had led his ragamuffin command in a headlong advance against Rome only to end as a French prisoner. Learning nothing from this *débâcle*, his plan for 1805 was to make a precipitate advance intended to block the roads through the Black Forest by which the French must emerge on their way to the Danube. He had the promise of support from 50,000 Russians under

Kutusov but decided not to wait for them. Nor did he realize that the Russians, who were still using the Julian calender, would be twelve days late on any date they suggested. Believing that Napoleon and the *Grande Armée* were still deployed on the Channel coast, Mack led the 45,000 men immediately available in a headlong rush westward starting on 5 September.

To speed the army's advance he decreed that no supply waggons should accompany the troops, who were to live off the country. This finally decided the Bavarian army of 25,000 men, whose country was being lived off, to join the French. Nor had Mack remembered to regulate the number of baggage carts brought by the officers so that a chaotic rabble of waggons followed the army. By the end of September the Austrian army, extremely short of food, had reached Ulm, 225 kilometres from their starting point. There they halted while Mack considered what he should do next.

As early as 25 August Napoleon had decided that the invasion of England was not, for the time being, a possibility and that he must take steps to curb the Austrian threat. Two days later he issued orders for the *Grande Armée* to move from its cantonments on the Channel coast (except for Bernadotte's I Corps in Hanover) to march to the Rhine. By 24 September the whole of Napoleon's striking force except VII Corps which had to march from Brest, was in position on the Rhine and in north Germany, having achieved one of the most notable moves in military history. Soult's corps, 40,000 strong, had marched from Boulogne to Speyer, more than 640 kilometres, leaving only thirty sick and stragglers on the road and Davout's III Corps claimed to have marched from Bruges to Mannheim without losing a man. It was a superb physical and administrative feat.

On 25 September the French, led by Lannes and V Corps, started to advance across the Rhine behind a heavy screen of cavalry. They moved at a steady 26 kilometres a day and in their rear came supply waggons loaded with nine days' rations. Napoleon's orders were that these supplies were not to be broached until contact was made with the enemy. Until that time the troops would live by foraging. The aim of the march was not Ulm but the stretch of the Danube north-east of the city, either side of Donauwörth. Having crossed, three corps turned south-west and swept to the south of Ulm.

Meanwhile Mack remained at Ulm concentrating his army. Archduke Ferdinand tried to induce him to move but the chief of staff was adamant. At one time he contended that the French were not interested in Ulm but would offer their flank to his army as they attacked Kutusov's Russian corps on the Inn. Later, when French troops were moving from east to west round the south of his position, he decided that the British had landed at Boulogne and that Napoleon was making a circuit of the Austrian position on his way back to France. On 11 and 14 October he made half-hearted attempts to send two corps away to the north but both failed and on the night of 14–15 October the Archduke took General Schwarzenburg and 6,000 cavalry and made a dash for safety. They succeeded in escaping with 1,500 men. Mack and the remains of the garrison surrendered on 20 October. The short

campaign had cost Austria 60,000 men. The French had lost 1,500 killed and wounded. 'Never' proclaimed Napoleon, 'has a victory been so complete and less costly.'

THE BATTLE OF AUSTERLITZ

When Mack surrendered at Ulm, Kutusov was at Braunau on the Inn river with 27,000 Russians while 27,000 more of his corps straggled across the Hapsburg Empire in his rear. There were 20,000 Austrians available to support him and, far away to the east, Buxhöwden was bringing a further 30,000 Russians to join the allied army. Napoleon decided that he must crush Kutusov before Buxhöwden could join him or Austrian reinforcements could come up from Italy or the Tyrol. The advance from Ulm started on 25 October and by 12 November Murat's cavalry rode into Vienna unopposed since, despite Austrian urgings, Kutusov refused to defend the capital. He was intent on joining Bux-höwden in Moravia and of stretching the French lines of communica-tions as far as they would go. He retreated with great skill, savaging Mortier's corps at Dürnstein on 9 November but losing most of his Austrian corps at Mariazell three days earlier. By 20 November the French had reached Brünn (Brno) but Kutusov was out of reach at Olmütz (Olomouc). He had picked up not only Buxhöwden's corps but a number of other Russian and Austrian divisions and his strength was up to 85,000 men.

The *Grand Armée* was at the end of its administrative tether. The troops had been continuously on the march for three months and, despite the vast quantity of stores they had captured in Austria — including sufficient muskets to re-arm the whole infantry — they could not go on marching eastward into Poland where the barns and store-houses had already been stripped bare by the Russians. If Kutusov continued his retreat for even a short distance Napoleon would have to turn back and leave the allied army in the field.

He was not allowed to do so. The Czar Alexander joined the army with Buxhöwden and determined to have a battle. He left Kutusov in nominal command but issued his own orders, relying on the advice of an Austrian, Major-General Weyrother, a tactical optimist who clung to the multi-column type of tactics that had proved so disastrous at Tourcoing and elsewhere. On 1 December, 70,000 Russians and 15,000 Austrians faced 80,000 Frenchmen on the position Napoleon had chosen near the village of Austerlitz. Late that evening a complicated set of orders was read over to the column commanders in German. Scarcely had they been translated into Russian and issued than the columns had to start their move in an attempt to turn the supposed right flank of the French. This was precisely what Napoleon had expected them to do and he held his main strength on his left. What he could not foresee was the chaos into which the Russians fell as they moved into the boggy valley of the Goldbach stream, held by part of Soult's corps. On to their flank fell the main weight of Napoleon's *mass de rupture*. The Russians resisted desperately and, on Napoleon's orders, the French bayonetted the Russian wounded:

A view of the battlefield of Austerlitz at 10 am in the morning, seen from the French left

Everywhere on this huge battlefield the ground was covered with Russian bodies. Whole companies, still in line, were lying in bloodsoaked heaps.

The allies lost one man out of every three engaged, some 27,000 men in all, 11,433 being prisoners. The French casualties were less than 8,000, of whom only 1,305 were killed.

Next day the Austrian Emperor sought an interview at which an armistice was arranged between his country and France. Before the end of the month the Peace of Pressburg was signed, Austria ceding Venetia to France. The Czar would have no part in the peacemaking and marched his army sullenly back into Russia.

CHAPTER SEVEN

The Conquest of Prussia

HAD PRUSSIA JOINED THE THIRD COALITION the history of the Ulm–Austerlitz campaign must have been different, but despite pressure from his Queen and the officers of his army King Frederick William had preferred to accept Napoleon's bribe to the chances of war. It was not until he heard that Hanover had been offered to Britain in an attempt to secure an Anglo–French peace that his sluggish pride was affronted. On 9 August 1806 he ordered the mobilization of his army and, two weeks later, called a Council of War to decide what should be done with it.

On paper the Prussian army had a strength of more than a quarter of a million men. Not all of these could be found in practice and after deducting some garrisons, the field force available amounted to 175,000, to which could be added 20,000 Saxons, that country having been overawed into concluding an alliance with her large northern neighbour. If ten years of ignominious neutrality had hurt the pride of her officer corps, it had not persuaded them to modernize their army to cope with the new conditions of war. As befitted the heir to the victorious traditions of Frederick the Great it was magnificently fitted to fight the wars of the mid-eighteenth century.

No other army kept its ranks so straight, manoeuvred in so precise (or so slow) a fashion, and fired such impressive (or such inaccurate) volleys. Learning from its experience in the War of Bavarian Succession (see p. 19), it had equipped itself with so elaborate a supply train that it regarded a day's march as being exceptionally satisfactory if 20 kilometres could be covered, a fifth less than any other major army. True to the eighteenth-century tradition it was largely composed of mercenaries and in 1806 at least 80,000 of its men were not Prussian nationals. Its commanders too were men of the Seven Years' War. The nominal head was Prince Ferdinand of Brunswick, nephew to Frederick the Great. He was 71 and had last seen action at Valmy. His chief subordinates, Prince Frederick of Hohenlohe-Ingelfingen and General von Ruchel were both in their sixties and the rising star of the army, Gebhard von Blücher, was 64. The King's chief military adviser, von Mollendorf, was 82, while Frederick William himself, who presided at the Councils of War, was only 36 but had all the indecision of a dotard.

This geriatric clique could not decide how the forces were to be employed. During September the army seeped southward until it came to rest on the north of the Thuringerwald in three groups. Prince Ferdinand had 70,000 men south-west of Leipsig, Hohenlohe with 50,000 Prussians and 20,000 Saxons was near Dresden, and 30,000 more, largely unenthusiastic Hanoverian conscripts, were north of Eisenach, with their right as far west as Göttingen. A reserve of 13,000 was stationed at Magdeburg. No attempt was made to co-ordinate operations with the Russians, with whom they had an alliance and who were building up a large army in Poland.

The Prussian mobilization had given the alarm to Napoleon and before the end of September he had six corps of the *Grand Armée* with the Guard, the Reserve Cavalry, and a Bavarian corps (193,000 in all) deployed to the south of the Thuringerwald with their right at Amberg and their left at Königshofen. Behind them ran the river Main, providing water transport for their supplies which were accumulated in depots at Würzburg, Forchheim, and Kronach. Everything was ready for war except that there was no coherent information about the Prussian movements. This was due not to lack of intelligence but to indecision among the Prussians. On 25 September, Brunswick had proposed an advance round the north-western tip of the Thuringerwald which would cut the French communications along the Main. Hohenlohe preferred an advance by the east bank of the Saale which would fall on the French right centre at Bamberg. Since the two princes would neither give way nor compromise and, conscious that a Prussian ultimatum had been delivered to Paris on 2 October, the King ruled on 5 October that both plans should be implemented at the same time, thus spreading his army over a front of 140 kilometres.

SAXONY INVADED

The Prussian ultimatum reached Napoleon at Bamberg on 7 October and next day he launched his army across the Thuringerwald. His orders, issued on 5 October, called for an advance in three columns with a front of only 60 kilometres so that each column could support its neighbour. They illustrate clearly the flexibility which the corps organization gave the French army. The orders issued to Soult read, in part:

I propose to invade Saxony with the army in three columns . . . You are to lead the right column with Marshal Ney's corps half a day's march behind you and 10,000 Bavarians a day's march in Ney's rear. Your column will thus be more than 50,000 strong. Marshal Bernadotte will lead the centre column, followed by Marshal Davout, the Reserve Cavalry and my Guard, making 70,000 men. The left column will be led by V Corps [Lannes] followed by Marshal Augereau, a total of 50,000 . . . The other columns will keep abreast of yours. I shall usually be at the head of the centre column. You will understand that with this great superiority of force on a narrow front, I shall take no chances and shall attack the enemy wherever he may be found. If you meet the enemy with a force not exceeding 30,000 men you may, in conjunction with Marshal Ney, concentrate and attack him, but act with prudence if he is in an entrenched position. On reaching Hof [the first town north of the Thuringerwald] your first task must be

PREVIOUS PAGE: Marshal Murat leading the Reserve Cavalry in the pursuit after Jena

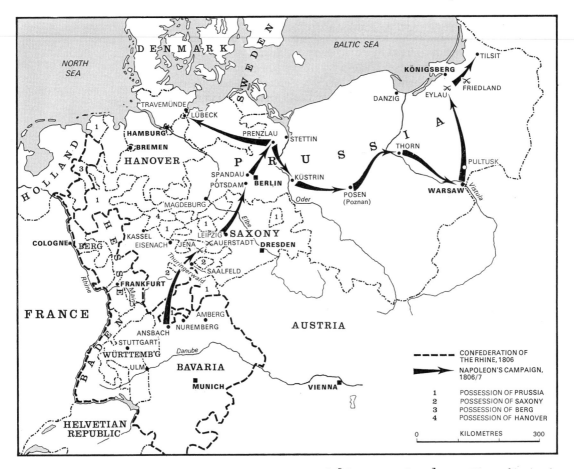

Napoleon's campaign of 1806/7

to establish communications with [*the centre column*] . . . *Your objective is Plauen. According to my latest reports the enemy seems to be moving towards my left, for his main body seems to be at Erfurt.*

It was only the uncoordinated wanderings of the Prussian corps that prevented Napoleon's campaign from being a textbook operation. As it was, the Prussian advance guards having been swept away, Napoleon moved his main strength, four corps and the Guard, westward across the Saale at Jena, believing that the bulk of the Prussian army could be engaged there. At the same time he ordered two corps, those of Davout and Bernadotte, up the river to Naumberg where they were to cross and cut off the Prussian retreat to Magdeburg. On 14 October, in the desperately fought battle of Jena, 96,000 Frenchmen finally routed 56,000 Prussians and Saxons under Hohenlohe. It was not until he returned to his quarters in Jena after the battle that Napoleon learned that the decisive battle had been fought 20 kilometres to the north at Auerstadt where Davout with 27,000 had fought and beaten 60,000 Prussians under Ferdinand, who died of his wounds. Bernadotte succeeded in missing both battles and failed to convince anyone, then or subsequently, that he had not done so on purpose.

95

With both main sections of the Prussian army heavily defeated, there followed the most effective pursuit in history led by Murat and the Reserve Cavalry but seconded by Bernadotte, smarting from a stinging imperial rebuke. It was Bernadotte who routed the Prussian reserve, their last unbroken formation, at Halle on 17 October and before the end of the month 19,000 survivors from Jena and Auerstadt surrendered to Murat at Prenzlau and Stettin. On 7 November Blücher, cornered at Travemünde, surrendered 10,000 men to Soult and next day Ney took Magdeburg and 20,000 men. The remains of the Saxon army lost no time in changing sides thus earning their Elector the title of King. King Frederick William had had his realm reduced to some isolated fortresses and the provinces on the east of the Vistula, and his field army to a single corps of 6,000 men.

IN PRUSSIA AND POLAND

Napoleon entered Berlin as a conqueror on 27 October and while he was there he received a delegation from the Senate in Paris urging him to make peace. That, he replied, was only possible when Russia was prepared to join him against England. At the same time he offered Frederick William peace on terms which were deliberately designed to be unacceptable.

The Czar was far from willing to make peace and was moving 100,000 men westward under the overall command of the 75-year-old Marshal Kamenskoï, a man of violent and unpredictable temper. The most forward corps, 56,000 men under Bennigsen, was approaching Warsaw at the end of October. The remainder, divisions which had fought at Austerlitz, were somewhere to the east and commanded by Buxhöwden. Against them the *Grande Armée* had 160,000 men under arms in November but this numerical superiority was more apparent than real. Western Prussia had to be garrisoned and a corps was needed to subdue the Prussian fortresses in Silesia. All these troops were badly in need of clothing, particularly boots and greatcoats, and there was a serious breakdown in discipline. The victorious army would barely obey orders away from the battlefield and, used to living off the countryside, was busy looting the barns and storehouses on which they would be dependent for a winter campaign.

Some of these shortages could be alleviated at the expense of Prussia. The kingdom was mulcted of 160 million francs beside huge requisitions of clothing, including 280,000 greatcoats and 250,000 pairs of boots. The whole French cavalry was remounted on Prussian horses. Reinforcements were demanded from Bavaria, Baden, Holland, and Württemberg. Spain was induced to send 15,000 of her best troops for garrison duty. The *Armée d'Italie* and the depots in France were called upon to send large drafts eastward. Napoleon's orders for their march throws an interesting light on the administrative limitations of warfare at this time:

Each man coming from Paris or Boulogne will start with a pair of shoes [on his feet] and two in his knapsack. At Mainz a new pair of shoes will be issued to replace that worn out on the march. At Magdeburg a further pair will be issued

Napoleon entering Berlin in October 1806. The population were not as enthusiastic as is suggested here

to replace that worn out between Mainz and Magdeburg. Thus each man will reach the army with one pair of shoes on his feet and another in his knapsack.

In all, during the 1806–07 campaign against the Russians, a campaign in which, compared to that of Ulm and Austerlitz, there was not a great deal of marching, the number of shoes [i.e. ankle boots for the infantry] required was 984,000. In contrast, the cavalry needed only 16,948 pairs of boots.

The front on which the coming campaign was to be fought was narrower than might be supposed since the partitions of Poland had left Austria in possession of south western Poland up to the line of the river Bug north east of Warsaw and, with the Hapsburgs resolutely neutral, the area of operations was confined to the gap of 240 kilometres between Warsaw and the Baltic. In this confined area there was some marching and countermarching by both the opposing armies which led to no

result and culminated in two very sharp actions at Pultusk and Golymin on 26 December. Both led to Russian withdrawals but both were indecisive since, as Lannes reported after Pultusk:

The battlefield was turned into a sea of mud through which soldiers and horses could only move with difficulty.

Davout, while noting that the battle had been preceded by a two-day thaw, wrote that:

The ground over which the army marched was slimy and marshy while the roads were frightful. Horsemen, infantry, and gunners could only move with extreme difficulty. It took two hours to march two and a half miles.

Another French general reported that Russian light infantry were able to beat off French cavalry by standing up to their waists in a marsh where the horses could not approach them. By mutual consent both armies withdrew into winter quarters, the bulk of the French being billetted north of Warsaw but Ney's corps held the area Mlava–Niedenburg while Bernadotte was allocated the huge area from Lobau to the Baltic at Elbing, since it was intended to besiege Danzig as soon as troops were available. A screen of cavalry posts covered the front.

Convinced that there would be no more fighting until the spring, Napoleon turned his energies to supplying his men with rations and clothing. It was an uphill task for the amount of food to be wrung from Poland in winter was never more than barely adequate and the clothing requisitioned from Prussia was disappointing:

The overcoats and shoes sent from Berlin are worthless. The overcoats from Leipzig ridiculously small. I have seen some which do not even reach to the knees. The shoes, especially those from Berlin, are of the worst possible quality.

Such administrative mishaps did not, however, stop him from issuing reassuring bulletins to the people of France:

The temperature remains between two and three degrees below freezing. This is the weather most favourable to the army . . . It is no colder than is desirable for the health of the soldiers.

The Russians were more used to winter weather and not inclined to halt the campaign. Before the end of the year Kamenskoi removed himself from the command of the army:

He went without his shirt into the streets and then sending for a surgeon, pointed out all his wounds, groaned as he passed his hands over them, and insisted on a certificate of his incapacity to serve.

Buxhöwden succeeded to the leadership of the army as senior corps commander and, at a Council of War held on 2 January to the east of Ostralenka, proposed an advance against the thinly-held French left.

Before this plan could be implemented the Czar superseded him with Bennigsen, a Hanoverian by birth and a man whom Jomini, who later served under him, described as 'a mixture of rash imprudence and irresolution'.

In mid-January he left two divisions to guard his left on the Narew river and moved along the north edge of the Johannisburg forest with 70,000 men and 500 guns. On 19 January, to his great surprise, his advance guard met and drove in a force of French cavalry at Schippenbeil, 65 kilometres east of where he first expected to meet any opposition. Napoleon was equally ignorant of the existence of French troops in that area until it transpired that Ney, ignoring the Emperor's order that 'all forward movements likely to rouse the enemy to activity are to be avoided', had led his starving corps forward on a foraging expedition. Angry as Napoleon was with the marshal, Ney's unauthorized foray showed that the Russians were offering an open flank to the French and, since Bennigsen continued his advance, the Emperor was able to plan a wheel northward by the right of the *Grande Armée* which should have destroyed the main body of the Russians. Four corps, the Guards and the Reserve Cavalry, were to swing up their right, cut in behind Bennigsen and fight a decisive battle near Allenstein [Olsztyn] These orders were to become operative on 1 February.

Bernadotte meanwhile had concentrated his corps to his right and, on 25 January, checked the Russian advance guard at Mohrungen, although his own baggage was seized and found to contain 10,000 ducats which he had deducted from the contribution levied on Elbing and was devoting to his own purposes.

By 31 January Bennigsen's army held a line running east and west from Graudenz [Grudiatz], where Lestocq's Prussian corps relieved a garrison of their compatriots on the lower Vistula, to Allenstein. For a short euphoric time he believed that he had achieved his aim and that the French would have to scurry back to the Vistula without fighting. On the following day a copy of Napoleon's orders was laid on his desk. Berthier had entrusted Bernadotte's copy to a newly commissioned officer who was captured by Cossacks with the letter intact. Thus not only was Bennigsen informed of the wheeling movement that the French were starting to execute against him but Bernadotte failed to get his orders to co-operate by driving in the Russians from Österode until a copy reached him on 3 February when it was too late.

The Russians immediately turned about and marched rapidly eastward, narrowly reaching safety before the French blow fell. Instead of a decisive action at Allenstein there was a sharp rearguard action at Inkovo on 3 February. Napoleon claimed that in one part of the field alone 12 Russian battalions were destroyed and 1,500 prisoners taken. In fact French and Russians alike lost about 1,500 men. Bennigsen was safe from interception. His only major concern was that Lestocq's corps became separated from the main force. Napoleon, hoping to isolate this last remnant of the Prussian army, detached Ney's corps, with orders to prevent Lestocq from rejoining his allies.

CHAPTER EIGHT

Eylau,
8 February 1807

NAPOLEON KNEW THAT HIS ARMY was in no condition to undertake an invasion of Russia but was anxious to inflict on Bennigsen a defeat sharp enough to make the Czar seriously consider making peace. He feared, however, that, having escaped from the Allenstein trap, the Russians would not make a further stand before they regained their own territory on the far side of the Pregel river. Nevertheless, he pressed them as closely as he could and was delighted when, on 6 February, they seemed to be making a stand at Landsberg. Their rearguard made a prolonged halt on the line of a marshy but frozen stream at the village of Hoff. Rather than let them slip away, he allowed Murat to try to pin them down with the cavalry, an expedient which failed until d'Hautpol's cuirassiers crossed the stream and drove back the Russian infantry. The Petersburg Dragoons attempted a counterattack but were so overmatched by the heavy armoured horsemen that they broke and fled, riding into two infantry regiments and breaking their formation to such an extent that when the cuirassiers charged them they were 'entirely trampled on or cut down'. The rearguard commander, Prince Bagration, was nevertheless able to make a new stand on a low rise where he beat off the attacks of Soult's infantry until nightfall, inflicting 1,960 casualties on Soult's men.

It had not been Bennigsen's intention to stand at Landsberg but he had been delayed by the usual incompetence of Russian staff work causing a jam of columns in the town itself, which took all that day to clear. Thanks to Bagration, the French were held off for long enough and, despite the disaster to the Petersburg Dragoons, the Russian losses were only 2,000 men and 5 guns, almost certainly lower than the French casualties.

Bennigsen's instinct was to make straight for Russian territory so that time and weather could destroy the French army but two factors induced him to modify this aim. The first was the political undesirability of abandoning Königsberg (Kaliningrad), now the temporary capital of Prussia and almost the last possession of the wretched Frederick William. Moreover, Königsberg was well stored with rations which, since the Russians had no transport, would have to be abandoned if he retreated. The second factor was the state of his own army. The

discipline of even the best armies deteriorates in a prolonged retreat and a Russian army 'was never by character of composition or system calculated to retreat'. By 7 February the commissariat service, never efficient, had completely broken down:

The soldiers had to prowl and dig for the buried food of the peasantry — so that between duty and the search for provision they had scarcely time to lay down, and when they did, they had no other bed than the snow, no shelter but the heavens and no covering but their rags.

All his senior officers urged him to stand and fight and, perhaps against his better judgement, he agreed. 'The map was therefore examined and Preussisch-Eylau [Bagrationovsk] selected as the field of battle.' By noon on 7 February the main body of the Russian army was in position on the high ground to the east of the town.

ABOVE: Napoleon and his staff during the battle, with the town of Eylau in the background

PREVIOUS PAGE: The Reserve Cavalry attacking Russian grenadiers during the battle

Napoleon followed Bennigsen with the centre column of the *Grande Armée* consisting of the corps of Soult (16,000) and Augereau (14,000) supported by the Reserve Cavalry (15,000) and the Imperial Guard (9,000), a total of 54,000 men. On his right Davout's corps (15,000) was, on 7 February, driving a Russian flankguard out of Heilsberg, while Ney (14,000), on the left, had been called in to Landsberg when there was a chance of a battle and had bivouacked a few miles west of the town. From there he marched towards Kreuzberg to resume his watch over Lestocq's Prussians.

On 7 February the centre column, following Bennigsen, made no contact with the enemy during the morning but at 2 pm the leading cavalry found Bagration's rearguard in position holding a gap, 900 metres wide between two frozen lakes about 2 kilometres to the west of Eylau. The lakes were sufficiently hard frozen to be able to support artillery but, since both were low-lying, they were not an attractive avenue of approach for the French infantry and their early efforts were directed to seizing a low height in the gap between the lakes, a position well sited to obstruct any force trying to deploy from the 14 kilometres long defile of woods which led back to Landsberg.

Since the cavalry had learned caution from their early repulse at Hoff, they waited until Soult's leading infantry came up, whereupon Soult launched two regiments, 18me and 48me *Ligne*, at the gap. The attack failed. The 18me on the left moved ahead of their comrades and were badly exposed to Russian guns on the lake. They swerved to their right and were taken in flank by the bayonets of a Russian grenadier regiment. While they were trying to fight off this onslaught the Petersburg Dragoons, burning to retrieve their reputation, charged in on them. Despite a counterattack by French dragoons, both battalions lost their eagles and the regiment was unfit to fight on the following day. The 48me also suffered heavily but withdrew in good order. It was not until the French brought up enough men to work round the outer ends of the lakes that Bagration pulled his rearguard back into Eylau, closely followed by French cavalry and Soult's infantry.

Eylau town stood about 400 metres in front of the ridge on which the Russian army was drawn up and it had been Bennigsen's intention to hold it as an advanced post to be garrisoned by a division under Barclay de Tolly. Barclay, however, misunderstood his orders and withdrew his men as soon as Bagration's rearguard had passed through the town. Equally, Napoleon had not intended to occupy Eylau as he believed the west side of the valley to be the strongest ground on which to resist a possible Russian counterattack. In the event French skirmishers pressed into the town on the heels of the withdrawing garrison and they were followed by the Emperor's servants, intent on finding shelter for themselves and their master for a bitter winter's night. Hardly had they entered and begun unpacking the imperial baggage when, on Bennigsen's orders, Barclay's men attempted to re-enter Eylau and skirmishing broke out in the streets. Both sides threw in reinforcements and a considerable battle broke out. As a French staff officer wrote:

Each street of the unfortunate town became a battlefield; they were covered with

dead and dying and
cemetery was taken and lost several times. The carnage was frightful.

It was at about 7 pm, when darkness had fallen, that Bennigsen decided that Eylau was not worth a high price and ordered Barclay to withdraw. At about the same time Napoleon, realizing that a major battle was to be fought on the following day, sent an ADC to Davout at Heilsberg ordering him to start the 30 kilometres march to Eylau. Then the Emperor, Murat, and Soult established their headquarters in the houses of the town and everyone else who could devise an excuse for doing so sought shelter there from the biting wind. 'The streets were so over-crowded that it was difficult to move about, even stepping between the corpses.'

PRELIMINARIES OF BATTLE

The battlefield of Eylau consists of the gently sloping valley of the Pasmar stream, running roughly south to north, which is crossed by the Königsberg road, immediately west of the town. The stream itself is inconsiderable but in places, notably south of the town, it widens into a number of lakes, all of which were solidly frozen and, like the rest of the

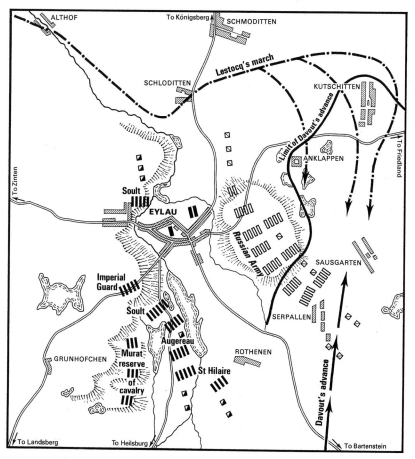

Nicolas Soult
(1768–1851)

landscape, thickly covered in snow, perhaps as much as one metre deep. The snow was everywhere passable for all arms except where it had built up in deeply-cut stream beds. On the evening of 7 February the temperature was −10°C but it fell to −16° on the morning of the following day and snow fell, sometimes very heavily throughout 8 February.

With 67,000 men and more than 400 guns, many of them 12-pounders, Bennigsen had decided to stand strictly on the defensive. The loss of Eylau town and the wounding of General Barclay necessitated some readjustment of his original dispositions and he gave his orders for these at a conference of generals held at Anklappen, his headquarters, at 10 pm. The main front was to be held by four divisions in 'small' (i.e. battalion) columns in two lines. The line followed the ridge on the east side of the valley and the right was to be somewhat to the north of the Eylau–Friedland road and the left 3 kilometres to the south at the hamlet of Serpallen. Two divisions in massed column acted as reserve to the centre and another, also massed, supported the left. Each flank was covered by cavalry and the rest of his horsemen stood behind the central reserve. Apart from the divisional artillery, three great batteries were formed, the largest, 70 guns, being on the high point of the ridge, opposite Eylau. A 60-gun battery was formed near the Friedland road and one of 40 guns supported the left flank. Near Anklappen a reserve of 60 horse artillery pieces was to be ready to move to any threatened sector. The only weak point of the line was the extreme right where the division responsible had had to give up a brigade to strengthen the left centre. This weakness was regarded as acceptable as Lestocq was expected early in the day to strengthen the right. The business of realignment was personally supervised by Bennigsen and was not complete at daybreak.

With 50,000 men, of whom a third were cavalry, Napoleon was determined that Bennigsen should not slip away. His intention, therefore, was to pin the Russians to their position with his central column until the 29,000 men in his two flanking columns could turn both of the enemy's flanks. Orders to bring in Davout from the right had been sent on the evening of 7 February but at dawn his divisions were between six and sixteen kilometres from the Russian left flank. Ney, on the other hand, was marching away from the field towards Kreuzburg and it was not until 8.30 am on 8 February that Napoleon sent orders to him to come to Eylau. This message did not reach him until 2 pm when he was at Pompicken, 16 kilometres north-east of Eylau, and engaged in a series of minor actions with Lestocq, who was between him and the battlefield. Bernadotte's corps should have been available to support Ney but, since his orders had miscarried, he was still near Möhrungen, 70 kilometres to the rear. French headquarters appear to have taken few steps to discover where he was or what he was doing.

Intent on keeping a solid body of troops intact for striking the decisive blow, Napoleon allocated responsibility for the pinning attack to Soult's corps but insisted that St Hilaire's division should hold the line south of Eylau and retained one brigade of Leval's for use 'à son fantasie'. The attack was therefore delivered by Legrand's division and a

The eastern armies

The uniforms of the Russian infantry private, 1812, (BOTTOM LEFT) and the Austrian grenadier, 1814, (BOTTOM RIGHT CENTRE) show little change, apart from the headgear, from the eighteenth century although both show how overloaded the infantryman was. On the other hand the Prussian private of *Landwehr*, 1813, (TOP RIGHT) set a new fashion. The tunic (*litewka*) worn over trousers with canvas gaiters and topped with a flat cap (*feldmütze*) was designed to be cheaply and easily produced but proved to be the prototype of all field uniforms for more than a century.

The Napoleonic wars saw the reintroduction of the lance after more than a century of disuse on western battlefields. The Cossack of the Russian Imperial Guard, 1812, (BOTTOM LEFT CENTRE) wore a slightly formalised version of traditional cossack irregular dress but the Austrian Uhlan (BOTTOM RIGHT) wore the traditional lance cap (*czapka*) of the Polish *Utan*, a fashion followed by the French when they acquired the Grand Duchy of Warsaw and, after Waterloo, by the British. The *czapka* was also worn by some Prussian Uhlan regiments but its only real function was to increase the wearer's apparent height.

OPPOSITE LEFT: Russian
Private, Mohilev
Musketeer Regiment
c. 1812

OPPOSITE RIGHT: Russian
Cossack, Don Cossack
Regiment of the Imperial
Guard c. 1812

RIGHT: Prussian Private,
1st Silesian Regiment
(Landwehr Infantry)
c. 1814

BELOW LEFT: Austrian
Grenadier 37th
(Hungarian) Regiment
Andreas Marriassy c. 1814

BELOW RIGHT: Austrian
Trooper, 1st Uhlan
Regiment c. 1806

brigade of Leval's at the northern end of the Russian position at what passed for daybreak when it was snowing very heavily. As the skirmishers moved forward the great Russian batteries opened fire. They:

played very heavily but rather at hazard as the French columns were principally concealed by the favouring swells of their ground and the town of Eylau. The French cannonade quickly followed with vigour and effect as every man in the Russian army was exposed from head to heel.

The most striking result of the Russian fire was a panic among the staffs and servants in the town of Eylau. For a while there were scenes of the greatest confusion and before order was restored and the Emperor was established in his command post at Eylau church, Soult had been driven back and Russian counterattacks were threatening to break his line. To divert Russian attention to the other flank Napoleon ordered Augereau's corps and St Hilaire's division to attack on the right, knowing that by this time Davout's leading division was close to that flank.

THE BATTLE

Augereau was a sick man that day and had sought, but been refused, permission to hand over command of his corps. At about 10 am he led his two divisions forward aiming to break through to the great batteries while St Hilaire covered his right and tried to contact Davout. The leading brigades were in line, the second brigades in column (or, according to some reports, in square) and it was unfortunate that, as they advanced, the heaviest snow of the day fell, reducing visibility to ten metres. In such conditions line was the most unsuitable formation in which to move and, before they knew what was happening, the disordered ranks blundered on to the muzzles of 70 Russian guns firing grape while St Hilaire's division veered away southward, leaving their right uncovered. Bennigsen launched a reserve division at their shaken front and Russian dragoons charged into both flanks.

Augereau's corps broke. They left more than 5,000 men dead and wounded on the ground and the rest dissolved into a mob of fugitives dashing for cover in the houses of Eylau. Only the 14me *Ligne* stood firm on a hillock until they were overwhelmed by a flood of Russians which swept into the eastern houses of Eylau. Napoleon himself was only saved from capture by a charge of his escort squadron of *Chasseurs à cheval de la Garde* who held up the Russians long enough for two battalions of the infantry of the Guard to arrive. In this desperate situation, with Soult on the left barely able to hold his ground, with Augereau's corps destroyed and St Hilaire falling back under attack from Russian cavalry, Napoleon decided to buy time by a desperate expedient. He ordered Murat to attack with the Cavalry Reserve backed by the cavalry of the Guard.

This mass of more than 10,000 horsemen — three divisions of dragoons, one of cuirassiers, together with *chasseurs*, *Grenadiers à cheval*, and mamelukes of the Guard, advanced in two great columns. According to French accounts they broke through two lines of Russian infantry, reformed and charged back through the same troops, after which the Guard cavalry performed the same feat. The Russian accounts, which

Murat ordering the
Reserve Cavalry to charge

E. BRISSET. 96

would naturally play down the exploit, make the event less spectacular and refer to a single regiment of cuirassiers which broke through a gap between two Russian formations and charged through to the rear where it was hunted down and destroyed by hussars and Cossacks.

The truth probably lies somewhere between these two versions. There is no doubt that on the right Grouchy's dragoon division drove off the Russian infantry and cavalry which was harassing the retreat of St Hilaire's division, while on the left the dragoons which led the advance were bloodily repulsed although the cuirassiers who followed them made some considerable progress and that most of them fought their way back. The Reserve Cavalry suffered about 2,000 casualties and the Guard cavalry also lost heavily, the *Chasseurs à cheval* alone losing twenty-one officers and 224 men. Nevertheless the cavalry achieved their purpose and bought time. When, about noon, they withdrew, Davout was beginning to press in on the Russian left.

Mobile artillery power

In 1792 the French started the wars with the newly-adopted, highly mobile artillery devised by Jean-Baptiste Gribeauval. Its mobility was due largely to the absence of limbers. The field guns, like the heavier models, had twin trails (instead of the usual block (T-shaped) carriages) which could be hitched to a pair of bogeys carrying the central shaft between the horses. The ready-use ammunition was carried in a wooden chest which, while in motion, rested between the trails supported by its carrying handles. For long journeys the barrel could be moved backwards to a second trunnion position allowing it to rest parallel to the ground.

Gribeauval's artillery also had a high level of interchangeability of parts and equipment between guns of various calibres thus keeping breakdowns to a minimum

Gun team and limber,
Artillery Company,
Neuchâtel Battalion
(Russian Campaign, 1812)

Davout advanced with two divisions forward and one in reserve and, as he described conditions:

There was a violent wind which blew almost all day. Swirls and gusts of snow prevented commanders from seeing what was happening and stopped the soldiers from hearing their orders. The instruction was given to close up the ranks and even the regulations about the gaps between the battalions were ignored as there were times when the dense squalls of snow made it impossible to see ten paces in front . . . The battle had all the characteristics of a night action.

The advance started well. On the left Morand's division, which had some support from St Hilaire's battered formation, took Serpallen while, on the right Friant, his open flank covered by Maraluz's light cavalry, seized Kleine Sausgarten, lost it to a counterattack and took it again. The Russians were fighting every inch of the way but Davout's pressure persuaded Bennigsen to wheel back his left on to a new line.

In performing this difficult manoeuvre a misunderstanding almost brought disaster. In the Russian army it was the custom for the colours to be carried one hundred yards to the rear before a charge was made and, for some reason, the ensigns retreated a hundred yards before the retirement began. When the troops began to retreat, the ensigns, still thinking that a charge was to be made, continued retreating to keep their distance from the columns but the troops pressed on to join their colours. Before stability could be restored the French again attacked and the extreme Russian right collapsed. At Anklappen they put up a stout resistance, losing the farmhouse, retaking it, and losing it again but the village of Kutschitten fell with scarcely a shot being fired. Thus the Russian right was bent back at an acute angle from their left centre and began to show signs of distintegration. As Robert Wilson, the British liaison officer, wrote:

Napoleon at Eylau; among his escort (*far right*) is his Mameluke bodyservant. Russian prisoners are being brought in on the left

Never was a change more sudden. The victors were yielding the field to the vanquished, and surprise and alarm were rapidly displacing confidence and exertion.

The French advance was, at this moment, checked by the fire of the reserve of 60 horse artillery guns and, before Davout's men could resume their advance, a new force came on to the field. Lestocq's Prussian corps, with two Russian regiments under command, had been on the march since 5 am and had fought several rearguard actions against Ney. Early in the afternoon they reached Althof, 5 kilometres downstream from Eylau, where the stream bed, deep and full of loose snow, was impassable except at the bridge. Here Lestocq left a grenadier battalion to hold the bridge and marched on with the remainder of his force, 5,584 men, with one and a half batteries of horse artillery. His orders were to take post on the right of Bennigsen's line now almost denuded of troops to bolster the failing left but, hardly had he reached this position when new orders urged him to march with all speed to the left. Passing through Schloditten, he could see the French around Kutschitten. He attacked them immediately.

Lestocq's attack was the finest feat of arms in the battle, a demonstration that, despite the disasters at Jena and Auerstadt, the Prussian army, of which this was the last remnant, had not lost the determination and discipline for which they had been famous. Advancing with one Prussian and one Russian regiment in column, linked in the rear by a Prussian grenadier battalion in line, they swept round Kutschitten and sealed the garrison, one and a half regiments, from all outside assistance. Only a few of them survived by dashing into the birch woods where they were hunted by Cossacks. Among the allied prizes were three Russian guns and the eagle of 51er *Ligne*.

Now the position on the French right was reversed. It was now Davout's men who were being turned and Lestocq exploited his opportunity to the full. He aligned his four infantry regiments, wheeled them to the right and marched on Anklappen and Kleine Sausgarten. As he wrote:

The infantry now advanced with drums beating and in impeccable order and resolution and, without firing a shot, directed itself on the wood [south-east of Anklappen] and on a column of infantry at least three times their number until within not more than fifty paces. Von Ruchell's regiment then inclined to their left and took a diagonal line on the enemy's right flank. Lieutenant Decker's half battery unlimbered at the same time somewhat to the left on a small height.

A brisk fire now commenced. The Prussian artillery was visibly superior and the musketry of the infantry, posted in a slight dip, caused prodigious loss among the massed enemy while his shot flew too high so that our infantry suffered little. After this tremendous exchange of fire had lasted for half an hour, we charged with the bayonet. The enemy was driven through the woods to Sausgarten and had to abandon the farm of Anklappen, which he set on fire.

By this time night was falling and with the Prussians joining hands with the Russian left centre, the position on this flank was stabilized. The

battle here degenerated into an increasingly desultory exchange of artillery fire.

The last of the fighting was on the Russian right where Ney, having overcome Lestocq's rearguard at Althof bridge, seized Schloditten, on Bennigsen's road to Königsberg from a small force of Russians and Prussians. Rather than leave it in enemy hands Bennigsen ordered an attack on the village by a grenadier regiment at 10 pm. Ney reported that this attack was driven off but that he subsequently evacuated the place. The Russians claimed that the attack succeeded.

At 11 pm Bennigsen, still on horseback, held a conference for his generals. He announced his decision to retire on Königsberg. His subordinates besought him to hold his ground and even to attack in the morning. He would not change his mind and there was no reason for doing so. The only food and ammunition for the army was at Königsberg and there was no way of bringing it to the army. The army must, therefore, go to their supplies. They had in any case denied Napoleon the victory on which he had set his heart. There was no possibility of the French being able to make any further offensive moves before a period of rest and re-equipment.

All battles are unpleasant but, partly because of the weather and partly from the determination with which both sides fought, Eylau has a peculiar unpleasantness. When it was over the ground was: 'entirely red

The vast column of the Reserve Cavalry breaking through the Russian position

with blood in the parts where the fighting had been most bitter'.

Bennigsen reported the Russian losses as 12,000 killed and 7,900 wounded, the latter figure probably being something of an underestimate, and the combined Russo-Prussian casualties were about 25,000, a third of the men involved. Napoleon's public announcement that: 'Our loss amounts to exactly 1,900 dead and 5,700 wounded, of whom 1,000 are wounded so severely as to be out of action' was a barefaced lie. Later in life he admitted to casualties of 18,000 but even this seems to be far short of the real total. The only firm figures available are those for Soult's corps (8,250 killed and wounded) and for Davout's (5,007). To these (and Soult was in the habit of understating his losses) must be added the almost total destruction of Augereau's corps and a very heavy loss in the cavalry while there must have been substantial loss in Ney's corps and the infantry of the Guard. It seems certain that the French loss was no less than that of the Russians and may well have reached 30,000.

Napoleon was able to claim a victory since his enemy retired but, even in the 58me *Bulletin de la Grande Armée*, his claim must have sounded hollow even to himself:

*Small perversities (*petites contrariétés*) in the weather, which would have seemed insignificant in other circumstances, much hampered the manoeuvres of the French command. Our cavalry and artillery achieved marvels. The Guard Cavalry surpassed themselves, which is saying a great deal. The infantry of the Guard was under arms all day, under a dreadful fire of grapeshot, without firing a shot or moving from their position since events did not justify it being required. Marshal Augereau's wound was an unfortunate accident which deprived his corps of leadership in the midst of a desperate* mêlée.

This was scarcely the language of triumph, and his infantry, which on the day after the battle was heard to be shouting *Du pain et la paix* rather than *Vive l'Empereur*, cannot have been much encouraged by the way in which the *Bulletin* ignored their own immense contribution while heaping praise on the Guard for doing nothing.

The Russians also claimed victory and at worst had the satisfaction of being the first army to have held the seemingly invincible Napoleon to a draw but the most apt comment on Eylau was that made by Marshal Ney when he saw the battlefield by daylight: *'Quel massacre! Et sans resultat'.*

FOOTNOTE

As David Chandler has written, 'None of the great Napoleonic struggles is surrounded by more doubt and uncertainty than the battle of Eylau. Fact, myth and propaganda are almost inextricably mixed'. Apart from deliberate misrepresentation, the heavy snow and the smoke of more than 700 guns on a narrow front made the fog of war thicker than usual so that the accounts of survivors are exceptionally contradictory. It is not even possible to establish which way the wind was blowing. Probability suggests an east wind but both sides say that it was blowing in their faces. The Russians say that when they fired Serpallen on evacuating the village, the smoke blew back in their faces, which suggests a south wind but Lestocq wrote that, as he was approaching from the north-east, he could see the gun flashes but could not hear the firing. This indicates a west or north-west wind.

CHAPTER NINE

War on Two Fronts

ON 25 JUNE 1807 NAPOLEON, Emperor of the French, and Alexander, Czar of all the Russias, met on an elaborately decorated raft moored centrally in the river Niemen to arrange the future of Europe and it appeared that the French Empire had reached its apogee. Eleven days earlier the Russian army had suffered a shattering defeat at Friedland (Pravdinsk) and its commander was convinced that only an immediate armistice could save it. If ever a commander could be said to have lost an important battle through his own incapacity it was Bennigsen at Friedland. Having moved to that town on information he found to be false, he stayed there with his army's back to an unfordable river and its front cut in two by an impassable millstream which he made no attempt to bridge until Napoleon had attacked his 46,000 men with 86,000. He lost 16,000 men and 80 guns and it was only the dogged resistance of his men and the initiative of his subordinates which saved the Russians from total disaster.

Friedland was no easy victory for the French, who lost 10,000 men, but it did much to revive the morale of the *Grande Armée* which had been severely shaken by the drawn battle at Eylau and the miseries of winter in Poland. Nevertheless the *Grand Armée* was changing. In August 1805, when it had set off eastward from the Channel ports, it had been a highly tempered force with three or more years of training behind it. Since then it had marched to Ulm, Vienna, Austerlitz, Jena, Berlin, and Königsberg and had fought five major and dozens of minor actions, almost all of which had cost it dearly in casualties. Napoleon was achieving his victories increasingly, by a crushing hammer blow, rather than the skilful manoeuvres of his earlier campaigns. Sometimes these hammer blows were ill-timed. Four days before Friedland, in an attempt to get between Bennigsen and Königsberg, he had launched a series of brutal frontal attacks on an entrenched Russian position at Heilsberg (Lidzbark). He incurred at least 11,000 casualties and gained nothing.

France, even with her new boundaries which included Belgium and much of north-west Italy, could not afford losses on this scale. The casualties at Austerlitz, Jena, and Auerstadt had been made good by anticipating the call-up of 1807 conscripts but even so Augerau's corps had to be disbanded and its place taken by a composite formation of

Poles, Italians, and Germans. Conscripts of 1808 were summoned to replace the more serious losses at Eylau. France was mortgaging her future manpower and henceforward she had to rely increasingly on her vassal states to fight her battles.

The treaty of Tilsit gave a promise of peace. With Russia an ally, Austria cowed, and Prussia under French occupation, the drain on French blood could be halted. Only Britain, Sweden, and Sicily were open enemies and their subjection would be more a problem for sailors than soldiers. Napoleon could not leave well alone. His restless ambition drove him to occupy the Iberian peninsula. The occupation of Portugal was achieved without a single battle casualty, though many men were lost when the occupation corps obeyed the Emperor's peremptory order to enter the country by a road which existed on a map but not on the ground. In May 1808, after eight months occupation of a sullen but quiescent country, the French had lost 3,000 men through disease, murder, and desertion.

The seizure of Portugal, a joint Franco–Spanish operation, could be justified by the need to stop British trade with Portugal and to deny to the Royal Navy its best overseas base, the all-weather harbour of Lisbon. The occupation could be maintained for just as long as France and Spain remained allies, for as long as the Spaniards could provide the bulk of the occupying army and could guarantee the security of the 644 kilometre line of communications between France and the Portuguese frontier. Napoleon's boundless ambition drove him to destroy this convenient arrangement and to try to force Spain into the status of a French puppet. Under pretext of reinforcing the army in Portugal he occupied Barcelona (29 February) and by a variety of stratagems seized the frontier fortresses of San Sebastian, Pamplona, and Figueras. These flagrant aggressions were submitted to by the Spanish government but the people saw themselves insulted. A riot outside the palace at Aranjuez secured the dismissal of Godoy, the detested minister and court favourite, on 17 March 1808 and next day King Charles IV abdicated in favour of his almost equally ineffective son, Ferdinand VII. With an army under Murat close to Madrid, Napoleon could not resist the temptation to intervene. He lured both Charles IV and Ferdinand VII on to French soil, extorted their abdications and set about substituting his brother Joseph Bonaparte as King of Spain and the Indies.

The Spaniards had been misgoverned for generations but, whatever illusory delights were offered by the usurper at the point of French bayonets, they preferred their own version of misgovernment. They took to their knives and their fowling pieces and set about achieving their own liberation, sending to Britain a stream of delegates demanding money and arms. At a blow the lifeline joining the French army in Portugal to the Pyrenees was ruptured. The Spanish troops in that country marched home to assist their compatriots leaving General Junot with 26,594 French troops isolated in Portugal. It was the opportunity that Britain had sought since 1793, an isolated French force within the reach of sea power. On 1 August 1808 the Royal Navy delivered Lieutenant-General Sir Arthur Wellesley and a corps of troops to the shore near Coimbra. Before the end of the month Junot was negotiating

PREVIOUS PAGE: The meeting of the two emperors on the Niemen

The main areas of action in the Peninsula

to have his men, defeated at Vimeiro, repatriated in British ships. The Royal Navy had recovered Lisbon and Britain was, at last, a permanent factor in the land war.

SPAIN AND PORTUGAL

To try to seize Spain was a serious misjudgement, to do it with too few troops and those of poor quality was a fatal error. Napoleon thought 'that troops would only be needed to maintain public order and to garrison the fortresses'. When he attempted his coup there were only 82,000 of his troops in Spain. Many of them, one in ten, were foreigners – Germans, Irish, Italians, or Swiss – and only 16,232, including 532 *Marins de la Garde*, were in regularly formed units. The rest were a hotch-potch of depot and provisional battalions and *régiments de marche*. It was a second-rate army commanded by second-rate generals and their position was made worse by Napoleon who, still thinking of providing garrisons, dispersed them all over Spain. The result was predictable. One column was repulsed from Valencia; a second found itself bogged

119

down in a seemingly interminable siege of Saragossa; a third set out to occupy Cadiz. On 19 July 1808 it was forced to surrender, 17,635 strong, at Bailen. Its adversaries, Spanish regulars, had for the past four years been besieging the British in Gibraltar.

The capitulation at Bailen, the first French defeat since the formation of the Napoleonic empire, stirred all Europe. Everywhere, and especially in Austria, men began to realize that war with France did not inevitably lead to defeat. The Spaniards were confirmed in their belief that they could drive the French out and King Joseph abandoned Madrid and went scuttling back to the Ebro.

The defeats in Spain and Portugal forced Napoleon to turn his full attention to the Peninsula:

The war can be finished by a single operation but it must be properly concerted and I must be there to arrange it.

He persuaded a reluctant Czar to keep Austria from moving and arranged for 100,000 men of the *Grand Armée* to move to Spain from Poland and Germany while every man who could be spared from the rest of Europe and Junot's repatriated corps from Portugal were set marching to the Pyrenees. By November 1808 the *Armée d'Espagne* had a nominal strength of 305,000 and could put 235,000 effectives in the field, this strength including two Italian, one Polish, and one German divisions but consisting in the main of battle-tried French troops in well established battalions, brigades, and divisions. To produce this array the army in the east was reduced to 120,000 men of whom barely half were French. The command there was left to Marshal Davout.

Napoleon, faced with a number of small and disunited Spanish armies, had no difficulty in marching to Madrid but on the way there one incident showed his increasing tendency to sweep away opposition regardless of casualties. The crest of the Somosierra pass over the Sierra de Guadarrama was held by 12,000 dispirited men, mostly recruits and, conventionally, Victor's corps was sent up the hills on either side to force them to withdraw. Impatient and anxious to reach the capital on the anniversary of Austerlitz, Napoleon ordered his escort squadron, 150 men of the Polish *chevau-légers*, to storm the pass. They charged up two kilometres of steep road, overwhelming four batteries protected by earthworks. As they approached the crest the Spaniards, already shaken by the approach of Victor's men, gave way. As a feat of courage the Polish attack was incomparable; as a tactical manoeuvre it was the trick of a spoiled child, gaining half an hour by the sacrifice of 81 brave men and 100 horses. The imperial entrance into Madrid was nevertheless a day late for the anniversary.

Established in the capital, orders were given for the subjugation of the rest of the country. Troops were sent to reimpose the siege of Saragossa, to relieve the garrison of Barcelona. To the east of Madrid divisions were accumulated for the invasion of Portugal. Napoleon had decided that the Spanish army were a *canaille* (rabble) and that the British would immediately re-embark. The *Bulletin* announced:

The English are flying towards Lisbon and, if they do not hurry, the French army will enter that capital before they do.

On the day these words were written, 12 December, Sir John Moore with 30,000 men was marching from Salamanca in an attempt to overwhelm Soult's corps, 17,000 strong, which had been left isolated to the north-east of Valladolid. He failed to do so and had to retire hastily to his transports but, by diverting every available man to intercept him, the Emperor distorted his strategy for the conquest of Spain and Portugal in such a way that it never recovered. Before Moore's army, flushed with victory over Soult at Corunna (16 January 1809), had buried their general on the ramparts and sailed away, Napoleon found that urgent business called him back to France. Taking courage from affairs in Spain, Austria was making preparations to renew the war. The Imperial Guard followed their master to Paris but the rest of the veterans withdrawn from the east remained in Spain, many of them for ever.

Napoleon carried two delusions back from the Peninsula. One was that the army could easily feed itself in Spain. There is, he wrote:

Sir John Moore mortally wounded at Corunna

no need to send provisions; there is plenty of everything. I have never seen an army so well fed or so lavishly supplied.

The second was that there was no communication problem in the country. From Paris and points east, he sent a stream of orders to his generals ordering them to march hither and thither as if they were manoeuvring on the plains of Lombardy. He must, wrote the disgruntled Marshal Jourdan 'have supposed that the roads were as freely passable as those from Paris to Lyons'.

NAPOLEON MARCHES EAST

Since the *débâcles* at Ulm and Austerlitz the Austrians had set about remodelling their army and had given the command to their best general, the Archduke Charles. His control, however, was far from complete. His brother the Emperor, who disliked him, kept in his own hands the right to appoint and supersede subordinate commanders, and the Aulic Council, a permanent committee of elderly reactionaries, could and did interfere with strategy. Nevertheless the size of the regular army had been increased from 200,000 (1805) to 340,000 and it had been formed into permanent corps on the French model. Behind the regulars stood a newly-formed militia (*landwehr*), largely German speaking, which, if its training and discipline were too sketchy for field service, could relieve the regulars in many garrison duties. A new drill book had been introduced which, belatedly, made some allowances for skirmishers although among 80 regiments of infantry there were only 9 *Jäger* battalions. The cavalry, 36,000 strong, still had a good reputation although it suffered from a frustrating shortage of remounts. The artillery, with 760 guns, was excellent at regimental level but could not produce senior gunner officers of even moderate competence.

Napoleon was hard put to it to raise an army sufficiently large to oppose this powerful new Austrian array. The *Armée du Rhin*, although 120,000 strong, had to find occupation forces in Poland and Prussia and could put only 75,000 men in the field. Only the Guard, 7,500, was withdrawn from Spain. Between September 1808 and January 1809, 270,000 additional conscripts had been called up, many of them men hitherto exempt from the classes of 1806–09 but 190,000 came from those not due to be summoned until 1810. By combing the depots (which had already contributed largely to the first *Armée d'Espagne*) and recalling veterans, a new *Grand Armée d'Allemagne* was called into being with a strength of 175,000. Of these 55,000 were Germans and Poles and 11,000 of the remaining Frenchmen were raw recruits who could not even load a musket when they marched off to join their battalions. Thanks to the demands of Spain only 311 guns were immediately available.

France was lucky that the Aulic Council wasted a month in tinkering with the Archduke's plans and it was not until 9 April 1809 that he struck into Bavaria. This was earlier than Napoleon had expected, he was still in Paris and the command in Germany was in the hands of Berthier, who had neither the talent nor the will to exercise it. Berthier's difficulties were not eased when an order sent by telegraph to his headquarters at Strasbourg was delayed by fog for six days and was overtaken by a subsequent order, dependent on the first, which was carried by courier. By 17 April he had succeeded in getting the two

RIGHT: Goya's vivid memorial to the brutally crushed revolt in Madrid, May 1808

BELOW: Moore's victory over Soult at Corunna, January 1809

Land Warfare

Since fleet actions were rare and almost non-existent in the last ten years of the war, I have used a different approach in dealing with the war at sea. Dividing the war into two periods – before and after the Peace of Amiens – I have devoted a chapter in each part to the ways in which France could hope to overcome 'the most powerful and most constant' of her enemies – by invading the British Isles or by strangling British trade and thus her ability to continue the war. I have linked these with a single battlepiece describing the usually neglected twin battles of Algeciras, the second of which is known in the Royal Navy's battle honours as Gut of Gibraltar.

The names of ships can easily cause confusion as not only did several navies use the same name for ships – there was a 'Venus' in the fleets of Britain, France, Holland, Denmark, and Russia while two 'Neptunes' and a 'Neptuno' fought at Trafalgar – but captured ships were frequently taken into service under their original names so that 'Northumberland' is confusingly to be found in the French line of battle and *Ça-ira* in the Royal Navy. I have therefore used small capitals for British ships and italics for those of other navies. Thus SWIFTSURE becomes *Swiftsure* when she was taken in 1801 but would have reverted to SWIFTSURE when she was recaptured at Trafalgar.

For the benefit of pedants I should remark that I am aware that the word 'battleship' was not used during the long wars with France as a shortened form of 'line of battle ship' and that the form 'ship or sail of the line' was more usual, although it was not unusual to refer to such ships as 'cruisers'. The occasional use of 'battleship', even if not contemporary, seems permissible on grounds of both brevity and clarity but I have frequently envied the French who, without ambiguity, could use the single word *vaisseau* for a line of battle ship.

FOREWORD

THE MAIN PURPOSE OF THIS BOOK is to describe and analyse the actions of armies and navies rather than those of governments. It is consequently my intention only to sketch in the backgrounds to the fighting which is the principal business of the text. To enable the reader to relate the actions described to the course of the whole war a *Chronology of the Wars 1792–1815* is included as an Appendix and those who wish to know more of the political, diplomatic, and economic background should refer to my *The Napoleonic Wars: An Illustrated History* (1979).

More important for this book is the way in which armies and navies fought, how they were commanded, how they were (or were not) supplied with food and ammunition, and, a much neglected subject, how the component parts of armies and navies communicated with each other. In an age when instant communication by radio or telephone is taken for granted it is all too easy to ignore the problems of a commander who, on land, could only communicate with his outlying subordinates by a written or verbal message carried by a horseman who was always liable to be lost, captured, shot, or merely delayed if his mount cast a shoe. The battles of Eylau and Friedland would not have been fought and the *Grande Armée* would not have lost 40,000 irreplaceable veterans if Marshal Berthier had not entrusted a vital message to an inexperienced staff officer who lost his way and was captured by Cossacks before he had time to dispose of his despatch. The worst repulse suffered by the British between 1793 and 1814 occurred two weeks after peace had been agreed; but news took longer than a fortnight to travel between Ghent and New Orleans. At sea the communication problem was even more difficult. Messages could only be passed between ships within visual range – about 24 kilometres on a clear day. At night there could be no communication beyond the call of a man's voice.

Rather than to attempt to describe, as an academic exercise, the tactics used on land and to illustrate them with disembodied examples, I have chosen to deal in some depth with six battles – Tourcoing, Castiglione, Marengo, Eylau, Salamanca, and Waterloo – and to use them as illustrations of the way in which the land war was fought. These battlepieces are linked with chapters giving an outline of events and developments between them.

7

Contents

wings of his army separated by 120 kilometres with only the thinnest screen of Bavarians between them. Fortunately Napoleon joined the army at Donauwörth that day and, thanks to an epic defence by Davout around Ratisbon, there was just time to hold the Austrian advance and bring them to battle at Eckmühl [Eggmühl] and Abensberg (20–22 April). Charles lost 30,000 men on those three days and retreated to the Bohemian mountains, leaving the way open for the French to reoccupy Vienna (13 May). Thereafter the Archduke moved his troops forward again and faced the French army from across the broad River Danube near the capital.

The Archduke Charles ordering an Austrian counterattack during the battle of Aspern-Essling

Although he had no idea of the Austrians' strength and position, Napoleon decided to deal with Charles' army immediately before they could be reinforced from Italy. Although warned that the Danube in spring was an unpredictable river liable to sudden floods, he ordered his army to cross, using Lobau island as a stepping-stone. A bridgehead was established on 21 May which included the villages of Aspern and Essling but the pontoon bridges were constantly broken by barges loaded with stone which the Austrians floated down on the strong current and the French could never build up sufficient strength on the far bank to deal with the attacks Charles constantly launched at them. After two days of bitter fighting Napoleon ordered a withdrawal, both sides having lost about 25,000 men. For the first time Napoleon had been defeated in person and he had only his own impatience and his underestimation of the enemy's strength to blame.

It was six weeks later that another attempt was made to cross the Danube. This time it was the Austrians who were surprised and, at the battle of Wagram (5–6 July), defeated. Nevertheless, it had been a narrow victory and the Austrians, having lost 37,000 men, were able to leave the field in good order, taking with them 7,000 French prisoners, 12 eagles, and 21 French guns.

Wagram induced the Austrians to make peace yet again but it cost France 40,000 casualties, a price she could no longer afford since she now had 288,000 men committed to Spain. The butchery at Wagram was greatly inflated by the desperate measure to which Napoleon had to resort to break the Archduke's will to continue the battle. He aimed at the Austrian line the most massive column ever seen in war, 8,000 men under General Macdonald. Four weak battalions were deployed in three-deep line with four more in support. On either flank was stationed a division in close column. In all twenty-three battalions advanced on a front of 365 metres. They were supported by the divisional artilleries and the guns of the Guard and there was cavalry on either flank. Macdonald, who won his marshal's baton for this attack, considered that the attack was a justifiable expedient to take the weight off other sectors of the French army but 'I was far from thinking that this demonstration (*montre*) was to be the main attack on the enemy's centre'. It was, in fact, a manoeuvre of desperation and, although it succeeded in making a break-in to the Austrian position, the cost was appalling, 6,500 fell — more than three-quarters of those taking part. In Macdonald's view success was not exploited since Nansouty could not be induced to charge with his cuirassier division through the gap which the infantry had made and the cavalry's only contribution was to close the open rear of the column when Austrian horsemen counterattacked.

This was the apotheosis of the attack in column (although technically Macdonald's formation was a huge *ordre mixte*), a battering ram of men used to beat a hole at a frightful cost and, although victory was secured, it was by no means overwhelming. The war was entering into a new stage. Napoleon's enemies were learning to ride the blows he dealt them while his own armies no longer had the strength, training, and coherence that had marked them four years earlier. There was a shortage of experienced officers at all levels and the men in the ranks were no longer sufficiently trained to fight as they had done at Austerlitz or Auerstadt. Napoleon recognized this and, to shore up his infantry, he reintroduced 'battalion guns', two to each battalion in the *Grande Armée d'Allemagne*, from the stocks captured in Austrian arsenals. As he remarked 'The worse the quality of the troops, the more they require guns'.

For the fourth time the Austrians had been beaten and induced to make peace but this was Napoleon's last victorious campaign and was marked by his increasing reliance on the knock-out blow. Strength was replacing subtlety in his tactics and he had already mortgaged France's strength.

OVERLEAF: The *Grande Armée* crossing the Danube on its advance to the battle of Wagram

CHAPTER TEN

Salamanca,
22 July 1812

T HE FRENCH FOUND A NEW TYPE OF WAR in Spain. They had little
trouble in defeating the Spanish regular armies who, after their
victory at Bailen, lost every sizeable battle for five years. But they never
succeeded in destroying them. However shattering the defeats they
suffered, the Spaniards would retire to their hills and, rearmed with
British muskets, would reappear to fight again. Nor, despite Napoleon's
belief, was food easy to come by. At best Spain lived at subsistence level
and the incursion of a quarter of a million Frenchmen, to say nothing of
British and Portuguese armies, meant that there was not enough food to
go round. The French generals pursued a ruthless policy of requisition in
an attempt to feed their men and the soldiers lost no opportunity of
supplementing their meagre rations by private looting.

It was the relentless search for food by the French that led Spaniards
of all ages and classes to leave their homes and form themselves into
guerrillas which harried their oppressors unmercifully. Increasingly, no
Frenchman was safe alone, no despatch could be conveyed without at
least a squadron as escort, no supply depot or magazine could be left
without a garrison and every foraging expedition had to be an operation
of war. Information could only be obtained under torture. The greatest
part of the huge French force in Spain was permanently engaged in
holding the ground they had seized. Only a fraction of the great army
could be used to combat the other menace which lay behind the
Portuguese frontier.

The British had maintained their hold on Lisbon even during the
dark days which followed the evacuation of Moore's army from Corunna
and in April 1809 Sir Arthur Wellesley returned there with reinforcements with which he quickly and competently ejected Soult's corps
from northern Portugal. Then, in an attempt to profit by the French
involvement with Austria, a joint Anglo–Spanish army attempted to
take Madrid. A bloody battle was won against Marshals Jourdan and
Victor at Talavera (27–28 July 1809) but the intervention of three more
French corps destroyed any hope of further progress. So the allies parted,
the Spaniards to indulge in further grandiose but ill-fated schemes of
liberation, the British to concentrate their strength on the protection of
their all-important base at Lisbon.

As soon as he had imposed peace on Austria, Napoleon determined to sweep the British out of the Peninsula. A steady stream of reinforcements crossed the Pyrenees and by the New Year of 1810 the *Armée d'Espagne* (which was soon to be divided into half a dozen uncoordinated armies) had 360,000 men on its muster rolls. This huge force contained substantial numbers of Italians and Poles and some Germans, Irish, and Swiss but more than 300,000 of the soldiers were native Frenchmen, a gigantic drain on the manpower resources of France. The greater part of this army was needed to hold down the parts of Spain which had already been overrun and all that could be spared as a striking force against the British was the *Armée de Portugal*, a force of 65,000 men with a promise of 20,000 more to follow. This number seemed more than adequate to Napoleon, who wrote that:

It appears from the returns of the English army extracted from the English papers, that their army consists of 23,000 English and Germans and 22,000 Portuguese. Marshal Massena should in consequence have more troops than he needs.

The Emperor had not greatly underestimated the numbers defending Portugal but he greatly underrated the difficulties facing Massena. Lord Wellington (as Wellesley had become in the aftermath of his victory at Talavera) had no intention of fighting on the frontiers but planned to retreat deep into Portugal, laying bare the country behind him, until he brought the French face to face with a formidable defensive system, the lines of Torres Vedras, which covered the immediate approaches to Lisbon. The *Armée de Portugal* was to be defeated by hunger rather than musketry. Nor did Napoleon, or Massena, appreciate that, thanks to the efforts of William Carr Beresford, the Portuguese army was being trained up to a standard at which they could take their place in the line beside the British.

INVASION AND STALEMATE

Massena started his invasion of Portugal on 24 July 1810. His army left the country on 5 April 1811 having achieved nothing but the loss of 25,000 men of whom only 1,500 died in battle. The year that followed was spent in disputing possession of the two fortresses, Ciudad Rodrigo and Badajoz, which command the only practicable roads between Portugal and Spain. Wellington's attempt to besiege Badajoz in the early summer of 1811 was frustrated by a combination of the *Armée de Portugal*, now under Marshal Marmont, and Soult's *Armée du Midi*, whose principal task was the occupation of Andalusia. Similarly an attempt to reduce Ciudad Rodrigo by blockade failed because of a junction of the *Armée de Portugal* and the *Armée du Nord*, whose task was to garrison Spain between Valladolid and the French frontier. Since Wellington's Anglo–Portuguese force was not strong enough to overcome a combination of the French armies it seemed, as winter came on, that stalemate had been reached.

Napoleon broke the deadlock by ordering all his armies in Spain to send large detachments to assist in the conquest of Valencia, an irrelevant dispersion of the already over-extended area of occupation. Wellington

PREVIOUS PAGE: British Dragoons being roused after a halt on the march in Spain

The Connaught Rangers storming the castle at Badajoz

took advantage of the weakness of his opponents to seize Ciudad Rodrigo (19 January 1812) and, three months later took Badajoz in a murderous attack (6 April) before Soult could march to its support. Marmont had proposed that he should take the *Armée de Portugal* to help Badajoz but received a peremptory order bidding him instead to concentrate at Salamanca, retake Rodrigo, and invade Portugal while Wellington was involved in the south. It was in vain for the marshal to try to explain to Napoleon the facts of military life in Spain:

If I concentrate my army at Salamanca it could not subsist there for two weeks and would create between Salamanca and Valladolid the kind of desert which already exists between Salamanca and Rodrigo and which inhibits the movement of the army. The emperor wants me to take the offensive towards Rodrigo but his Majesty does not realise that the smallest movement in these parts expends great quantities of resources, especially of horses. Such a move is the equivalent of fighting a great battle . . . The army could not cross the Agueda which is unfordable at this season and it could not live for three days near Rodrigo for lack of food . . . None of our magazines contain four days' rations and we have no transport. To make requisitions on even the poorest village we have to send a detachment of two hundred men and, to be able to live, we have to scatter over great distances.

The Emperor refused to be convinced by this glimpse of reality and merely reiterated his original order. Marmont did his best to obey. Napoleon was by this time increasingly preoccupied with the prospect of a campaign against Russia but he dared withdraw only 27,000 men from Spain for his eastern army. He did, however, establish a long overdue supreme command in Spain (16 March 1812). Unfortunately he gave it to his brother Joseph, whose military experience was minimal, assisted by Marshal Jourdan who had a clear strategic brain but, despite his eighteen-year-old victory at Fleurus, was not taken seriously by his brother marshals. They continued to pursue their own diverse concerns.

The prospect facing Joseph and Jourdan was not encouraging. They were responsible for a huge force, 243,832 men under arms in May 1812, but its wastage rate was very high, 50,000 men had been struck off the effective list in the past six months apart from those the Emperor had withdrawn. Leaving aside the men needed to hold eastern Spain and the small reserve at Bayonne, there were four armies who could be called upon to resist an Anglo-Portuguese thrust into Spain. At the northern end of the Portuguese frontier was Marmont with 50,000 of the *Armée de Portugal*, one division of which was, on the Emperor's orders, stationed in the Asturias. The southern end of the frontier was the responsibility of Soult's *Armée du Midi*, 60,000 men largely concerned with occupying Andalusia and prosecuting the two-year-old siege of Cadiz. Behind the junction of these two forces was Joseph's own *Armée de Centre*, 18,000 men, the garrison of Madrid and its surroundings. Finally there was General Cafarelli's *Armée du Nord*, 35,000 strong, which guarded the communications between Valladolid and Bayonne.

Seeing that Wellington had the option of striking through either Rodrigo at Marmont or through Badajoz at either Soult or Madrid, Jourdan issued orders that whichever front line army was not attacked should send help to the one that was. Marmont agreed to this, Soult would have nothing to do with it:

The Armée du Midi *cannot send* [a corps] *to the valley of the Tagus without being obliged to evacuate Andalusia within two weeks.*

The implication was quite clear to Jourdan who wrote:

If Lord Wellington, who has 60,000 men apart from the Spanish armies and the guerrillas, moves against either the Armée du Midi *or that* de Portugal, *whichever he attacks will be unable to resist him. As things stand, only disaster can be expected.*

Realizing that if Marmont was defeated Soult would have to evacuate Andalusia or be isolated, Wellington decided to strike at the *Armée de Portugal*. Having left 18,000 men to watch Soult from around Badajoz, he could put into the field a force of 48,000 men, including 17,000 Portuguese and 3,000 Spaniards:

I think I can make this move with safety, excepting always the risk of a general action. I am of opinion that I shall have the advantage in such an action and that this is the period of all others in which such a measure should be tried.

Lieutenant-General (Acting General) Lord Wellington. He never wore uniform if he could avoid it

The allied army started marching eastward from Ciudad Rodrigo on 13 June, a day on which Wellington heard that Marmont's army was now 54,000 strong, outnumbering his own, but wrote 'I propose to continue our movement'. In fact only two divisions of the *Armée de Portugal* were immediately available and Marmont withdrew them, leaving 800 men as a garrison for three fortified convents which dominated the Salamanca bridge over the Tormes. It took ten days to take the convents during which time Marmont was able to assemble most of his divisions but, to Wellington's disappointment, he declined to attack the covering force and, as soon as the siege ended, retreated north to the line of the Douro where he was joined by his division from the Asturias, making his field strength 49,000 men of whom 3,500 were cavalry. There were 78 guns.

Little help was forthcoming from the other French armies. Cafarelli, who promised 8,000 men, found himself so harassed by guerrillas and seaborne raids by Royal Marines that he could with difficulty be induced to part with a weak cavalry brigade and a battery. Soult, as was to be expected, did not move a man and from Madrid, where Jourdan believed that Wellington had only 18,000 British troops with him, came a letter dated 30 June, asking why Marmot had not attacked the allied army:

His Majesty [Joseph] believes that you are strong enough to win a victory and to take advantage of the present circumstances to fight Wellington while he has not got his full strength in hand.

From 2 to 15 July Wellington and Marmont faced each other across the broad Douro. With some British reinforcements, Wellington now had 52,000 men, including 4,000 cavalry and 54 guns, but he made no attempt at an assault crossing since he knew that Marmont could not feed his army on the north bank and he saw no point in incurring casualties to force his enemy to make an inevitable move.

The break came on 15 July when, with great skill, Marmont feinted with his right and struck with his left at Tordesillas. He caught Wellington off balance, came close to entrapping his right wing and to capturing both Wellington and Beresford who had to draw their swords to defend themselves against French cavalry. The situation was soon restored and that night Wellington learned from a captured letter that King Joseph was marching to Marmont's aid with 13,000 men from Madrid. It was typical of the difficulties under which the French laboured in Spain that of the three copies of this letter sent by Jourdan all were taken by guerrillas and one reached Wellington within six days of despatch.

For the next six days the two armies marched towards Salamanca on parallel courses, always close to each other, sometimes within 'half musket shot'. When the British reached the city on 21 July, Wellington had decided that, with reinforcements joining Marmont from both Madrid and the *Armée du Nord*, he would not be justified in risking a battle. It would be better:

to cross the Tormes, if the enemy should; to cover Salamanca as long as I can; and above all, not to give up our communication with Ciudad Rodrigo; and not to

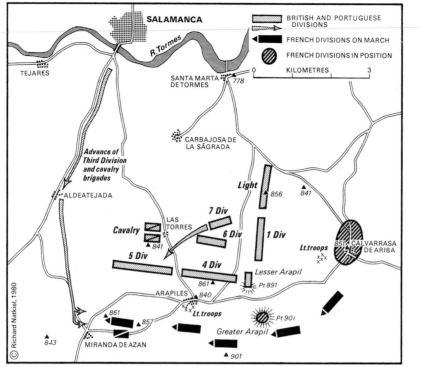

The battle of Salamanca

fight an action, unless under very advantageous circumstances, or if it should become absolutely necessary.

He gave orders for his baggage train to start withdrawing on the following morning while the rest of the army held its position to ensure that it got safely away. This would leave him with the opportunity of utilizing any 'very advantageous circumstances' that might occur.

At dawn on 22 July the allied army was astride the Tormes at the fords of Santa Marta with most of the troops on a north-south ridge which swung sharply west at a height known as the Lesser Arapil. Facing this ridge on the east was another ridge on which allied light troops were skirmishing with Marmont's *tirailleurs* around the chapel of Nuesta Señora de la Peña.

The French had forded the river during the night at Huerta, some miles to the east, and were pressing forward through the scrubby woodland behind Nuestra Señora. Marmont was up with his leading units and rode to the high ground near Calvarrasa de Ariba to view the allied position. There was little to be seen. Most of the troops were concealed behind the ridge but he saw Wellington and his staff watching the French advance and the dust raised by the movement of columns out of sight. Away to the west was a larger dust cloud raised by the baggage column with its escort of a single regiment of Portuguese dragoons. This he took to be a body of fighting troops. As he wrote:

All the indications were that the enemy intended to occupy a position at Tejares, a

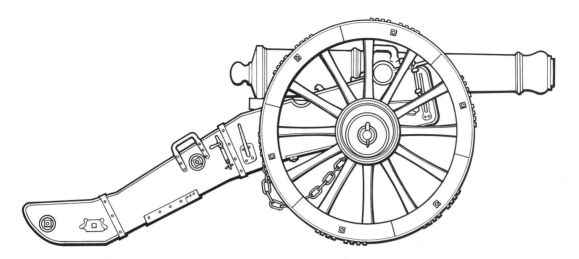

ABOVE: French 12-pounder
field piece. Napoleon
adapted the Gribeauval
System which had
introduced
standardization and
mobility, by replacing
many lighter pieces with
12-pounders

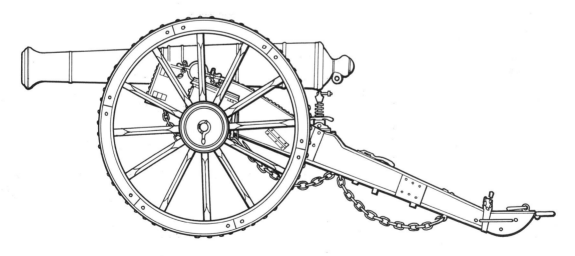

French 9-pounder.
Although capable of firing
nine rounds a minute these
guns threw out such clouds
of smoke only two rounds
of aimed fire were
practicable

league in rear . . . but since his move on Tejares could be difficult in the presence of the whole French army, I thought I ought to concentrate my army so that I would be able to act as circumstances suggested and permitted . . . It seemed likely that there would not be a battle but a brisk rearguard action with all my forces against only a part of the English army in which I could, late in the day, score a point.

Although Marmont was the youngest of the marshals, aged only 38, he was a very experienced soldier, a gunner of dash and distinction as he had demonstrated at Castiglione and Marengo. Nevertheless, he had never won a battle in independent command and was naturally anxious to do so. Like most French commanders he believed that Wellington was a cautious general, adept at choosing good defensive positions but not a man to take the offensive. The French had grown unused to opponents as daring as themselves. It occurred to the marshal that it might be possible to turn the southern flank of the allied rearguard.

Wellington was in no hurry to abandon Salamanca but during the morning he moved much of his strength to the ridge that ran west from the Lesser Arapil. His position was now L-shaped and lying outside it, to east and south, was another L-shaped ridge across which the French were slowly spreading. Within the angle of this outer, French ridge, there stood an isolated height, the Greater Arapil, and, had he not been anticipated by the French, Wellington would gladly have occupied it as an advanced post. Instead he left two divisions facing east and formed his striking force, four divisions on a front of two with independent Portuguese brigades on their flanks, facing south with their left on the Lesser Arapil. Two cavalry brigades and the Spanish force were in their rear. A final reserve was the Third Division, commanded by Wellington's brother-in-law, Edward Pakenham, which was crossing the Tormes at and near Salamanca and making for Aldeatejada on the extreme right.

Noon was well past and Wellington was still reluctant to give the order to retire and decided to have a belated midday meal. While he was eating it a staff officer reported that the French were moving steadily westward. Dashing to his telescope, Wellington saw that not only were the French marching in force along the outer ridge but that their divisions were becoming spread out. There was a fleeting chance that, if he acted quickly enough, the *Armée de Portugal* could be destroyed. 'By God,' he said, 'that will do.'

WELLINGTON'S ATTACK
Wellington's orders for retreat were immediately countermanded and the 27,000 men waiting on the ridge west of the Lesser Arapil were ordered to deploy. The leading line consisted of Fifth Division (6,500 men) on the right and Fourth Division (3,900), which was less one brigade which was left to guard the height, on the left. Both divisions formed in two two-deep lines and the Sixth Division (5,500) was in rear of Fourth while Seventh (5,000) covered the Fifth. The two cavalry brigades moved to the right rear of Fifth.

While they were deploying, Wellington galloped to his right to

The charge of Le Marchant's brigade at Salamanca. They are depicted as wearing the new dragoon headdress which was not in fact issued until the end of the 1812 campaign

meet Third Division which had reached Aldeatejada. They were to move in two columns with all possible speed to block the head of the French advance at the point where the outer ridge falls away above Miranda de Azan. They were to be flanked by two cavalry brigades, one Anglo–German, one Portuguese. 'My orders,' wrote Pakenham, 'were to head them and drive everything from the heights they occupied.'

Third Division had an hour's march ahead of them and, as they went forward, Wellington rode back to Fifth Division so that the main striking force's advance could be timed to coincide with Edward Pakenham's attack.

It was about 4.30 pm when Thomières, commanding the leading French division, saw the threat to his front and gave orders to form to resist the unexpected attack. One of his battalions, moving to its left to prolong the front, was surprised and broken by Portuguese dragoons. But almost simultaneously French dragoons charged the open flank of Pakenham's leading brigade before they could form square. A volley emptied many saddles but the dragoons came on and:

Ranks were broken and thrown into confusion. Several times the enemy rode through us cutting down with their sabres all that opposed them.

The arrival of the Anglo–German cavalry soon ended this menace and meanwhile the rest of the leading brigade was ready to attack. They had been advancing in open column of companies at deploying distance and moving across the front of Thomières' men. As the leading company came level with the French left, Pakenham gave the order 'Left Form' and each company swung up to make a perfect two-deep line, a drill movement requiring great skill and, since the brigade did not halt during the manoeuvre, one beyond the evolutions laid down in the Drill Book.

As the lines came up the hill they were greeted with a heavy fire which checked them in some places, as Sergeant Morley, Fifth Foot, recalled. The massed enemy on the crest:

seemed capable of sweeping everything before it. Still we advanced — the fire became stronger, there was a pause, a hesitation. Truth compels me to say that we retired before this overwhelming fire, but slowly, in good order, not a hundred paces . . . General Pakenham approached and, very good-naturedly, said 'Reform' and in about a moment, 'Advance', adding, 'There they are, my lads, just let them feel the temper of your bayonets'.

This time there was no hesitation and Thomières division broke and fled.

Less than a kilometre from Pakenham's left the Fifth Division was sweeping forward in line. Their opponents, Maucune's division, expected to be attacked by cavalry and had formed square. They held their fire until they saw the British bayonets come down for the charge and fired a single volley:

In an instant every individual was enveloped in smoke and obscurity. No struggle for ascendancy took place: the squares were penetrated, broken and discomfited.

As Maucune's division disintegrated a terrible fate overtook it. The British heavy cavalry brigade charged obliquely into the gap between the Third and Fifth Divisions:

We quickly came up with the French columns and charged their rear. Hundreds of them threw down their arms, their cavalry ran away, and most of the artillery jumped upon their horses and followed the cavalry. One or two charges mixed up the whole brigade, it being impossible to see for dust and smoak, but this attack threw the French into confusion and gave our infantry time to get another battle at them.

The cavalry charges completed the destruction of the two leading French divisions which lost about 4,000 men including 1,500 prisoners.

To make the French situation worse, Marmont had been seriously wounded by a British shell and it was about twenty minutes before the next senior unwounded general could be found to take command. When he did so, Bertrand Clausel acted with splendid decision. Seeing that the flank of Fourth Division had been uncovered when Pack's Portuguese brigade was repulsed in an attempt on the Greater Arapil, he launched a counterattack which almost succeeded in rolling up Wellington's line from the left. With cavalry supporting his infantry there was momentary chaos in Fourth Division. The commanding officer of the Fifty-Third Foot wrote:

Unsupported we were attacked by the enemy's heavy dragoons; we retired in good order, in line, and twice stopped their advance by halting and firing. At last a circular rocky hill, about two hundred yards in the rear, offer'd an advantage to profit by it; the dragoons being too near and the ranks being too thinn'd to attempt a square, we made a dash for the hill. The dragoons came thundering on in the rear, and reached the hill just as our people faced about. The fire checked them, and it was soon obvious that they would make no impression.

The crisis did not last long. Beresford brought up a Portuguese brigade which checked the French advance and Sixth Division, sweeping down from the ridge in line, scattered the counterattack and went on to assault the outer ridge. As a lieutenant of the Queen's wrote:

At 7 o'clock the light companies of the Queen's, 32nd and 36th, with a regiment of Portuguese Caçadores, were ordered to turn the enemy's right and the 6th Division was ordered to advance to take the height, which was a second Bunker Hill. We all advanced under a terrible war of artillery and, before 8 o'clock, had carried the hill, notwithstanding terrible losses. On gaining the height the division halted but our light companies and cavalry dashed on and followed them up for two or three miles.

Sixth Division suffered 1,600 casualties but they destroyed Clausel's last hope of standing his ground. Under cover of their last intact division the French swarmed away towards Alba de Tormes. If a Spanish general had not abandoned the fort which he had been ordered to hold, since it commanded the only crossing over the Tormes, the whole of Clausel's army must have been trapped. As it was, Wellington directed the pursuit towards what he believed to be the only escape-route open to the enemy, the fords of Huerta. The Light Division led the way and Wellington himself rode with them. It was only in the early stages of the pursuit that they met any resistance. As an ensign of the Forty-Third described it:

it was quite dark and our skirmishers opened upon them upon the brow of a hill and the French immediately returned it, which mostly passed over our heads. We had express orders not to fire until ordered. Our regiment was well prepared to give them an excellent charge but they had received another lesson that afternoon that they will not forget in a twelvemonth. We advanced in line ½ a mile over corn and ploughed land. Then we formed sections of a company, keeping our distance, and marched 2 or 3 miles over bushes and ploughed land. We halted and slept until sunrise.

If Wellington was denied the triumph of capturing the whole French army he at least had the satisfaction, on the following day, of wrecking their last unbroken division. Early on 23 July the French rearguard was found near Garçia Hernandez. Their supporting cavalry fled when British light dragoons advanced and Foy's infantry division formed squares. Undeterred, the two dragoon regiments of the King's German Legion, consisting of exiles from French-occupied Hanover, dashed straight at the nearest squares, attempting the near-impossible feat of breaking formed infantry. The French fired a volley but one mortally wounded horse fell forward on to the bayonets and, kicking in its death

The Anglo-Portuguese Army fording the Mondego in 1810, in the bottom right-hand corner is one of the Portuguese bullock waggons on which the supply of the army depended

agonies, opened a gap through which the dragoons poured, destroying the square from the inside:

We dashed in like madmen, and our blades carried the bloody revenge we had so long owed them. In less than half an hour we had 1,500 prisoners and 200 more towards evening. The French were formed in a ridge of hills, and we charged up a hollow way. Our loss is great, 150 men either dead or so badly wounded that we are burying them every minute.

The Hanoverians broke not one but two squares, the second of which, shaken by the destruction of the first, they overcame after a 300 metre gallop uphill and, to crown their achievement, they rode down two battalions of 6me *Léger* whose colonel, unwisely, had formed them into column so as to march for the safety of the hills.

On 25 July Clausel reported that he had only 22,000 men in the ranks out of the 48,000 with which the *Armée de Portugal* had started the battle three days earlier. Many stragglers later rejoined but the permanent loss was some 14,000 men of whom half were prisoners. Wellington's army suffered 4,762 casualties, of whom 1,627 were Portuguese and 6 were Spaniards. They had captured 20 guns and 2 eagles.

Salamanca changed the whole face of the war in the Peninsula. Napoleon had invaded Russia confident that his armies in Spain were large enough to hold those parts of Spain which had already been occupied even if they could not extend the area of French rule. The disabling of Marmont's army, the principal force committed to containing the Anglo–Portuguese army, changed the whole face of the situation. The Emperor had assumed, as had most of his subordinates, that Wellington was no more than a highly competent defensive general. Salamanca showed that he could be equally competent on the attack. Napoleon also underestimated the effect of this unexpected defeat on his own troops. Already they detested service in Spain; after July 1812 they came to believe that they would be beaten by Wellington wherever and whenever he brought them to battle.

The secret of Wellington's success lay in his adaptation of the basic tenets of eighteenth-century military thought to meet the needs of the new form of warfare which followed the French revolution. Leading a comparatively small army of British and Portuguese soldiers who had been trained to the precision of peacetime regulars, he was able to fight in the classic eighteenth-century line formation, using two ranks instead of three to enable every musket to be brought to bear on the enemy. Alone among his contemporaries, he took care always to take advantage of the ground to shield his tenuous line from enemy artillery and skirmishers until the last possible moment. From the lessons of revolutionary warfare he learned to employ his own skirmishers with a skill and on a scale that the French could not match. One man in five of his infantry was trained and employed in the skirmishing role and among them were the superb riflemen of the Sixtieth and the Ninety-Fifth supported by a proportion of the light troops of the German Legion and the Portuguese *caçadores* who were also armed with the rifle which Napoleon had discarded for his own army.

Behind the lines the Anglo–Portuguese army had an administrative machine which had no rival in Europe. He had learned how to supply an army in the field in the arid wastes of India and he knew that 'an army which is not fed is actually worse than no army at all.' Not the least of his Peninsular triumphs was his success in making that ramshackle offshoot of the Treasury, the Commissariat, a department that operated efficiently in conditions that its Whitehall masters had never contemplated. While French troops in Spain had constantly to plunder for their bare subsistence, the British were supplied so regularly with rations that it was a noteworthy day if the bread supply was short.

What is generally overlooked is the contribution of the guerrillas to the victory. It was they, with some assistance from the Royal Navy, who kept Cafarelli from reinforcing Marmont and it was they who kept Marmont utterly cut off from Madrid and ignorant that reinforcements were on their way to him in a strength that would have convinced Wellington that a battle should not be risked. By their occupation of most of Spain and the ruthlessness of their requisitioning, the French had handed the British an alliance which more than compensated for the smallness of their own army. As Wellington said:

It is true that [the French defeat in Spain] may in part be attributed to the operations of the allied armies in the Peninsula; but a great proportion of it must be ascribed to the enmity of the people of Spain. I have known of not less than 380,000 men of the French army in Spain at one moment & yet with no authority beyond the spot where they stood, & their time passes & their force expended by the mere effort of obtaining subsistence.

CHAPTER ELEVEN

The Big Battalions

WHILE THE WRECK of the *Armée de Portugal* was trailing away from Salamanca, Napoleon was approaching Vitebsk, 3,060 kilometres to the east. He was commanding an army of 600,000 men – 40 divisions of infantry, 25 of cavalry, supported by 1,500 guns. Of this ·horde only 270,000 could be called Frenchmen and these included Belgians, Dutchmen, Frieslanders, Hanoverians, Genevans, Piedmontese, Genoese, Tuscans, and Romans, whose homelands had been annexed to France. There were scarcely more Frenchmen in the *Grande Armée* than there were in the French armies in Spain. The bulk of the Emperor's force consisted of more or less willing allies. Since they dare not do otherwise, the Austrians contributed 34,000 men, the Prussians 25,000, The puppet kingdom of Italy sent 45,000, the Grand Duchy of Warsaw 35,000. From the French-created kingdoms of Bavaria, Saxony, and Westphalia came contingents each of about 20,000. Smaller formations came from Anhalt, Baden, Berg, Croatia, Dalmatia, Denmark, Hess-Darmstadt, Illyria, Mecklenberg, Naples, Switzerland, and Württemberg. There were even two regiments each from Spain and Portugal, men who had been shanghai'd into the French service in 1808.

Operating on a front nearly 480 kilometres long Napoleon was faced with two problems – supply and command – on a scale never previously contemplated and which the technological facilities available – horses – could not solve. The supply problem was the most unyielding. Contrary to accepted belief it was not Napoleon's custom to plunge blindly into an enemy's country assuming that his supply problems would be solved at the enemy's expense. Elaborate arrangements were always made for the opening of the campaign, as witness the careful logistic planning which got the *Armée de Réserve* over the Alps on its way to Marengo. It was after the breakthrough was made that improvisation became the order of the day since it was physically impossible to feed an army at more than a few days' march from its depots. Beyond a certain point the draught animals would be eating their payload. Quick and decisive victories stemmed from Napoleon's genius but they were essential if his army was not to starve.

The supply arrangements for the invasion of Russia were made with extreme care. A chain of nine huge depots was established from

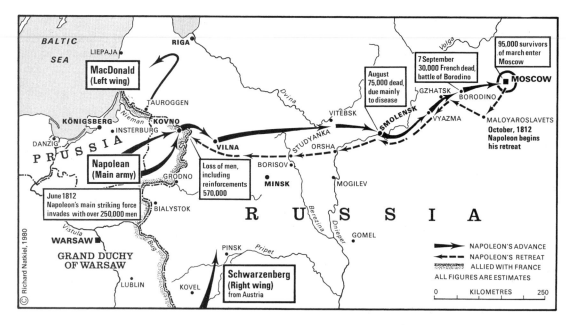

Königsberg to Warsaw, largely at Prussia's expense. The depot at Danzig alone held rations for 400,000 men for 50 days. To bring these rations forward a supply train was built up (again, largely at the expense of the Prussians) comprising 5,424 horse-drawn and 2,400 ox-drawn waggons, and giving a lift of 6,936 tonnes. These waggons required 200,000 draught animals (apart from 110,000 horses for the cavalry and artillery) and each horse needed 9 kilograms of fodder a day. Thus 1,800 tonnes a day was required to keep the waggon train moving – nearly a third of its payload. Nevertheless, given the short sharp campaign to which Napoleon was accustomed, the supply situation might have been contained and, as he said just before the army crossed the Niemen into Russian territory: 'In less than two months' time the Russians will be suing for peace'.

SCORCHED EARTH

The reality was very different. Two months after crossing the frontier the *Grande Armée* had passed Smolensk, more than 480 kilometres from its depots, and there was no sign of a decisive action. Behind the lines there was chaos. As the Emperor's Master of the Horse wrote in his diary:

Our waggons, built for metalled roads, were in no way suitable for the country we had to traverse. The first sand we came to overwhelmed the horses . . . The emperor was always anxious to obtain everything with the least possible expense and the result was that, to move large depots, everything had been loaded on waggons in the hope of being able to commandeer horses from the countryside. This had always been done in previous campaigns but in Russia there was no means of doing so. Horses, cattle, inhabitants had all fled and we found ourselves in the middle of a desert.

ABOVE: Napoleon's invasion of Russia

PREVIOUS PAGE: Marshal Ney, the *brave des braves*, with the rearguard on the retreat from Moscow

Vast quantities of carefully collected stores had to be dumped by the roadside and the army had to do without them. Medical supplies were non-existent and typhus and dysentery, aggravated by near-starvation, stalked the army. By the time the army reached Smolensk the central striking force, which started more than quarter of a million strong, had lost 75,000 men, of whom not one in ten was a battle casualty.

The command difficulties made the supply problem worse. The means of communication available – the ADC on his horse – were so slow that it was impossible to control so large an army on so wide a front. Accustomed to control manoeuvres in person, Napoleon was now dependent on others and opportunities to take advantage of Russian mistakes were frequently missed either because subordinate commanders were too unenthusiastic, like Schwarzenberg at the head of the Austrian corps, or too incompetent, like Jerome Bonaparte, King of Westphalia.

It was not until 7 September that Napoleon had, at last, his chance of a decisive battle when Kutusov drew up his army to fight at Borodino. The command failure at Borodino was Napoleon's own. Disregarding Davout's plan for turning the Russian left, he insisted on making a series of crude frontal attacks using his infantry in column against the 640 Russian guns. When at last the great Raevsky Redoubt, dominating the Russian centre, was captured largely by the use of massed heavy cavalry there was a gap in the Russian position, which, if he could exploit it, must ruin the enemy army. His only reserve was the infantry of the Imperial Guard, 30,000 incomparable soldiers. He could not bring himself to commit them:

I will not have my Guard destroyed. When you have come eight hundred leagues from France you do not wreck your last reserve.

Napoleon during the retreat from Moscow

Equally when you have come eight hundred leagues to destroy the Russian army it is unwise to throw away your only opportunity for doing so. The Russians lost 44,000 men that day but they retired in good order on their supplies and reinforcements. The *Grande Armée* lost more than 30,000 men at Borodino and, a week later, entered Moscow 95,000 strong, remnant of a quarter of a million.

Napoleon could not stay in Moscow because he could not feed his troops through the winter and, after five weeks in the city, he had to retreat. When the final stragglers had recrossed the Niemen the loss of men, including those who had reinforced the original *Grande Armée*, was 570,000. Of these 370,000 were dead, some in battle, some in hospital, some in the snow beside the road. A further 100,000 more died as prisoners of war.

Once the wreck of Napoleon's army was back on the west bank of the Niemen the rest of the war was a matter of mathematics and will power. Once mass armies, a French expedient to resist the crisis days of the beleagured republic, became the rule it could only be a matter of time before France's enemies overwhelmed her, provided that they could agree a common policy. Coalition after coalition had collapsed through disunity but, by 1813, Napoleon's incessant bullying had driven the

rest of Europe to a state where they must unite or perish. Once they united their armies must prevail. The population of France, 28 million in 1800, had increased by annexations to 35 million with the Kingdom of Italy adding nearly 5 million more. Against her were 28 millions in the Hapsburg Empire, 8 million in Prussia, 40 million in Russia, 14 million in Spain and Portugal, and 15 million in the United Kingdom. In the end, numbers would tell.

DEFEAT AND ABDICATION

Napoleon's raising of a new army for the campaign of 1813 was one of his greatest administrative feats. In December 1812 he had only 40,000 French and allied troops on the eastern front. Austria sank into a wary neutrality. Prussia changed sides by March 1813 but by that time

ABOVE: A bivouac on the early stages of the retreat from Moscow before the snow had started

ABOVE RIGHT: The battle of Smolensk, Napoleon's only opportunity to cut the Russian armies off from Moscow. The picture shows in a stylized form the skirmishers of the two armies engaging each other

Napoleon's army in Germany was 200,000 strong, of whom 145,000 were available as a field army with 400 guns. This imposing array was, once more, raised by mortgaging the future. The conscripts of 1813 were already in training. Those of 1814 were called up in February 1813. Twenty-four battalions were formed from sailors and 80,000 National Guardsmen were compulsorily embodied in the regulars. Only 16,000 men were withdrawn from Spain and the army there still had 240,000 men on their muster rolls and 195,000 available for action. They were opposed by a British army of 30,856 effective rank and file (15 April) backed by 28,000 Portuguese and an uncertain number of Spanish regulars but, above all, the French army in Spain could not be reduced because of the lethal hostility of the Spanish people.

On the eastern front the Russians and their new Prussian allies were slow in building up their strength and in May, Napoleon, with a considerable numerical superiority, was able to win two great battles at Lützen (2 May) and Bautzen (20–21 May), but his weakness in cavalry, legacy of the Russian *débâcle*, prevented him from exploiting them and on 4 June he willingly agreed to an armistice which, in the event, lasted until 17 August.

The armistice of Pleischwitz gave the allies the time they needed to build up their strength and to add to their allies. On 12 August, Austria decided to join them and, a month earlier, the Swedes also adhered although their leader, the Prince Royal, continued for some months to demonstrate his talent for being absent from battles. This talent had made him a contemptible figure when, as Marshal Bernadotte, he had commanded one of Napoleon's corps. The allies also received good news. On 21 June, Wellington, after a brilliantly conceived march of 480 kilometres, routed Joseph Bonaparte at Vitoria. Before the end of that month the French were defending their own frontier on the Pyrenees.

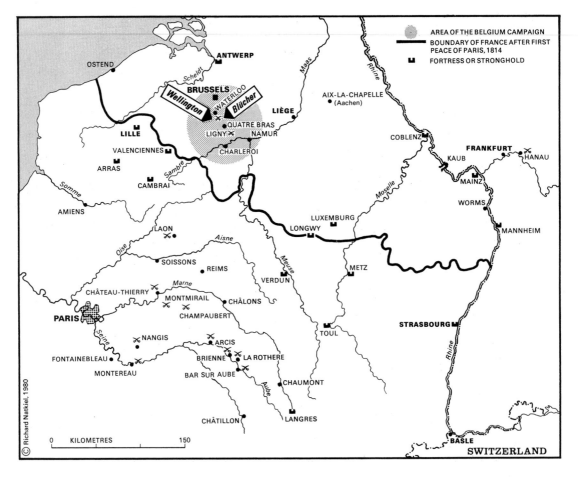

ABOVE: The Eastern
campaigns of 1814/15

Napoleon also used the time to build up his strength and, by
mid-August, could put 375,000 men in the field. Against him were
three allied armies consisting of 435,000 with a reserve army of 60,000
in Poland and 300,000 more men becoming available. Almost more
important, the allies decided to appoint a supreme commander and their
choice fell on Prince Schwarzenberg. He was not a brilliant commander
and his position was made no easier by the presence at his headquarters
of the Czar, the Emperor of Austria, and the King of Prussia. He had,
however, a genius for coordinating his allies and he laid down one
admirable guiding rule. Whichever of the allied armies was attacked by
Napoleon in person should retire while the others would advance and
deal with the subordinate French commanders.

There followed six weeks of indecisive fighting in which Napoleon
scored a victory at Dresden while his subordinates suffered a series of
shattering defeats. The French army lost 78,000 men in battle alone and
achieved nothing. In desperation Napoleon took up a defensive position
at Leipzig so as to draw the allies towards him and defeat them in detail.
He misjudged the manoeuvre and between 16 and 18 October he was
attacked from north and south. When on the third day Bernadotte

decided that it was safe to bring his own troops into battle, the allies had a superiority of 335,000 to 175,000, the result was predictable. To try to compensate for his shortage of numbers Napoleon, a week before the battle, ordered his infantry to fight in two ranks, writing to Marmont on 11 October:

It is my intention that you form your troops in two ranks instead of three. The third rank does no good while firing and is even less useful with the bayonet.

This was a difficult though sensible reform to introduce in the middle of a campaign, requiring as it did a change in basic foot drill, since three-deep and two-deep are not easily interchangeable formations as any soldier will understand. Some corps commanders made no attempt to conform with the instruction. Even had they done so the outcome of the battle can scarcely have been in doubt. The French were bound to be crushed between the northern and southern arms of the allied pincers and, to make matters worse, they had no room to manoeuvre since the position Napoleon had chosen had, in its rear, an unfordable river crossed by a single narrow bridge approached by a causeway 3 kilometres long. Late on 18 October the Emperor ordered a phased withdrawal which might have been largely successful had not the bridge been blown prematurely, leaving 33,000 men and 260 guns on the east bank. During the battle almost all the remaining German auxiliaries took the opportunity to change to the allied side. Only 60,000 French troops succeeded in crossing the Rhine and, although 40,000 more straggled in later, typhus accounted for 30,000.

Once more a new *Grande Armée* had to be raised and the New Year of 1814 found 100,000 Frenchmen, many of them 16-year-olds, facing 350,000 allies on the eastern front while, to the south, Wellington already had his headquarters on French soil. The campaign that followed was as brilliant as any Napoleon had ever fought, comparable to that in Italy in 1796, but his task was hopeless. For a time he managed to hold the allies at bay, marching and countermarching his small and increasingly weary army first to one side then to the other. It could not last, for the enemy had an overwhelming superiority in numbers as well as generals, especially Blücher, with a determination to finish the business. On 31 March the allies marched into Paris to the cheers of the war-weary inhabitants and on 6 April Napoleon abdicated. On that day Wellington defeated the *Armée d'Espagne* for the last time and, next day, entered Toulouse. The overwhelming numbers of the allies had, at last, triumphed.

OVERLEAF: Allied artillery
at the battle of Leipzig.
The uniform of the
artillerymen seems fanciful
and the direction in which
the cannon are pointing
improbable

CHAPTER TWELVE

Waterloo,
18 June 1815

T HE CAMPAIGN OF WATERLOO, the four days of sharp fighting which
ended the Hundred Days of Napoleon's reign after his return from
Elba, is probably the most described military operation in history.
Rather than attempt yet another detailed description, the intention of
this chapter is to illustrate the strengths and weaknesses of the armies of
the participants.

Napoleon was under no illusions that his former enemies would
allow him to retain his throne unless he could prove that to remove him
would cause more trouble than it would be worth. During the summer
massive armies, 662,000 men, would close on France in a great arc from
the English Channel to the Riviera and there might be a further threat
across the Pyrenees. To counter this massive show of force France had a
standing army of 200,000 which could easily be raised to 280,000 by
recalling men on half pay and leave. The restored Bourbons had
abolished conscription but, although it could not be immediately
reintroduced, it was considered possible to call back to the colours the
150,000 men of the class of 1815 who had been called up by imperial
decree in October 1813 but sent back to their homes as soon as the war
ended. These, however, would not be ready for field service until the late
summer of 1815 and it was not certain that they could be armed and
equipped since stocks were barely adequate to provide for the existing
army on a war footing.

The options open to Napoleon were either to wait until the allied
invasion developed or to strike immediately at the only enemies within
his reach, Blücher's 117,000 Prussians around Liège and Wellington's
motley collection of 110,000 British, Netherlanders, and Germans who
were based around Brussels.

The decision to adopt the second course was taken in early May and,
having allocated covering forces to the other frontier, a striking force of
122,721 men with 366 guns, the *Armée du Nord*, was available for the
attack on Belgium. This force outnumbered either of the two allied
armies it was to assail but was, of course, greatly fewer than their
combined strength. The numerical calculation was misleading since the
allies would have to provide a large number of garrisons and both
included some very suspect troops. Blücher had 14,000 Saxons,

French and British infantry

The most conspicuous changes in infantry dress between 1792 and 1815 concerned the head and legs. Breeches and gaiters were abandoned for active service and replaced by trousers secured at the ankles by various improvisations.

The cocked hat which, in a variety of shapes, had been almost universal military headwear for a century gave way to a peaked cap of more or less cylindrical shape, the shako. The French adopted a bell-topped design while the British favoured a stovepipe model (shortened in 1812–13), their light infantry wearing a slightly tapered shako. Regimental officers wore cocked hats until 1810–12 and staff officers continued their use for many years after Waterloo. These changes are shown by the figures at

TOP LEFT, privates of battalion companies of 45th Foot, 1811, (*left*) and 14th Foot, 1794, (*right*). Below them are a private, 43rd Light Infantry, 1810, (*left*), and a captain of grenadiers, 28th (North Gloucestershires), 1814. Both wear 'wings' on their shoulders, the badge of light infantry and grenadiers.

Wings are also worn by the French grenadier officer of 54me *Ligne*, 1809 (BELOW LEFT). The *fusilier* (private of battalion company) of 86me *Ligne*, 1812, wears the bell-topped shako and the *capote*, the greatcoat always worn over the tunic by French infantry irrespective of the climate.

It is clear from these pictures that infantrymen of both armies carried too many accoutrements (about 28 kilograms) for comfort.

converted into Prussians by the Congress of Vienna, who mutinied in May and had to be removed. Wellington's army included at least 9,000 Belgians, many of whom had willingly fought for Napoleon in the past and, in the opinion of both Wellington and Napoleon, would do so again.

The French had an advantage in quality. Almost every man in the *Armée du Nord* was a veteran and many of them had spent years in British or Russian prisoner of war camps and had a burning desire for revenge. Too many of the allied regiments were newly formed and in Wellington's army there were thirty battalions of militia while Blücher had twenty-two of *landwehr*. Even the regular units of British and King's German Legion infantry which had seen service in the Peninsula had replaced more than half their time-expired men with recruits.

If Napoleon was to succeed, he must strike two knock-out blows, one at each of the allies, in quick succession. It was in his favour that both armies were widely dispersed. From their junction south of Brussels the Anglo–Netherlands army stretched 64 kilometres west to Audenarde while the Prussian left was 96 kilometres eastward at Liège. It must take them three days to close on their centre so that it should be possible, by striking at their junction, to put the French army between them before they could concentrate. It was Napoleon's misfortune that he was opposed by the two allied commanders who had been most effective against his armies up to 1814 and, although their characters were diametrically opposed, the two men liked and trusted each other so that, except when Blücher was temporarily incapacitated, allied cooperation was excellent.

On the French side there was a shortage of sound subordinates. Since Berthier had committed suicide, the job of chief of staff was given to Marshal Soult who had many military virtues but whose only experience as a staff officer had been a three month spell of duty in 1794. Soult not only made errors on his own account but failed, as Berthier would not have failed, to draw attention to the Emperor's own mistakes and omissions. Only two other marshals went with the army. Michel Ney was belatedly appointed to command the left wing. He was the bravest and most admired man in the French army but, at his best, had never been a great military brain. The right wing was entrusted, after the campaign had begun, to Emanuel Grouchy, newly promoted to marshal. A talented cavalry general, he had no experience of commanding infantry in battle. Two much abler marshals, Suchet and Davout, were not included. The first was appointed to command the *Armée des Alpes*, the second to the Ministry of War.

Since the allies were not at war with France, they were forbidden to patrol across the frontier and Napoleon was able to concentrate his whole force on a front of 30 kilometres around Beaumont by the night of 14 June and the allies had no serious suspicion of its presence. The concentration had been admirably administered and executed but when the advance started on the following day the staff work revealed flaws, the most serious being that III Corps (Vandamme) received no orders to move and seriously obstructed the advance of VI Corps (Lobau) in their rear. Fortunately the Prussians made little resistance on the line of the

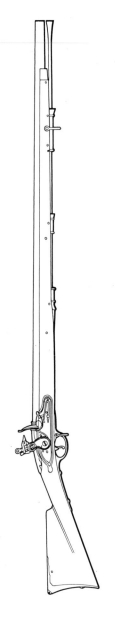

PAGE 152:
A French representation of the Union cavalry brigade charging the French guns at Waterloo

unfordable Sambre and the two bridges at Charleroi were captured without difficulty. Had they been stoutly defended the French march tables would have been irretrievably disorganized.

Wellington in the western sector, had convinced himself that the attack would come not through Charleroi but through Mons. Unfortunately the few and uninformative messages that reached him from the Prussian front on 15 June did nothing to disillusion him. It was not until 1 am on 16 June that he learned from his own advance posts that the French had been across the Sambre for 12 hours and that French cavalry was probing up to Quatre Bras. As a result he almost left ordering the concentration of his army until too late and might well have done so had not one of his subordinates, an Eton-educated Dutchman, disobeyed his orders and moved troops to Quatre Bras. The early breakdown in communication between Blücher's forward corps and Wellington came very close to wrecking the campaign before it was properly started.

On 16 June it was the French who suffered most from communications. Napoleon's strategic plan, as explained in a letter to Ney, was:

For this campaign I have adopted the following general principle. I shall divide the army into two wings and a reserve. Your wing will consist of I [D'Erlon] and II [Reille] Corps, two light cavalry divisions and two divisions of the Cavalry Corps. This should not be far short of 45–50,000 men and Marshal Grouchy, on the right wing, will have about the same. The Guard will form the reserve and I shall bring it to either wing as circumstances may dictate . . . Also, according to circumstances, I shall draw troops from one wing to strengthen my reserve.

That day the plan was for Grouchy to drive in the Prussians (whom Napoleon believed to have only 40,000 men in hand) beyond Fleurus, while Ney was to take Quatre Bras and then detach men to his right to fall on the Prussian flank.

Largely because their orders failed to emphasize the need for speed, the two wings moved very slowly and both found themselves faced with larger forces than had been anticipated. The Emperor, who was with Grouchy, found himself faced with 84,000 Prussians at Ligny and, since both he and Soult forgot that Lobau's corps was waiting without orders at Charleroi, demanded troops from Ney.

There followed the tragi-comedy of marching and countermarching by D'Erlon's 20,000 men. Forming part of Ney's wing, this corps was moving towards Quatre Bras when one of Napoleon's ADCs, using the convention whereby an ADC spoke with the authority of his general, ordered D'Erlon to turn about and march towards Ligny. Neither he nor D'Erlon thought to tell Ney what had happened and when the marshal, always a hot-tempered man, discovered that his rear corps, on which he was counting to make a breakthrough, was marching away from him, he exploded with rage. Not only did he send a peremptory order to D'Erlon demanding his return but he berated another of the Emperor's ADCs, who had at that moment arrived, to such an extent that that officer forgot to deliver a letter from Napoleon telling Ney to:

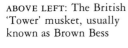

ABOVE LEFT: The British 'Tower' musket, usually known as Brown Bess

ABOVE RIGHT: French Charleville musket

Direct your march on the heights of Brye and St Armand [on the right flank of the Prussian position] so as to cooperate in a victory that may well turn out to be decisive.

ABOVE: Napoleon on the morning of Waterloo surrounded by the Imperial Guard. In fact, all the French infantry would have been wearing their *capotes* (greatcoats)

As a result D'Erlon's only contribution to the day's fighting was to cause a panic in the left wing of the French engaged at Ligny when his men, clad like the Prussians in blue uniforms and bell-topped shakos, arrived unheralded behind their comrades.

The result of the two battles on 16 June was that Ney was held to a draw at Quatre Bras, thus giving Wellington time to complete his concentration. At Ligny, Blücher was eventually defeated, suffering 16,000 casualties and 21 guns while he himself was unhorsed and ridden over, thus being for some hours out of touch with his headquarters. The Prussian army, meanwhile, lost a further 9,000 men, mostly *landwehr*, who took the opportunity to desert and streamed away eastward for Liège and home. Never have deserters done their country a greater service, for Napoleon, hearing from a cavalry general that a swarm of Prussians were making for Liège, assumed that this was the direction taken by the whole of Blücher's army.

On 17 June Napoleon was so convinced that he had driven the allies

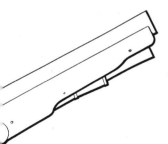

apart and that he now had only to contend with Wellington that he relapsed into lethargy in the early part of the day. The first orders to Ney, issued at 8 am, told him to take Quatre Bras if it was only held by a rearguard but adding: 'Today is to be devoted to mopping up, completing with ammunition and rallying the stragglers.' It was not until 11 am that Ney was told to make an all-out attack on Quatre Bras. Soon afterwards Grouchy was told to pursue the Prussians eastward 'in the direction of Namur and Maastricht'.

Napoleon's dilatory behaviour on the morning of 17 June lost him his last chance of attacking Wellington while he was isolated. During the night the allied communications had again broken down and when night fell the only news from the Prussians was that at 6 pm their front at Ligny was still intact. A further messenger was sent but was wounded and failed to reach Wellington. At 3 am an ADC was sent with an escort of hussars to discover where Blücher was. At 7.30 am he reported that he had contacted the Prussian rearguard who said that the army was marching on Wavre, a town not shown on any map at Wellington's headquarters. This news was confirmed by a letter which arrived from Blücher at 9 am. By that time most of the wounded were on their way to the rear, carried on the backs of cavalry horses. At 10 am the main body began to follow them and, soon after noon, Wellington was able to say, 'There's the last of the infantry gone and I don't care now'. Covered by the cavalry, the horse artillery, and a thunderstorm, the army fell back to the ridge of Mont St Jean, soaked but safe. They numbered less than 60,000 with 154 guns. During the night the *Armée du Nord* arrived on the ridge to the south of them, 72,000 with 246 guns. 33,000 more under Grouchy were painstakingly following the Emperor's explicit orders and chasing Blücher in the wrong direction.

At dawn Napoleon was delighted to see that the allies were still in their position. He had feared that Wellington would slip away in the night and, when he saw that he had not, remarked:

We have not less than ninety chances in our favour and less than ten against . . . We shall bombard them with my great weight of artillery, charge them with my cavalry, so that they show themselves, and, when I am quite sure where the English troops are, I shall march straight at them with my Guard . . . It is impossible for the Prussians to join them in less than two days.

THE FINAL DEFEAT

At 6.30 that morning, 18 June, Wellington received a letter from Blücher promising that he would join him as soon as possible with at least two corps and, at Mont St Jean, the orders were given that the army would stand its ground and fight till the Prussians arrived. To Napoleon such trust between allies was incomprehensible and he prepared to smash the Anglo–Netherlands army with a series of hammer blows, postponed only while the ground dried out sufficiently to allow the great 12-pounders to be moved into position.

In the hope of drawing off Wellington's reserves, the French left launched a diversionary attack on the château of Hougoumont, but the serious business started at about 1 pm when forty-four 12-pounders and

George III Light Dragoon pistol. Cavalry pistols had little effect on the battlefield except at the closest range

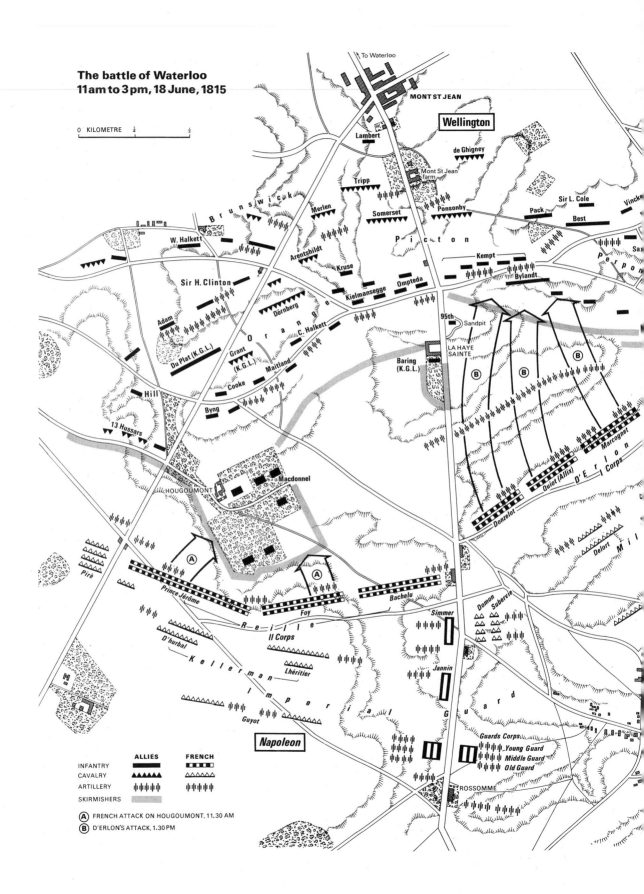

The battle of Waterloo
11am to 3pm, 18 June, 1815

0   KILOMETRE   ½

To Waterloo

MONT ST JEAN

Wellington

Lambert

de Ghigney

Mont St Jean farm

Tripp

Merlen

Somerset

Ponsonby

Pack

Sir L. Cole

Vinck

Best

B r u n s w i c k

W. Halkett

Arentshildt

Kruse

P i c t o n

Kempt

Bylandt

Sir H. Clinton

Kielmansegge

Ompteda

95th   Sandpit

La Haye Sainte

P e r p o n

Sax

Dörnberg

O r a n g e

C. Halkett

B

B

B

Adam

Grant (K.G.L.)

Maitland

Baring (K.G.L.)

B

B

Du Plat (K.G.L.)

Cooke

Marcognet

Hill

Byng

Quiot (Allix)

D'Erlon Corps

13 Hussars

Donzelot

Delort

Mil

Macdonnel

HOUGOUMONT

A

A

Bachelu

Pirè

Prince Jérôme

Foy

Domon

Subervie

Simmer

R e i l l e

Jannin

D'hurbal

II Corps

Lhéritier

G u a r d

K e l l e r m a n   I m p e r i a l

Napoleon

Guyot

Guards Corps

Young Guard

Middle Guard

Old Guard

ROSSOMME

	ALLIES	FRENCH
INFANTRY		
CAVALRY		
ARTILLERY		
SKIRMISHERS		

Ⓐ FRENCH ATTACK ON HOUGOUMONT, 11.30 AM

Ⓑ D'ERLON'S ATTACK, 1.30 PM

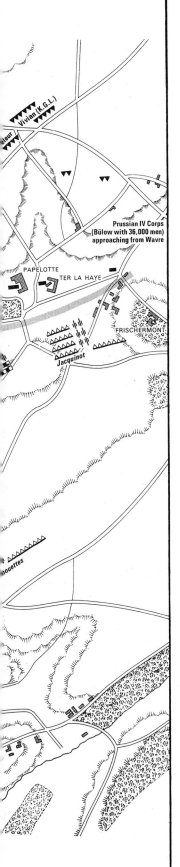

forty 8-pounders opened fire on the allied centre. They made a most impressive noise and covered the battlefield in white smoke but they had very little effect. The allied line was lying down 'about forty paces behind the crest of the position' where no roundshot could reach them. Apart from the skirmishers and the garrison of the farm of La Haye Sainte, a very solid building, the only troops on the forward slope were a Netherlands brigade, whose commander was used to serving under Napoleon, deployed in full view of the enemy. Under cover of this bombardment, the entire French army deployed themselves within range and sight of Wellington's guns.

Nothing is more striking in the campaign of Waterloo than the attitudes of the three commanders to incurring unnecessary casualties. At Ligny Wellington, while visiting Blücher before the fighting started, remarked to the Prussian staff that:

According to my judgment, the exposure of the advanced columns, and, indeed, the whole army to cannonade, standing as they did so displayed to the enemy's fire, was not prudent. I said that if I were in Blücher's place with English troops, I should withdraw all the columns and get more of the troops under shelter of the rising ground. However, they seemed to think that they knew best, so I came away.

Two days later at Waterloo, Napoleon, who knew the capability of artillery better than anyone living, drew up his own army on the forward slope where they suffered heavily. Under Napoleon's bombardment, the British suffered scarcely at all and, in one battalion, Sergeant Morris slept 'as comfortably as ever I did in my life'.

The first of Napoleon's hammer blows was struck as soon as the cannonade was judged to have done its work. D'Erlon's corps, 16,800 infantry, supported by two regiments of cuirassiers, advanced upon the allied centre. D'Erlon, who had met the British many times in the Peninsula, chose to send three of his four divisions forward in divisional columns on a battalion front (*colonne de bataillon par division*). This gave each division a front of about 160 men and a depth of 24 ranks with an interval of four paces between each battalion. Thus of every 4,000 and more men only 320 could fire their muskets at the enemy and each great mass of men presented a magnificent target to artillery and even muskets could scarcely miss. Wellington must have been reminded of a remark he made four years earlier, 'I do not desire better sport than to meet one of their columns *en masse* with our line.'

Despite their vicious formation, Napoleon's last army fought with such ferocity that they almost achieved a break-in. Although 'the enemy's artillery shot could plough through us to the depth of twenty ranks', two divisions reached the crest and attempted to deploy. In one place they were driven back by the superlative musketry of Kempt's brigade of Peninsular veterans but in another it needed Wellington's presence to restore the situation:

I saw about two hundred men of the Seventy Ninth who seemed to have had rather more than they liked of it. I formed them myself about twenty yards from the flash

of the French columns, and ordered them to fire and, in a few minutes, the French went about.

As the French started to fall back two brigades of British heavy cavalry charged home into the flanks of the French columns which, from their formation, were unable to form square to resist them.

D'Erlon's corps dissolved in something approaching rout but the Household and Union brigades, like all British cavalry, were uncontrollable once their charge had succeeded. They dashed on until they reached the French gun line before, scattered and blown, they were counterattacked by French horse. They lost half their horses and a third of their men, a poor exchange for the 2,000 French infantry they had captured and the 20 guns they had wrecked.

While this was going forward, Napoleon could see the advance guard of the Prussians appearing to the east. If Wellington was to be beaten, he had to be beaten quickly but Napoleon seems to have had no idea how this was to be achieved. Nor was he prepared to take his only alternative – to retreat. Instead D'Erlon's corps was rallied and sent forward again, an attack that was beaten off with ease. Meanwhile, Reille's corps on the left was becoming increasingly sucked into the attack on Hougoumont, a diversion which diverted less than two battalions of Wellington's reserves, and Lobau's corps had to be detached to check the Prussians. Ney, therefore, had little disposable infantry but he had, under his immediate command, about 4,000 cavalry and when Wellington withdrew his infantry behind the shelter of the ridge, from which it had emerged to beat off D'Erlon, the marshal took it into his head that the allied army had set off on a retreat. He ordered his cavalry forward to turn the supposed retreat into a rout.

Seeing this mass of horsemen going forward at 'a stately trot', Soult turned to the Emperor and remarked 'Ney has compromised us once again'. Napoleon replied that, although the charge had started an hour too early, 'Since it has happened, we must support him'. He ordered the rest of the heavy cavalry – dragoons, carabiniers, and cuirassiers – not even excluding the heavy cavalry of the Guard, to add their weight to the attack.

The allied infantry formed into twenty squares as the danger approached and no man in them ever forgot the sight of 8,000 cavalrymen sweeping steadily up the slope towards them:

I can compare it to nothing better than a heavy surf breaking on a coast beset with isolated rocks, against which the mountainous wave dashes with furious uproar.

As a French general was to remark about a later cavalry charge *C'est magnifique, mais ce n'est pas la guerre.* Garçia Hernandez (see pp. 139–40) remained the single example of cavalry riding down unbroken infantry formed into square. The artillery, firing canister over roundshot, brought down scores of men and horses at each discharge so that the corpses of those in front blocked the way for those who followed. Those who survived could make no impression on the squares. The French heavy cavalry, that incomparable body of horsemen, retired a wreck.

PREVIOUS PAGES:
Napoleon ordering forward the Imperial Guard. When Wellington saw this painting he is said to have remarked: 'Very good, not too much smoke'

Napoleon's position was now becoming desperate. The pressure on his right was building up and he was making no progress to the front. He ordered Ney to capture La Haye Sainte, the key to Wellington's centre, at all costs and, with two weak battalions of 13me *Légere*, a company of sappers and a handful of horsemen, *le brave des braves* obeyed his orders, helped by the fact that the defenders had run out of ammunition and could not be resupplied. Immediately Ney brought up a battery to break open the allied centre and sent to the Emperor for reinforcements to exploit his success. Both efforts were unsuccessful. On the crest behind the farm were the Ninety-Fifth Rifles, who were not short of ammunition:

They began serving out grape to us; but they were so very near that we destroyed their artillerymen before they could give us a second round.

When Ney's ADC rode up to Napoleon and asked for support, the only reply he received was:

Troops? Where do you suggest I get them from? Would you have me manufacture some?

Yet the Emperor had infantry in hand. Some of the Guard had been sent to help keep Blücher at bay, but there were still twelve battalions unemployed. It was an hour before Napoleon could bring himself to put them into the battle.

An hour was enough for Wellington to plug the gap in his centre and when the Guard did attack the assault was made by only five

battalions and they were directed to the wrong place, not to the vulnerable centre but further to the west where they could be enfiladed from Hougoumont. At this point to make matters much worse they attacked in a rough arrowhead of battalions, four of them in column, one in square.

The result could have been foreseen. Blocked in front by the British Guards, they were taken in flank when the Fifty-Second Light Infantry wheeled up their right:

When the regiment was nearly parallel to the enemy's flank, [*Lieutenant-Colonel*] *Sir John Colborne gave the word,* Charge, Charge! *It was answered by a steady cheer and a hurried rush to the front. In the next ten seconds the Imperial Guard, broken in the wildest confusion and scarcely firing a shot to cover its retreat, was rushing towards the hollow road in the rear.*

With the repulse of the Guard, Napoleon's last army disintegrated. Individual units, notably two battalions of the Old Guard, fought on bravely but the great majority became a mass of fugitives. At the town of Genappes in the rear it took Napoleon and his remaining staff officers an hour to force their way through the struggling mob of unarmed men. The French casualties have never been accurately assessed but can scarcely have been less than 30,000 and, although it might have been possible for Napoleon to have raised another army, the French people had had enough. They had given their Emperor a second chance and he had led them straight to overwhelming defeat.

Wellington, whose army had lost 15,000 men (of whom 8,445 were from the British troops), and Blücher, who lost 6,700 at Waterloo, led their armies to Paris and supervised the second restoration of Louis XVIII. The long war was finally over.

NAPOLEONIC WARFARE: QUEST FOR THE DECISIVE BATTLE

What had changed in warfare on land between 1792 and 1815? The most striking feature was the quest for a decisive battle, of which Waterloo was the most impressive example. It was a result that Napoleon always sought and, occasionally, achieved – Austerlitz, Jena, Friedland, and Wagram all led directly to peace treaties since the beaten side felt the war could not be continued. Equally he had his failures – Aspern-Essling, Borodino, and Waterloo – where the search for a knock-out blow led to incurring such heavy casualties that either the battle had to be broken off or such advantages as had been gained could not be exploited. It was the search for the knock-out that led Napoleon and many of his marshals to use attacks in column. As has been seen (p. 14) manoeuvring in line was a slow business and it was hard to produce a quick, final decision in an offensive linear battle unless the enemy made serious mistakes. In the early days of the wars French columns had frequently made spectacularly successful attacks against enemies who were less than wholly steady but, as Wellington remarked before sailing for Portugal in 1808:

If what I hear about [*the French*] *system of manoeuvres be true, I think it a false*

The final stand of the Old Guard at Waterloo

one against steady troops. I suspect all the continental armies were more than half beaten before the battle was begun. I, at least, will not be frightened beforehand.

Napoleon's enemies learned much of the art of war from his hands and, given time, reorganized their tactical systems so as to be able to ride the whirlwind blows that he struck at them. The French had a long and well-merited run of victories but eventually the evidence built up – Eylau, Bailen, Aspern-Essling, and a series of defeats in Portugal and Spain – that French armies were not invincible. From that grew up a school of generals who refused to 'be frightened beforehand'. It was Napoleon's ill-luck that at Waterloo he was faced with the two most conspicuous members of this new breed, Wellington and Blücher.

Nevertheless the need for the quick victory remained and many French commanders clung to the hope that it could be achieved by the use of the heavy columns. Twentieth-century historians have claimed that since the French drill books laid down that attacks, except those against fortified posts or salients, or on narrow fronts, should be made in line or in *ordre mixte*, that linear attacks were the norm in Napoleon's army, that Borodino and Waterloo were aberrations, and that the constant attacks of French columns against Anglo–Portuguese lines in the Peninsula were the result of a consistent series of errors by the French generals in misjudging the moment to deploy. This theory argues a

standard of incompetence on the part of French generals which is not borne out by their other actions. The truth is that columnar attacks continued to be used because they offered the only hope (even if it was a fading hope) of achieving instant victory.

Instant victory had become a necessity to Napoleon's army because it had grown so large. This was the other most notable change in war between Valmy and Waterloo. Conscription had swollen armies to a size undreamed of in the eighteenth century. At Valmy the armies of both sides totalled less than 100,000 men altogether. At Leipzig the opposing armies amounted to half a million. Even in the most fertile area in Europe a vast mass of men cannot live for more than a very few days and only quick victory could give the opportunity to move on into unravaged areas where more food could be found. A drawn battle only increased the quartermaster's problems.

After Eylau, Bennigsen was forced to retire if his army was not to die of starvation, but Napoleon had to withdraw his own troops almost immediately for the same reason. Armies had increased five-fold but the means of supplying them remained exactly the same or decreased. Although agriculture had become more efficient during the eighteenth century, the conscription took away more farm workers and, even if the food was grown and harvested, the means of moving it was still in waggons, drawn by horses or oxen which shrank in number during the war as they were killed by overwork or battle. Even Britain, with a small army, money to buy supplies and, thanks to her sea power, the means to import food from North Africa, Ireland, Sicily, and the United States, found it a hard struggle to maintain the supply of rations to Wellington's army in the Peninsula. For the French armies in Spain the effort to keep the soldiers alive consumed as much energy as fighting their enemies. Before the invention of the railway every army had to adhere to the maxim 'Scatter to live, concentrate to fight'. But the growth in the size of armies meant that they had to scatter ever more widely and could afford to concentrate only for a matter of days and in those days a decisive battle had to be won. Hence the attempt to achieve it by the use of columns of attack.

ABOVE: Congreve rockets in action. They would have been a most effective weapon had they been even remotely reliable

Chasseur, 2ᵉ Chasseurs à Pied de la Garde Impériale
Waterloo Campaign, 1815

Rear view of the French Voltiguer of the line in full
marching order *c.* 1812

In most other ways the battlefield was remarkably unchanged after twenty-three years of almost continuous war. Muskets had undergone only the slightest of modifications, the rifle (which had been in use in the American Revolution) had been reintroduced and improved but its use was confined to a small minority of the infantry owing to the time which it took to reload, a defect which induced Napoleon to withdraw all rifles from his army in 1807. The cavalry armament remained unchanged, except in details of sword design, but the lance was reintroduced on a limited scale after more than a century of disuse. The artillery pieces of 1792 were almost unchanged in their essential features in 1815 but there was a tendency for guns to be bigger. Their projectiles continued to be largely ineffective and the only improvement was a British development first used at Surinam in 1804 — the spherical case-shot, commonly known by the name of its inventor, Colonel Henry Shrapnell. No other army succeeded in copying this, the first effective airburst weapon, until many years after Waterloo.

Another British invention in artillery was the Congreve rocket, a wildly inaccurate weapon which did some good service, largely by luck, at Leipzig and on the retreat to Waterloo. As early as 1810 Napoleon had offered a reward to anyone who could copy Congreve's invention and a French artillery officer had made a detailed plan and section of one in Portugal, but nothing came of the idea. In communications, there was even less improvement, apart from the semaphore telegraphs on a strictly limited number of routes. All messages, unless they were simple enough to be conveyed verbally, had to be written out, copied, and entrusted to a man on a horse. The only small improvement which did occur was the introduction of a primitive form of carbon paper which Wellington was using in 1809.

Despite so much that was the same, war in 1815 was a very different business from war in 1792. The changes lay almost wholly in two features which made the whole business of manoeuvring, both strategically and tactically, much quicker. At the higher level all armies had adopted the organization of permanent formations greater than the regiment. Now divisions and corps, each with permanent staff officers, formed part of the war establishment of every major army, thus enabling the field force to be commanded and manoeuvred with a speed and efficiency unknown when commanders had to give their orders to a collection of regiments or, at best, brigades, and separate instructions to artillery. At the lower level, and possibly even more influential than the establishment of higher formations, was an improvement in the system of foot drill which made movement on the battlefield so much quicker than it had been in the wars of Frederick the Great since it made it possible for infantry to deploy and concentrate with an unprecedented speed. When only the French army used this more flexible drill, they won their battles with monotonous regularity. When their opponents equalled them in flexibility the result became more open and, in the end, there were not enough French troops left to be able to hold back the vast numbers of their enemies, despite the skill of their Emperor.

PART TWO

War at Sea

The Conditions of War at Sea

NAVIES DID NOT HAVE TO DEPEND on the horse but they suffered from all the other disadvantages endured by armies and several more besides. Naval armament, though greatly more plentiful, was quite as inefficient as military with the additional drawback of being fired from a moving platform. Naval signalling facilities were even less satisfactory than those available to armies. On land the movements of armies were circumscribed by rivers and mountains but these were known features; the movements of fleets was dependent on the incalculable wind. In a dead calm no sailing ship could move; in a gale all thought of the enemy had to be abandoned while the crew fought to save their ship. No ship could sail directly into the wind and no large warship, all of which were square rigged, could sail less than six points ($67\frac{1}{2}°$) off the direction of the wind. Fleets operated over gigantic distances and the first task of any admiral was his most difficult – to find his enemy. The Atlantic is 4,800 kilometres across and the longest view which could be expected even in clear weather was 25 kilometres from masthead to masthead. In fog or at night darkened ships would be lucky to see one another at a distance of one kilometre.

Since the main armament of any ship had to be mounted aiming at right-angles to the direction in which the ship was sailing, it was the custom for fleets, like armies, to fight in line so that the maximum fire-power could be brought to bear. As a British naval writer of 1744 had laid down:

A line of battle is the basis and formulation of all discipline in sea fights, as is universally practised by all nations that are masters of any power at sea. It has had the test of long experience, and stood before the stroke of time, pure and unaltered, handed down by our predecessors.

The Fighting Instructions issued to the Channel Fleet by Lord Howe in 1799 included an explanatory note that:

The chief purposes for which a fleet is formed in line of battle are: that the ships may be able to assist and support each other in action; that they may not be exposed to the fire of the enemy ships greater in number than themselves; and that every ship may be able to fire on the enemy without the risk of firing into the ships of her own fleet.

The drawback to fighting in line was that it was almost impossible to produce a decisive result. It was most unusual for the whole of two opposing lines to come to grips and most sea fights degenerated into a number of ship-to-ship duels, fought broadside-to-broadside, from which, even when a clear victor emerged, she was likely to be so damaged as to be useless for days, weeks, or months to come.

As early as 1763 a French authority had declared that 'There are no longer decisive battles at sea' and Nelson commented, 'No day can be long enough to arrange a couple of fleets and fight a battle according to the old system'. This was little different from Guibert's comments on battles on land (see p. 16).

Another drawback to fighting in line was that the guns were hammering away at the strongest timbers in the opposing ship. Even when ranges were very short (and at the 'Glorious First of June' BRUNS-WICK was pressed so close to *Vengeur* that her lower-deck gun ports could not be opened and were blown off by her own guns firing through them), it was unlikely that serious damage would be done to the enemy unless at least one mast could be brought down. The most effective form of fire was to rake the enemy, to fire down the length of his ship, preferably from the less well-protected stern. Since ships did not have transverse bulkheads, a shot fired through the stern would go from end to end of the enemy, clearing away all the men and equipment which stood in its way. Unfortunately it was a condition of fighting in line that the enemy could not be raked unless, by accident or design, he swung out of line.

At the battle of the Saints (12 April 1782) Admiral Sir George Rodney opened a new era of sea fighting. His flagship FORMIDABLE luffed and cut through the French line of battle, thus turning what would have been an indecisive skirmish into a decisive action which saved the British possessions in the West Indies. It is irrelevant that, in the opinion of Admiral Lord St Vincent:

Rodney passed through the enemy's line by accident, not design, although historians have given him credit for the latter.

Henceforward the more forward-looking officers of the Royal Navy aimed to break through the enemy's line so as to give themselves the chance to capture or destroy a significant portion of the enemy fleet. In Nelson's words:

It will surprise and confound the enemy. They won't know what I am about. It will bring on a pell-mell battle, and that is what I want.

Such tactics were the exact equivalent of those practised by French generals who hurled a column of men at the enemy line aiming to break it and bring on a 'pell-mell battle'. The difference lay in the fact that

PREVIOUS PAGE: The battle of the Saints, 1782 which opened a new era of sea fighting

columnar attacks on land could be undertaken with partially-trained soldiers while at sea the requirements of a pell-mell battle called for highly trained officers and ratings working as an experienced team.

Any departure from fighting in line at sea brought out the weakness of naval signalling, for it was difficult in the extreme for an admiral to make his intentions clear to his subordinates. For almost a century before the American Revolution the Royal Navy had gone into battle with only seven signal flags – red, white, blue, striped red and white, striped red, white and blue (the Dutch jack), the Genoese ensign, and the Union flag. Each of these flags could be differentiated by being hoisted in different positions on different masts but the number of signals in the *Fighting Instructions* was strictly limited by the fact that not more than two flags were used in any one signal. Admirals Vernon, Anson, and Boscawen had introduced seven more flags, and guns were sometimes used either to emphasize or differentiate a signal. In his *Additional Instructions*, Boscawen laid down that he would fire 'one gun for every point of the compass I would have the course altered'. But such signals could give rise to confusion if used in the presence of the enemy. It was not until 1782 that Lord Howe, commanding the Channel Fleet, promulgated a code of 230 pre-arranged flag signals which gave a fairly wide selection of possible messages which could be speedily communicated to a large fleet, given good visibility. The transmission of specific words, letters, and numbers had to wait until 1803 when Captain Home Popham's *Marine Vocabulary* was taken into service but even this could do nothing to help in the sending of signals at night or in fog. In darkness a few simple instructions could be passed by different arrangements of lanterns hoisted on the masts. But in fog there was no way of passing orders or information beyond the distance at which a man with a speaking trumpet could be heard.

Rodney's manoeuvre at the Saints, opening as it did new avenues in tactics, required new signals and, soon after the news of the battle reached England, Howe added a new one (No. 235) to his code.

When fetching up with the enemy to leeward, and on the contrary tack, to break through their line and endeavour to cut off part of their van or rear.

At almost the same time Admiral Pigot, who succeeded Rodney in the West Indies, introduced two new signals for his fleet.

For the leading ship to cut through the enemy's line of battle.
For a particular ship specified to cut through the enemy's line of battle and for all other ships to follow her in close order to support each other.

In 1790 Howe, reappointed to the Channel Fleet, added yet another signal. This instructed each ship to cut through the line independently, thus by a single manoeuvre putting the entire fleet on the further, unprepared side of the enemy and giving each ship, as it cut the line, the opportunity to rake her opponent.

The effect of raking fire was much increased by the introduction of carronades. These were the invention of General Sir Robert Melville

Admiral Lord Howe
(1726–99)

OPPOSITE: Royal Naval types by Rowlandson. A Captain (TOP LEFT); carpenter (TOP RIGHT); seaman (BOTTOM LEFT); and midshipman (BOTTOM RIGHT)

ABOVE: The 'Glorious First of June', 1794. BRUNSWICK in action with *Vengeur*

BELOW: The battle of Cape St Vincent, 1797. Nelson's CAPTAIN(74) boarding *San Nicolas*(80). The boarders pushed on and also captured the *San Josef*(112) which lies behind the *San Nicolas*

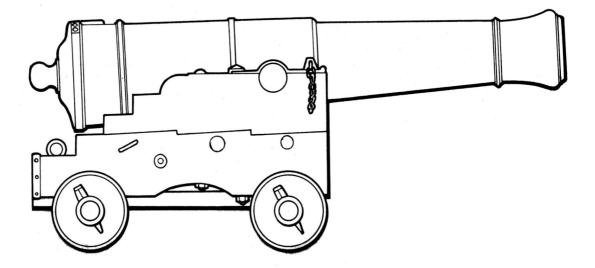

who produced his first practicable model in 1774. The carronade was essentially a short range weapon, being useless at more than 360 metres. The barrel had no trunnions but was held to its carriage by a central lug on the underside and its carriage consisted of a heavy slab of wood which was clamped to another along which it was permitted to slide but the friction between the two slabs of wood absorbed the greater part of the recoil. The comparative absence of recoil meant that it could be manned by a very small crew, two or three was the usual number, and the burden on the gun-numbers was also lightened since the balls, though the same size as those for 'long guns', were hollow and thus lighter. This hollowness meant that it would fragment on impact and the flying pieces were extremely dangerous to opposing sailors. The carronade itself was much

TOP: English 24-pounder naval gun and BOTTOM: French 36-pounder naval gun. It took a gun crew of twelve to achieve the maximum rate of fire for both guns. The English gunners were far superior due to the blockade which kept French crews trapped in port and unable to practice

lighter than a comparable long gun, Sir Robert's original model, an apparent 68-pounder, weighing only $1\frac{1}{2}$ tonnes compared to the 3 tonnes of a 32-pounder long gun.

The short range of the carronade made it unsuitable as a main weapon for ships of the line, though some smaller vessels were entirely armed with them, and battleships and frigates carried them in the 32- or 24-pounder models as additional artillery mounted at the bows and on the quarterdeck. They were therefore usually not counted in the 'rating' of the ship (i.e. as a 100- or 74-gun ship), a sore point with naval officers since a captain's pay depended on the rating of his command and to include the carronades would have increased his pay.

One other factor must always be remembered when considering warships built before the middle of the nineteenth century. The weather and accidental fire were far more dangerous to them and their crews than any human enemy. Between 1793 and 1815 the Royal Navy lost a total of 32 ships of the line but of these only 5 were lost to the enemy while 17 were wrecked, 2 foundered, and 8 were burned by accident unconnected with battle. In all 473 ships of all sizes were lost but only 152 of these casualties were due to enemy action.

CHAPTER THIRTEEN

Insurrection and Invasion

WHEN THE YOUNG FRENCH REPUBLIC declared war on Great Britain and Ireland she had some hope that her new enemy would destroy herself from within, but the prospect of a British revolution soon faded even if Ireland remained a promising field for stirring up and supporting a revolt. France, therefore, was faced with two ways in which she could conquer her island enemy. She could invade her – via Ireland seemed a promising route – and conquer the kingdom, or she could throttle British commerce and undermine the financial strength on which British resilience rested. Neither the Republic nor the subsequent Empire could ever decide which of these courses they wished to pursue and, since either course called for a separate naval preparation, they failed to implement either policy with any degree of success.

At the revolution France possessed the second navy in the world and, a few years earlier, in the American War, her ships had shown themselves to be the best designed, the handiest, and the fastest in any fleet while her admirals and crews were as competent as any. This promising basis for a further war was destroyed almost wantonly. From 1789 to 1792 mutiny was regarded by the authorities as a legitimate demonstration in favour of 'natural liberty' and when the navy was required its discipline had been destroyed. Many officers had been removed because of their aristocratic lineage, many more had left since they could find neither credit nor utility in commanding crews who would not obey orders. Three-quarters of the officer corps, including almost all the senior officers, had quit the service by July 1791 and desertion among the trained ratings was on a huge scale since the more experienced a seaman was the more keenly he would realize the danger of sailing in a ship with an ill-disciplined crew. Those who remained or were drafted on board were anxious to leave, since the revolutionary government was incapable of paying, feeding, or clothing their sailors. Unlike soldiers, sailors had no opportunities to make good the administrative deficiencies by private looting. To make matters worse the Convention, in an excess of idealistic stupidity, insisted on abolishing the corps of marine artillery, a splendid body of non-commissioned officers and men, on the grounds that such an *élite* corps smacked of aristocracy. To replace the skills they had driven away the Convention resorted to exhortation:

Disdaining skilful evolutions, our seamen should think it more fitting to attempt those boarding actions in which the French always conquer.

Threats were enacted to reinforce exhortation. In February 1794 a decree prescribed the death penalty for a captain and his officers if a ship was surrendered before it was in a sinking condition. Later that year the same penalty was decreed for any captain who allowed the line of battle to be broken.

Courage was seldom if ever lacking in the French navy but it could be no substitute for skilled seamanship and the experience and team-work which alone could make a warship safe and effective. In June 1793 Admiral Morand de Galles, the first republican commander of the Brest squadron, remarked:

I have sailed in the most numerous fleets but never in a year did I see so many collisions as in the month this squadron has been together.

In 1793–94 France had need of all the naval skill she could muster for she was facing a monstrous naval coalition. She herself had 76 ships of the line (of which 27 were in commission in January 1793) and 13 more building. Against her was, primarily, the Royal Navy with 113 of the line (26 in commission January 1793; 91 two years later) with 12 building, apart from stationary harbour ships. In support were the Spaniards with 76 battleships, of which two-thirds were fit to go to sea, the British-trained Portuguese navy with 6, Naples with 4, and the Dutch with 49. To this array might at any time be added the fleets of Russia, 40, and Denmark and Sweden with 20 each.

Nor were the first three years of the naval war encouraging for the French battle fleet. The allied occupation of Toulon cost her thirteen of the line and it was little consolation that it was only the incompetence of the Spanish demolition teams that saved 14 more. Three brushes with the Royal Navy, the 'Glorious First of June' and actions off Lorient and Genoa, cost 13 more while the perils of the sea accounted a further 7, the most disastrous event occurring at the New Year of 1795 when Admiral Villaret-Joyeuse attempted to take the Brest fleet to sea. At an early stage *Républicaine*(110) struck a rock and sank before leaving Brest roads. This decided Villaret to recall the remainder but before the ships could beat back into port a gale blew up and *Scipion*(80); *9ᵐᵉ Thermidor*(74) and *Superbe*(74) foundered while *Neptune*(74) was so badly damaged that she had to be beached and became a total loss.

To balance this loss of 33 ships of the line, 3 British battleships were taken, 1 was lost at sea, and 4 were accidentally burned. France, in fact, might well have ceased to be a major naval power had she not acquired the Dutch fleet by conquest and the Spanish by alliance.

The Republic was not deterred by its misfortunes from producing plans for invading the British Isles. The first schemes (1793–4) aimed at seizing the Channel Islands but in 1796 a start was made with building a flotilla of landing craft at Dunkirk. However the most promising plan, constantly reverted to, was the invasion of Ireland. There is no doubt that the French greatly over-estimated the amount of local support they

PREVIOUS PAGE: The battle of Camperdown, 1797

would receive there — one of their agents reported that 150,000 men were armed and ready to rise as soon as the French landed — but it is equally certain that, had they secured a foothold, they would have been able to call on much sympathy and some useful assistance from the disaffected Irish. Nor would the British have found it easy to expel a French army with local support from Ireland since, as the Duke of York, Commander-in-Chief, wrote:

Almost the whole of the recruits of the infantry of the line are Irish and it would be by no means a politic measure to send any of the regular battalions to Ireland.

The first scheme, put forward by the Directory, for the invasion of Ireland was one of great complexity. Warships containing 5,000 regular troops were to be detached from a convoy sailing for the East Indies and ordered to land in Galway (*Galloway*) Bay from where they were to seize both banks of the Shannon estuary and the whole of Connaught (*Connacie*) except Leitrim. To consolidate this extensive beachhead two further expeditions were to join the regulars. The first was to sail from Holland and would consist of 5,000 foreign deserters dressed in captured British uniforms. They were to be joined by a division from Brest consisting of 6,000 men formed into *corps francs*, 'by which means' said the directive, 'it will be possible to rid France of many dangerous individuals'.

The overall command was given to General Lazarre Hoche, an excellent soldier but one whose genuine zeal to invade the British Isles did not prevent him from remonstrating against this absurd scheme. His protests were successful and a new plan was devised in which he held a double commission as general and admiral. On 16 December 1796 he sailed from Brest with 14,750 regular soldiers, complete with field and siege artillery, who were accommodated in 17 ships of the line, 1 cut-down battleship (*rasé*), 13 frigates, 4 corvettes, 6 *flûtes* (warships with their guns removed), a lugger, and a brig loaded with powder. Hoche and the senior naval officer, Morand de Galles, embarked on the frigate *Fraternité*(40).

There are three entrances to Brest roads. Directly to the west is the broad Iroise channel while to the north is the difficult and dangerous Canal du Four. To the south is the easier but narrow Raz de Sein, a long strait between the coast and the mass of reefs, shoals and islets of the Chausée de Sein. Morand des Galles believed that a squadron of five British frigates was watching the Iroise channel and gave orders for the fleet to leave by the Raz de Sein. They started to do so shortly before dusk on 16 December. Just at that time the wind, which had been fresh from the east, veered southerly and, hoping to take advantage of the last of the light, Morand signalled for the fleet to use the Iroise channel. Only the ships close to *Fraternité* saw this signal and Morand tried to emphasize it by firing guns and despatching a corvette to hail the leading ships. At this juncture *Séduisant*(74) struck a rock at the entrance to the passage and was wrecked. Her distress signals did nothing to make the admiral's orders more widely understood and, to add to the confusion, INDEFATIGABLE(44), Captain Sir Edward Pellew, sailed into the fleet, firing her guns and illuminating the darkening scene with flares.

At dawn on 17 December, Hoche and Morand found only one battleship, 2 frigates, 3 corvettes, and 2 *flûtes* in company with *Fraternité* while a thick fog prevailed. Nevertheless every captain had been given sealed orders and 35 ships reached a pre-arranged rendezvous off Bantry Bay on the morning of 21 December. Unfortunately *Fraternité* was not among them and the naval command devolved upon Admiral Bouvet while the senior soldier was General Emmanuel Grouchy, a *ci-devant* marquis and a future marshal of the Empire.

The sealed orders called upon them to wait at the rendezvous for five days but Bouvet soon became nervous and it was with difficulty that Grouchy persuaded him to move into the bay and attempt a landing. It was unfortunate that the wind was now blowing steadily from the east and since, by a minor navigational error, the squadron had arrived somewhat to the west of the bay, which runs east-north-east, it was extremely difficult to enter. Wolfe Tone, who was aboard *Indomptable* (80), wrote in his diary:

I believe we have made three hundred tacks, and have not gained a hundred yards in a straight line.

It was not until 24 December that fifteen ships carrying 6,400 soldiers and seven light guns had anchored near Bear Island within Bantry Bay. That night the east wind rose to a gale which continued to blow throughout Christmas day. Several ships dragged their anchors and, led by Bouvet, ran for Brest. The remainder, including the ship on which Grouchy was sailing, hung on in the bay until 27 December when, the wind veering south and threatening another gale, they decided to make for home. Meanwhile *Fraternité*, with both the commanders of the expedition on board, was alone in the Atlantic. The small group of ships in company with her had been forced westward by the appearance of some ships believed to be British and driven further still out into the ocean by the easterly gale in which all the ships had become separated. It was not until 29 December that the frigate sighted two of Bouvet's ships, one sinking, the other heavily damaged, and learned that the main body had set off for Brest. Hoche and Morand reached that port on 13 January to find that most of the rest of the expedition had docked on the previous day.

THE ROLE OF THE ROYAL NAVY

It must be asked what the Royal Navy was doing throughout this period. The answer must be very little, to any useful purpose. The fleet's prime task was to prevent the invasion of the British Isles and this meant that their first responsibility was to keep a guard on Brest, the largest and most northerly of all the French bases. They could not, however, neglect the other naval bases of France and her allies so that squadrons had to be detailed to watch Rochefort, Toulon, the Texel, Hellevoet-sluis, Ferrol, Cadiz, and Cartagena. Nevertheless, some thirty ships of the line were available to the Channel Fleet, the force primarily responsible

Emmanuel Grouchy.
(1766–1847)

for Brest. It was unfortunate, though understandable, that the first two commanders of this fleet, Lords Howe and Bridport, believed that keeping their ships constantly at sea would destroy them from wear and tear. They therefore kept their main strength at Spithead, where there were excellent dockyard facilities while a squadron of seven or eight of the line, with an advanced guard of lighter ships cruised off Brest. The disadvantages of this disposition were that it was 240 kilometres from Spithead to the approaches to Brest and that the French needed a south-east wind to leave Brest and that if such a wind was blowing the first and second raters of the Channel Fleet would be unable to sail the first 5 kilometres from Spithead to St Helens. Howe and Bridport believed that these drawbacks must be accepted since the alternatives were so unattractive. Falmouth, only 160 kilometres from Ushant, is a bad anchorage for large ships; Plymouth Sound was dangerous in south-westerly gales before the great breakwater, started in 1812, was completed after Waterloo; Torbay, 217 kilometres from Ushant could not be left with a strong south-easterly wind.

Towards the end of 1796, Bridport had heard that an expedition was preparing at Brest and had doubled the watching squadron to fifteen of the line commanded by Vice-Admiral Sir John Colpoys. Colpoys, a competent but unimaginative officer, believed, like most of his colleagues, that it was dangerous to keep ships of the line too close to Brest since the prevailing westerly wind should drive them into the bay itself from where his three deckers in particular would only be able to extract themselves if the wind changed. He therefore gave as his rendezvous a position 32 kilometres west of Ushant and entrusted the close watch to a light squadron, three frigates and a hired lugger, under Captain Sir Edward Pellew.

It was on 15 December that Pellew saw the first of the French squadron coming through the Goulet which connects the inner harbour of Brest with the roadstead and he immediately detached one frigate to inform Colpoys. By that time the easterly wind which allowed the French to come through the Goulet had driven Colpoys eastward and he did not receive Pellew's message until 19 December, by which time he was 80 kilometres west of Ushant and the main body of the French was another 80 kilometres west of him and turning north for Bantry. Three days earlier, when the whole French squadron was in the roadstead, Pellew sent another frigate to Colpoys and on 17 December, by which time the bulk of the French had gone through the Raz de Sein, he sent his cutter with despatches to Spithead. With his own ship INDEFATIGABLE he tried to follow the French, only to lose them in the fog. He therefore made for Falmouth, hoping to find some of the Channel Fleet.

It must be emphasized that neither Pellew nor Colpoys could know Hoche's destination. Ireland was certainly a strong possibility but so was Lisbon, the base of the British Mediterranean Fleet, and it was not improbable that the French were making for the West Indies or the Mediterranean. Moreover Colpoys did not learn from Pellew's second frigate that the French had actually put to sea until 22 December, a day after Bridport got the news from Pellew's cutter at Spithead. Colpoys decided that his best course was to rendezvous with the Channel Fleet.

Droits de l'Homme(74) being engaged by INDEFATIGABLE(44) and AMAZON(36) on the night of 13 January 1797

This Bridport took to sea and cruised off Brest in the hope, unfulfilled, of intercepting some returning French ships.

The French, however, did not escape unscathed. Three frigates, the *rasé*, and four *flûtes*, were lost at sea. A fourth frigate had the misfortune to meet a 64-gun ship off the Irish coast and was captured as were two brigs. But their most serious loss, apart from *Séduisant*, was *Droits de l'Homme* (74). She had failed to reach Bantry but had arrived off the mouth of the Shannon where she took a richly laden merchantship and cruised until 9 January in the hope of meeting some of her consorts. Then her commander, Commodore La Crosse, decided to make for Brest and was approaching that port when, on the afternoon of 13 January, she was sighted by Pellew in INDEFATIGABLE who had AMAZON(36) thirteen kilometres astern. By remarkably bad luck a sudden squall, just as the French sighted Pellew, carried away the *Droits de l'Homme*'s fore and main topmasts. Thus, when INDEFATIGABLE attacked, the Frenchman's superior armament was largely offset by his lack of manoeuvrability. His fire-power was also cut when the wind rose and made it impossible for him to open his lee gun-ports.

Nevertheless La Crosse handled his ship brilliantly although his gunners were no match for those on the two frigates who succeeded in bringing down his mizzen mast. The fight continued all night in appalling conditions of wind and rain and it was not until 4.20 am that all three ship's commanders realized that they had been driven into the bay of Audierne, at the southern end of the Passage du Raz. INDEFATIGABLE was able to haul off, and just weathered the southern headland but AMAZON, damaged aloft, had to wear to the north and was unable to keep off the shore. Three of her men had been killed in the fight but all the remainder except six got safely to the beach and were made prisoners. La Crosse was less fortunate. *Droits de l'Homme*, with 549 soldiers on board, was greatly overcrowded and the damage to her masts made her barely able to manoeuvre, the more so since she had already suffered 103 killed in the fighting. She drove on to a sandbank and, a gale blowing for the next forty-eight hours, 400 more of her complement died before they could be rescued.

But for the difficulties in communication and the perversity of the wind there had been nothing to stop Hoche's expedition landing at Bantry Bay. The same factors had completely frustrated the British attempts to intercept them. Had even a slight shift in the wind allowed Grouchy and his 6,400 men to land there was little to stop them from seizing Cork. If that had led to a sizable Irish rising the whole island might have been lost to the British with incalculable consequences to the future course of the war. As it was it clearly demonstrated to the French that the invasion of Ireland was a practicable operation.

An invasion was also becoming more practicable since France and her allies now had a clear numerical superiority at sea. *Séduisant* and *Droits de l'Homme* were the only capital ships lost by the French navy in 1796 and 1797 so that their building programme at last could begin to make some headway and in 1797 the fleet had more than 50 of the line while the Spaniards could contribute as many again in sea-going shape and the Dutch, despite some losses when they declared war on Britain, could send 40 of the line to sea. Thus the alliance could produce 140 of the line against the 108 that Britain had in commission. The immediate strategic questions were whether the allied strength could be concentrated on the invasion front and whether the numerical advantage of the French was sufficient to overcome the Royal Navy's undoubted qualitative superiority.

Another factor which told in the alliance's favour was that the French land victories in Italy had deprived the British of all their sea bases in the Mediterranean so that their fleet in that sea had, in December 1796, been forced to withdraw and use Lisbon as a home port. During the withdrawal two 74-gun ships had been lost, one in a gale off Gibraltar, the other on a sandbank in the Tagus. Despite reinforcements from Britain Sir John Jervis, the commander-in-chief, could only muster 15 of the line (2×100s, 3×98s, 1×90, 8×74s, 1×64), 4 frigates, and 3 smaller ships, in early February 1797.

Meanwhile the main Spanish fleet was summoned from Cartagena to concentrate with the main French squadron at Brest, picking up more Spanish ships at Cadiz on their voyage. Under Admiral de Cordoba, the fleet sailed on 1 February with 27 ships of the line (1×130, 6×112s, 2×80s, and 18×74s) and 12 frigates. It was an imposing armada but to some extent it was misleading. The Spanish fleet had greatly deteriorated under the government of Charles IV and Godoy, there were only 60 or 80 trained seamen in each crew and, in Nelson's words, they were 'ill-manned and worse officered'.

To make matters worse they had very little luck. On 11 February MINERVE(38) sighted their rear as they passed Algeciras and immediately sailed to warn Jervis. The admiral, however, did not get the information until 13 February by which time Cordoba would have been safely in Cadiz had not a strong easterly carried him out too far into the Atlantic and it was not until the morning of 14 February that he was able to approach the coast and, off Cape St Vincent, caught sight of some

British ships. These were not unexpected as Cordoba had spoken to an American merchant captain who had told him that there were nine ships of the line off Cadiz. This force Cordoba considered to be too small to interfere with his fleet.

There was mist in the early morning of St Valentine's day and, according to the log of the British flagship, VICTORY(100) it was 6.30 am before she 'discovered a number of strange ships to windward, believed to be the Spanish fleet' and 9 am when she 'counted 20 sail of the line and 31 sail altogether'. Thereafter the captain of the fleet continued to report increased estimates of the enemy's numbers:

'There are twenty sail of the line, Sir John.'
'Very well, sir.'
'There are twenty five sail of the line, Sir John.'
'Very well, sir.'
'There are twenty seven sail of the line, Sir John.'
'Enough, sir, no more of that; the die is cast; and if there are fifty sail, I will go through them.'

The Spaniards, hastening for the safety of Cadiz, were taking few tactical precautions and were moving in two irregular huddles of ships, one of six battleships to leeward, another of nineteen, with two more tagging along far astern, to windward. Jervis formed his own fifteen battleships into a single column 'ahead and astern of the flagship as convenient' and sailed between the two Spanish groups before turning the head of his column to engage the larger of the two. The opening of the battle is described in VICTORY's log:

Admiral Sir John Jervis, later Lord St Vincent (1735–1823)

At 11, the enemy forming the line on the larboard tack. The PRINCE GEORGE, BLENHEIM, CULLODEN *and* COLOSSUS *a little ahead and forming as most convenient. 11.20 Hoisted our colours. 11.29. The signal to pass through the enemy's line. At 11.31,* CULLODEN *began to engage. ½ past 12, the action became general from van to centre. At noon, the fleet engaging the enemy on different tacks. Moderate breezes and hazy. Employed passing through the enemy's line and engaging to windward. ½ past [12] a Spanish vice admiral attempted to pass ahead of* VICTORY. CULLODEN *and* BLENHEIM *on the larboard tack and passing to windward of our line.* PRINCE GEORGE *passing to windward of our centre. The Spanish vice admiral forced to tack close under* VICTORY's *lee. Raked her both ahead and astern; he appeared to be in great confusion [and] bore up as did six others of the enemy's ships.*

The battle had begun well but, as Jervis had slightly misjudged the timing of the fleet's turn, the action could only have been indecisive since the British rear would have taken time to come into action. The day was turned into a victory when the third ship from the rear, CAPTAIN(74), flying the broad pennant of Commodore Nelson, cut off the corner. On Nelson's order she wore to port, cut across the tail of the line between the last two ships, came up with the British van and plunged into the centre of the main Spanish group which was already engaged with CULLODEN(74), BLENHEIM(98), and PRINCE GEORGE(98). When Collingwood in EXCELLENT(74), the rear ship of

CAPTAIN having lost her foremast, boarding the *San Nicolas*

the fleet, followed CAPTAIN there were five British ships in a position to head off the Spanish retreat. The result was as pell-mell a battle as Nelson could have wished in which he set an example by boarding and taking *San Nicolas*(80) and from her deck going on to board *San Josef*(112) which had run foul of her consort after a heavy battering from PRINCE GEORGE. By nightfall four Spanish ships (2×112s, 1×80, 1×74) had been taken for a cost to the British of 73 dead and 227 seriously wounded. The battered remnants of Cordoba's fleet reached Cadiz but the Spanish navy was never again a serious menance to Britain.

News of the victory off Cape St Vincent reached London on 3 March and gave a much needed boost to the British morale. Not only had news been received of Bonaparte's victory at Rivoli and the surrender of Mantua but French troops had actually landed in Britain, causing a financial panic worse than any in the worst moments of the American war. Consols fell to 51 and the government had been forced to abandon gold payments.

It had not been a very menacing invasion. Even the French regarded it as a *chouannerie*, a guerrilla operation, rather than a serious attempt to gain a foothold. The commander was an American, Tate, who had been badgering the Directory with a plan for conducting *une enterprise de flibusterie* against Bermuda. Instead he was given the rank of brigadier and the command of the 2me *Légion des Francs*, a regiment of which Hoche, from whose command they were drawn, wrote that they consisted of:

600 men drawn from all the prisons in my district and gathered in two forts or islands from which they cannot escape. I have added to them 600 galley slaves (who are still in irons).

This desperate crew were given muskets and 200 rounds a man and Tate was ordered to land at the mouth of the Severn and burn Bristol. Should this prove too difficult he was given the option of landing in Cardigan Bay, marching across Wales and burning Liverpool. The French navy contributed two frigates, a brig, and a lugger for transport.

In the event the escort burned a few coastal vessels off Ilfracombe and landed the expedition midway between their alternative goals at Pencarn, near Fishguard, on 22 February 1797. Next day Tate surrendered to the Castlemartin troop of the Pembrokeshire Yeomanry. Both the frigates were captured on their way back to France.

Despite St Vincent, the early months of 1797 were a difficult time for Britain. In April the fleet at Spithead broke into mutiny and hardly had a settlement been reached by well-merited concessions than another, more serious mutiny occurred at the Nore. Although the mutineers declared their willingness to take the fleet to sea if the French should threaten invasion, Britain's sea defences were in poor shape between April and the middle of June. Meanwhile a large French squadron was being prepared at Brest. Even without the expected Spanish reinforcements, detachments from Toulon had brought the fleet there up to 30 of the line with 14 frigates, 13 corvettes and, for the transport of troops, 29 *flûtes*.

If this concentration of ships could have been got ready for sea during the period of the mutinies there would have been little that the Royal Navy could have done to stop them. In fact the inadequacy of Brest defeated them. Situated in the extreme west of France in a lightly populated region, it was difficult to obtain food there and, thanks to the activities of generations of shipbuilders, impossible to find timber. Thus the great concentration of ships could not be repaired nor could they be stocked with provisions. For the single sortie they did make the fleet could only be provisioned for fifteen days, instead of the usual six months, and even this was only achieved by raiding the stores carried by the ships from Toulon. Nor could crews be found around Brest. Of the 24,000 sailors needed only 15,616 were available.

Simultaneously a squadron of sixteen of the line was concentrating at the Texel. Here again there was difficulty in obtaining stores but even more time was wasted in discussing whether the troops they were to carry should be Dutch or French. Their objective was agreed to be Scotland but when, on 11 October, the squadron, without its transports, put to sea, Admiral Duncan was waiting for them with the North Sea Fleet, his ships manned almost entirely with men who had mutinied at the Nore.

The two fleets were not unequally matched. Duncan also had sixteen of the line (7×74s, 7×64s, 2×50s) against De Winter's 3×74s, 1×72, 5×68s, 2×64s, 3×56s, 1×44 (*rasé*), and any advantage the British had in weight of broadside was offset by the number and armament of his lighter craft. Certainly De Winter was confident of his chances and courted a battle, forming his battleships in line, with frigates and brigs in second line, about 14 kilometres off Camperdown (Kamperduin). Duncan sailed down on him in two columns but, seeing the Dutch formation, signalled to form line abreast, each ship to engage her opposite number. Since the two lines were not parallel, the weight of the attack fell on the Dutch rear and centre but, at the end of one of the most hard-fought battles of the war, 9 of the line (1×74, 1×72, 4×68s, 2×64s, 1×54) and 2 frigates were in British hands. The prizes were of little use. The Dutch fought them so stubbornly that every one of them was:

either dismasted outright, or so injured in their masts that most of the latter fell as soon as the wind and sea began to act powerfully upon them. As for their hulls, the ships were like sieves and only worth bringing into port to be exhibited as trophies.

Six days after Camperdown, peace was concluded between France and Austria and the Republic was able to turn her whole attention to the problem of defeating Britain. Bonaparte was appointed to the command of the *Armée d'Angleterre* (26 October 1797), and orders were placed for the construction of 170 gun-brigs (*chaloups canonières*) in the ports of northern France together with more in Holland. 20,000 tonnes of merchant shipping for the transport of 30,000 troops (apart from 10,000 to be transported in naval vessels) were chartered. 56,000 troops, many of them veterans from the *Armée d'Italie*, were concentrated on the invasion coast and further warships were ordered to Brest from the Mediterranean.

The result was anti-climax. As early as February 1798 Bonaparte decided that the operation was impracticable:

Whatever efforts we make we cannot gain naval superiority for some years to come. To invade England without such supremacy would be to embark on the most daring and difficult task ever undertaken . . . Our navy is no more ready than it was four months ago.

The ships were there but, thanks to the inadequacies of Brest, they could not be got ready for sea. Of 34 ships of the line in the port only 13 were seaworthy and stored by the end of March.

THE WAR IN THE MEDITERRANEAN
As an alternative the Directory sent Bonaparte, at his own suggestion, on the abortive expedition to Egypt. This was a serious error of judgment based on the belief that the Royal Navy, having left the Mediterranean, would not dare to return. In fact they were most anxious to do so, both to re-establish the profitable Levant trade and to keep a watch on Toulon which, they suspected, might be used as a base for the invasion of Ireland. On 9 May 1798, Admiral Jervis, now Lord St Vincent, sent Rear-Admiral Nelson with three 74-gun ships, 2 frigates, and a sloop, sailing eastward from Gibraltar.

Meanwhile a great fleet had been assembled at Toulon. 224 chartered merchantmen carrying 24,000 infantry, 4,000 cavalry, and 3,000 gunners, set sail on 19 May under escort of 13 of the line (1×120, 3×80s,

9×74s), 6 frigates, and smaller vessels. Only bad luck and bad weather prevented Nelson from intercepting them almost as soon as they sailed but they reached Alexandria and landed their troops. It was not until 1 August that Nelson, reinforced to thirteen 74-gun ships, one 50-gun, and a brig, sailed into Aboukir (Abu Q'ir) Bay and caught the French fleet unprepared. Before morning the French flagship, the 120-gun *L'Orient* had blown up, *Timoléon*(74) had been burned by her crew to avoid capture and 9 more of the line (2×80s, 7×74s) had been captured. Two French frigates were also lost. The survivors, 2 battleships and 2 frigates, had the satisfaction a few days later of capturing LEANDER(50) in which Nelson had sent home his despatches. But British naval superiority in the Mediterranean was decisively re-established and siege was laid to Malta which, when it was eventually captured, gave Britian the unassailable base in that sea which she had hitherto lacked.

While Bonaparte was wasting time, ships and men in Egypt, France missed a great opportunity elsewhere. In May 1798 rebellion broke out in Ireland but the main trouble was settled on 21 June when the rebel army was defeated at Vinegar Hill. No French assistance had reached them since the Brest fleet was incapable of getting to sea. However a force of four frigates from Rochefort sailed on 6 August and, without meeting a single British ship, reached Killala Bay, County Mayo, sixteen days later. There they landed General Humbert, a survivor from the wreck of *Droits de l'Homme*, with 1,150 soldiers and four light guns. They found little Irish support but by splendid discipline and effrontery they defeated a British force, partially composed of regulars, at Castlebar on 27 August. It was not until 8 September that they were cornered by a huge concentration of troops at Ballinamuck, 128 kilometres from their starting place. It was an astonishing achievement and there was little exaggeration when Humbert wrote, on the day after Castlebar:

The battle of the Nile

194

If you can send me 2,000 reinforcements, I can promise you that Ireland will be free within a month of their arrival.

If all had gone well 2,841 reinforcements (accompanied by 17 wives, 7 children, and 26 servants) should have joined. With an escort of one battleship, 8 frigates, and a schooner, they should have sailed at the same time as Humbert but ill-winds and the usual delays of preparing ships at Brest kept them there until 16 September. They were sighted by frigates as they slipped out of the Passage du Raz but, although they were lost to sight in a gale, a strong squadron under Commodore Warren found them off Tory Island on 12 October. *Hoche*(74) and three frigates, were taken that day and 3 more frigates were captured before they reached France. Yet another expedition, 300 soldiers with 6,000 muskets and 2 field guns, set out from the Texel on 24 October aiming for Galway (Gaillimh) embarked in a frigate and a corvette. They had not covered 50 kilometres before they were captured, in succession, by SIRIUS(36).

In all, France lost fourteen battleships in 1798 while the British lost only one, COLOSSUS(74), wrecked off the coast of Sicily. From the naval point of view the following year was little better. The Anglo–Russian expedition that landed in north Holland in August 1799 achieved nothing on land but it did succeed in capturing much of the Dutch navy including seven battleships (1×70, 3×68s, 3×64s), and eighteen smaller ships of the war, thus making any serious attempt to invade the British Isles impossible for some time to come.

Earlier than this the strength of the Brest squadron had been temporarily reduced when the Directory attempted to re-establish French control of the Mediterranean and to rescue the army in Egypt. In April, twenty-three of the line managed to put to sea and, picking up two more from Rochefort, headed for the Mediterranean while Lord Bridport, who had an unhappy facility for making the wrong guess, deployed the Channel Fleet to guard the approaches to Ireland. Joined, belately, by fifteen Spanish ships the French established an almost two to one supremacy in the Mediterranean but achieved very little. They delivered some stores to Genoa and, by a detachment of three frigates which were later captured, provided Bonaparte with some ships' guns for the siege of Acre. But their commander could not convince himself that he would not be attacked and overwhelmed by the Royal Navy and, on 13 August, brought the whole Franco–Spanish fleet back to Brest where the usual deficiencies prevented it from making any contribution to the rest of the war.

Ten days after they crept back into Brest, the Royal Navy missed its greatest opportunity of the war. On 23 August Bonaparte sailed from Alexandria in the ex-Venetian frigate *Muiron*(40) with another frigate, and two brigs in company. Evading the British blockade of the port he reached Ajaccio on 1 October and, eight days later, landed in France. A month later, in the *coup* of 18 *Brumaire*, he became the effective ruler of France. Henceforward that country was to be ruled by a single powerful intelligence instead of a series of incompetent and corrupt committees.

CHAPTER FOURTEEN

Destroying Fictitious Wealth

Two weeks before France declared war on Britain in 1793 a spokesman for the Ministry of Foreign Affairs told the National Convention that:

The credit of Britain rests upon fictitious wealth; the real riches of the country are scattered everywhere . . . The public future of England is found almost wholly in its Bank, and this edifice is entirely supported by the wonderful activity of their maritime commerce. Asia, Portugal, and Spain are the most advantageous markets for the products of British industry; we should shut these markets to the English by opening them to the world.

The extent of the failure of the Republic to destroy the 'wonderful activity' of Britain's maritime commerce is best demonstrated by the figures for the islands' trade. Between 1790 and 1800 exports more than doubled and imports increased by 64 per cent. The French made every effort to bring this trade to a standstill. A high proportion of their naval strength was devoted to this purpose. In 1798, when warships were badly needed to support an invasion of Ireland, a report to the Directory pointed out that 26 out of 46 frigates, 16 out of 19 corvettes, and 2 out of 6 brigs, much more than half France's naval strength in lighter craft, were 'entrusted to privateers (*armateurs*) for commerce raiding (*faire la course*)'. All this activity gained them some measure of success. According to Lloyds, 3,466 British merchant ships were captured between 1793 and 1800. This represented no more than $2\frac{1}{2}$ per cent of British trade.

Although some larger (44- and 50-gun) and many smaller types of ship were used in commerce protection, the main weight of the task fell on the frigates, fast, handy, single-deck vessels mounting between 28 and 44 guns. In the early days of the war the guns were mostly 12-pounders but as time passed the 18-pounder became more common while the 44-gun frigates, at first unique to the French navy, mounted 24-pounders. There were, of course, never enough of them. Nelson remarked that 'Want of Frigates' would be found engraved on his heart when he died. He was referring to the shortage of such craft to work with the battle squadrons. One of the reasons for the shortage was the need of frigates for protecting convoys and patrol work.

The Royal Navy had only 42 frigates in commission at the outbreak of war and most of these were of the smaller 28- and 32-gun types mounting 12-pounders. France, at the same time could deploy 79 frigates of which 15 mounted 40 or more guns, and it was one of these that won the first decisive naval action of the war. On 27 May 1793 HYAENA(24) was cruising off the coast of Hispaniola (Haiti) when she fell in with *Concorde*(40), the leading ship of a considerable French squadron:

As soon as she discovered the character of her pursuers, HYAENA *put before a light air of wind but, being unable to make way against a heavy sea, was rapidly gained upon. As* Concorde *approached her on the quarter,* HYAENA *fired a few of her main-deck guns and then, without waiting, it would appear, to receive any fire in return, hauled down her colours.*

Three weeks later a more equal fight took place in the English Channel. On 17 June NYMPHE(36) sailed from Falmouth commanded by Captain Edward Pellew. NYMPHE was typical of the larger British frigates having 26 long 12-pounders, 6×6-pounders, and 8×24-pounder carronades, a total of 40 guns (though rated as a 36) and early on the following morning, 'the Start Point bearing east by north, distant five or six leagues', she sighted a ship to the south-east. Pellew gave chase and, coming up with her, found her to be *Cléopâtre*(36), *Capitaine de Frégate* Mullon, armed with 28 long 12-pounders, and 8 long 6-pounders.

Seeing that he was being outsailed, Mullon shortened sail and stood to fight and, at 6 am, as NYMPHE closed:

The captains mutually hailed. Not a shot had yet been fired. The crew of NYMPHE *now shouted 'Long live King George' and gave three hearty cheers. Captain Mullon was seen to address his crew briefly, holding a cap of liberty which he waved before them. They answered with acclamation, shouting* Vive la

PREVIOUS PAGE: The Danish moored hulks and floating batteries being engaged by Nelson and his squadron at Copenhagen, 1801

BELOW: NYMPHE capturing *Cléopâtre*. The latter is hauling down the old French naval ensign with the tricoleur in one quarter of a white flag

république. The cap of liberty was then given to a sailor who ran up the main rigging and screwed it on the masthead.

These formalities over, Pellew put on his hat, a pre-arranged signal for NYMPHE to open fire, and both ships began to pound each other, both 'running before the wind; within rather less than hailing distance'. The French had the worst of the duel and, before 7 am:

Cléopâtre, *from the loss of her mizen-mast and wheel, being rendered unmanageable, came round with her bow to* NYMPHE's *broadside, her jib-boom pressing hard against the main-mast. Captain Pellew, supposing that the enemy were going to board, ordered the boarders to be called to repel them; but the disabled state of* Cléopâtre *was soon evident and he at once gave orders to board her. Immediately the boarders ran to the forecastle, a division of them boarding through the main-deck ports, fought their way along the gangways to the quarter-deck. The republicans, though much superior in numbers, could not resist the impetuosity of the attack. At 10 minutes past 7 they had all fled below or submitted, and the pennant of* Cléopâtre *was hauled down.*

Out of her crew of 240 men and boys NYMPHE suffered 50 casualties while *Cléopâtre* lost 63 killed and wounded out of 320. All her officers were casualties and Mullon, who had fought most gallantly, had lost 'the greater part of his hip from a roundshot'. He was found dying on his quarterdeck attempting to eat his copy of the secret French coast signals. Unfortunately he had selected the wrong piece of paper and was chewing his own commission. For this first victory of the war Pellew was knighted and *Cléopâtre* was bought into the Royal Navy under the name of OISEAU, the reason for this being that there was already a CLEOPATRA in the service.

The action between NYMPHE and *Cléopâtre* set a pattern of light ship engagements which persisted throughout the war. Between 1793 and 1801 the Royal Navy lost a total of 36 frigates of which only 6 were lost to the enemy. Three of these were taken by greatly superior force and another, NEMESIS(28) was seized by a frigate and a corvette while in the neutral port of Smyrna. The fate of the other two was less creditable. HERMIONE(32) was commanded by a brave man and skilful sailor, Hugh Pigot, whose brutality to his crew was so extreme that he can scarcely have been sane. In September 1797 the crew, driven beyond endurance, rose, murdered all the officers except one midshipman and handed the ship over to the Spanish governor of La Guaira in what is now Venezuela.

Faults in the captain were also responsible for the loss of the other frigate. Captain Henry Jenkins of AMBUSCADE(32), with 32 long 12-pounders and 8×24-pounder carronades, had a most indifferent crew which he had been permitted to leaven with thirty experienced seamen from a ship of the line on which he had served as first lieutenant. Since he showed them unbounded favouritism they proved a source of weakness. On 14 December 1798 AMBUSCADE was cruising off Bordeaux when she sighted another ship but, since she was expecting to be joined by another frigate, she failed to make recognition signals. The other ship was the corvette *Baionnaise*(24), homeward bound from the West Indies and carrying, in addition to the strong crew common to all French ships of war, a platoon of regular soldiers. Jenkins did not realize that he was in the presence of an enemy until the Frenchman, seeing that he was greatly outgunned, suddenly went about. AMBUSCADE went in pursuit and, getting within range, started to damage her opponent seriously when one of her 12-pounders burst, wounding eleven men.

The result was a panic which affected Jenkins and most of the seamen and his opponent decided to seize his opportunity to ram and board. As *Baionnaise* came straight at her opponent Jenkins took no evasive action so that AMBUSCADE was struck on the starboard quarter. Her mizen mast fell and her wheel was cleared away, whereupon, preceded by a disciplined volley from their soldiers, the French boarded. Their only opposition came from Marines while most of the sailors, ignoring the efforts of the purser, who was the senior unwounded officer, took shelter below decks. At this juncture a second explosion shook AMBUSCADE when carelessly handled cartridges took fire and the French soon took possession. On the British side 10 were killed and 36 wounded out of a complement of 190. *Baionnaise* suffered 60 casualties out of 250 on board. In due course Jenkins was brought before a court martial which acquitted him though the nature of his wounds, the top of his thigh bone had been shot away, was widely believed to have swayed the court in his favour.

During the period in which Britain lost 30 frigates to the sea and 6 to her enemies, the French lost 84 to her enemies and 18 to the sea beside one which was broken up for firewood in beleaguered Malta. The Royal Navy captured 82 of these frigates and also took 20 from the Dutch and 13 from the Spaniards. Among the captures were five of the six frigates which had been lost. The sixth, renamed *Embuscade* was not retaken until after the end of the Peace of Amiens when she was unfortunate enough to fall in with VICTORY(100) off Rochefort.

It was not the case that all these captured enemy frigates were taken in single-ship actions like NYMPHE and *Cléopâtre*. Most of them were taken by greatly superior force and 17 of them were captured in harbour (11 at Toulon, 5 at Alexandria, 1 at Malta). One that was taken in a ship-to-ship duel was *Insurgente*(36). In December 1796 the Directory made a series of ill-considered gestures to the United States as a result of which a Navy Department was formed in Washington in April 1798. War was not formally declared between the two countries but each began attacking the merchant ships of the other. On 9 February 1799, *USS Constellation*(38), cruising off Nevis in the Leeward Islands, sighted *Insurgente* which had lost her maintop-mast. *Insurgente* seems to have been unaware of any hostility between the two countries and, as *Constellation* approached, hailed her in a friendly fashion. As soon as the American ship ranged alongside, she opened with her broadside, a formidable onslaught since, despite her rating, she carried 28 long 24-pounders, 10 long 12-pounders, and 10×32-pounder carronades. *Insurgente*, taken by surprise, fought back for over an hour before she was forced to strike, having lost 29 killed and 44 wounded against 3 wounded in her opponent. *Constellation's* captain was much commended and received, among other testimonials, 'a handsome piece of plate' from the merchants of the City of London. The same captain, Commodore Thruxton, tried, a year later, to play the same trick on *Vengeance*(40) but this time the French were not taken by surprise and *Constellation* lost her mainmast and had to break off the action. In the following year, the American government having changed, Thruxton was appointed sheriff of Philadelphia and, at about the same time, France and the United States composed their differences.

WAR AGAINST MERCHANT SHIPPING

It was not only France that had troubles with neutrals. While French raiders stopped $2\frac{1}{2}$ per cent of British trade, British naval superiority brought French overseas trade to a virtual standstill. London, moreover, though anxious to encourage British trade with France and her allies, was determined to ensure that no warlike supplies reached them. She therefore claimed the right to search all neutral shipping, allowing those carrying permitted goods, largely British and colonial produce, to enter the continent after paying dues to Britain, while warlike stores were confiscated. The neutrals, not unnaturally, resented this interference but, since seaborne trade could only be carried on with the consent of the Royal Navy, usually confined their protests to words.

In July a British flotilla, 3 frigates, a sloop, and a lugger, intercepted in the North Sea a Danish convoy escorted by *Freya*(40). Captain Thomas Baker of NEMESIS(28), the frigate that had been taken in neutral Smyrna and subsequently recaptured in equally neutral Tunis, told the Danish captain that he intended to search his convoy. The reply was that he would be fired upon if he did so. It is not clear who fired first but the upshot was that after two Danish and four British seamen had been killed, *Freya* was taken into the Downs with her convoy, the Danish ensign still flying, and searched. *Freya*'s damage was repaired at British expense. The incident would have been passed over had not Czar Paul, mad and disillusioned with his British alliance, decided to aggravate the dispute. Although Russia had agreed to Britain's right to search neutral ships, he reactivated the Armed Neutrality of the North of 1780 whereby Russia, Sweden, and Denmark sought to close the Baltic to British trade. Even had Britain been prepared to waive her right of search, she could not afford to lose her trade with Russia and Sweden since from them came most of the timber for her warships. Her answer was the dispatch of Hyde Parker's fleet to the Sound and Nelson's engagement with the shore batteries and moored hulks off Copenhagen on 2 April 1801. This, together with the murder of Czar Paul, was sufficient to break up the Armed Neutrality although the Danish sea-going fleet, twenty of the line, was scarcely affected, only two battleships being captured.

The trade of Britain's enemies was further reduced by the laborious capture of their colonies. The cost in British lives of these conquests was vast since fever struck down ten and twenty men for every one who fell in battle. The gain was equally immense. British trade greatly increased and Britain was able to build up the wealth that was to sustain her and her allies in the long years of war ahead. It also reduced the strain on the navy. When Cape of Good Hope was taken in 1796, the gains included two of the line and four frigates and the loss of Trinidad cost Spain four battleships and a frigate. The conquests also reduced the number of bases from which commerce raiders could operate. Nevertheless in 1796–97, 45 out of 119 frigates still had to be deployed on the East and West Indian and Canadian stations, together with 41 other 'rated' ships.

As important as the stopping of the enemy's overseas trade was interference with his coastal shipping. At a time when roads were, at best, indifferent and the insatiable demands of the army made horses in short supply, coastal shipping was a vital activity for France and nowhere was it more important than for the supply of Brest, perched out on the Breton peninsula and far from all the main centres of French production. Jersey was an ideal base for intercepting convoys to Brest and in 1795 the squadron there consisted of 5 frigates commanded by Captain Sir Richard Strachan. At dawn on 9 May a convoy of 13 sail was seen running along the French coast and the frigates put to sea. Strachan in MELAMPUS(36) headed the convoy which ran close inshore under the protection of 2 gunboats and a powerful shore battery. Strachan therefore sent in the boats of the squadron covered by the frigates' guns. In a very short time they captured 10 merchant ships, averaging 180 tonnes, loaded with ship-timber, powder, guns, and cordage. They also captured the two gunboats and burned a brig which had run ashore. The British loss was 2 killed and 17 wounded. Two months later Sir Richard succeeded in taking 6 out of 10 merchantmen, loaded with naval stores, and a brig.

Somewhat to the east of the Channel Islands, Captain Sir Sidney Smith decided to establish his own base on French territory. In DIAMOND(38) he seized the two small islands of St Marcou, $4\frac{1}{2}$ kilometres from the coast and on the coasting route from Le Hâvre and Cherbourg. These the Admiralty commissioned as HMS BADGER, named after a Dutch hoy with 4 guns which was attached to the garrison of 500 sailors and marines, many of them unfitted for sea service by wounds and injuries. A few ship guns were also landed. In 1798 the French, galled by the depredations caused by BADGER, attempted to recapture the islands. They brought up 33 of the flat-bottomed boats which had been designed for the invasion of England and assembled 5,000 soldiers. On 7 April their first attempt was deterred by the presence of British ships but a month later there was a windless night and the flotilla set out again supported by 7 brigs and some armed fishing boats, all of which could be rowed with sweeps while the larger British ships in the vicinity were immobilized. On 7 May the defenders, at dawn, saw the flotilla some 320 metres from the beach and opened fire with the only 17 guns which would bear. The French replied with 80 guns but 6 of the landing craft were soon sunk and the remainder withdrew having lost more than 1,000 soldiers killed or drowned. HMS BADGER remained in British hands until the Peace of Amiens.

BRITISH COMMAND OF THE SEAS

As British superiority at sea gradually asserted itself, the Royal Navy, finding few French ships at sea, took to going in to cut them out from their anchorages. In July 1801 a frigate squadron off Brest saw the corvette *Chevette*(20) moored under the shore batteries in Camaret Bay, immediately south of the entrance to the Goulet. It was decided to capture her but a first attempt on 20 July miscarried and only succeeded in alerting the enemy. *Chevette* was moved further up the bay and 'moored close under some heavy batteries, one in particular on a point of land off her larboard and inner bow'. She also embarked some soldiers, bringing her complement up to 339 and she 'loaded her guns almost up to the muzzle with grapeshot'. A gunboat, armed with 2 long 36-pounders, was stationed at the entrance to the bay and field guns in earthworks were unlimbered on the shore nearby.

At 9.30 pm on 21 July 280 officers and men from ROBUST(74), DORIS(36), BEAULIEU(40), and URANIE(38) set out, but six boats, led by the lieutenant in command of the expedition, allowed themselves to be diverted into a wild-goose chase after a guard boat. The rest waited for them until the senior remaining officer, Lieutenant Keith Maxwell:

considering that the boats had at least six miles to row and that the night was already far advanced, resolved, notwithstanding that the force was reduced to less

The naval war in European waters 1793–1813

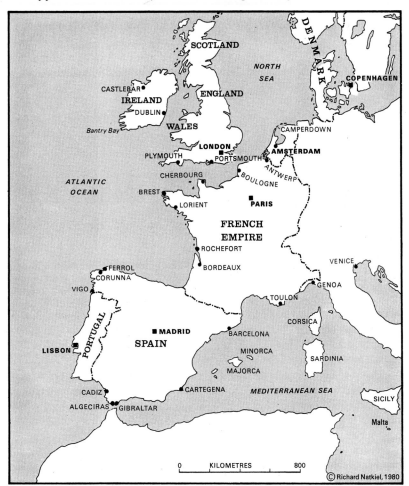

The recapture of *Hermione* in Puerto Cabello, 1799

than 180 men, to proceed. He gave orders that, while one party was engaged in disarming the enemy's crew on deck, the smartest topmen of BEAULIEU *should fight their way aloft, and cut loose the sails with their sabres; and others, who were named, should cut the cable. He appointed Henry Wallis, quartermaster of the* BEAULIEU *to take charge of the corvette's helm.*

The boats approached *Chevette* at 1 am and were greeted with musketry and grape, they were however undaunted and they pressed on, attacking from two directions:

The attempt to board was most obstinately resisted by the Frenchmen, armed with firearms, sabres, tomahawks and pikes; and who in their turn boarded the boats. Notwithstanding this formidable opposition and that, in their efforts to overcome it, the British had lost all their firearms, the latter, with their swords alone, effected the boarding.

The topmen swarmed up the rigging, cut the sails free, the cable was cut and 'a light breeze having sprung up from the land, the ship began to drift out of the bay' with the severely wounded Wallis at the helm. The batteries opened on her but, the wind stiffening, she was soon out of range. Her capture cost the boat crews 11 killed, 57 wounded, and 1 missing presumed drowned. The French casualties were 92 killed and 62 wounded, most of the rest of the crew being taken prisoners.

Almost as satisfactory was the recapture of *Hermione*, the frigate which had been handed over to the Spaniards by the mutineers (see p. 199). She had been taken into the Spanish navy and rearmed as a 44-gun ship with a complement of 393. In July 1799 she was moored in the harbour at Puerto Cabello (Venezuela) under the protection of heavy batteries. Sir Hyde Parker, then commanding on the Jamaica station, considered an attempt to cut her out to be too hazardous an operation and therefore he merely stationed a frigate off Puerto Cabello in the hope of capturing *Hermione* if she came out of the harbour.

This task was entrusted to SURPRISE(28), formerly *Unité*, but when after months of patrolling, her provisions began to run short her captain, Edward Hamilton, decided he would cut her out despite his orders. On the night of 24 October 1799 he detailed boarding parties of 107 officers and men, leaving only 90 aboard SURPRISE. He was so short of officers that one of the boats was entrusted to the command of the surgeon. The French were on the alert but the boarding was successful although Captain Hamilton was first stunned by a blow on the head from the butt of a musket so severe that the musket broke. He was then wounded successively by a cutlass, a boarding pike, and, as *Hermione* sailed out of the harbour, by a grapeshot from the shore guns. The entire Spanish crew, less 119 dead, were sent ashore in a captured schooner since they could not be fed and the frigate was taken in to Jamaica where she was taken back into the Navy as RETRIBUTION since, while she had been in enemy hands, another ship had been named HERMIONE.

Hamilton was knighted but, on his way back to England to convalesce from his wounds, the packet boat in which he was sailing was captured by a privateer and he became a prisoner of war until he was exchanged for six French midshipmen. It was unfortunate for the reputation of so brave a man that in 1802 he was found guilty by court martial of inflicting excessive and illegal punishment on the gunner and his mate of his then ship TRENT(36). He was dismissed the service but reinstated a year later since it was widely believed that he had been deranged by the blow to his head. The Prince Regent made him captain of the Royal Yacht and he died a full admiral in 1851.

AN UNDERSEA THREAT

While Britain was establishing an unchallengeable domination of the sea, France was toying with a scheme which might have broken British supremacy. Late in 1797 an ingenious American, Robert Fulton, offered the Directory a submarine. He offered to build the machine at his own expense if the French would pay him 4,000 francs a gun on the rating of every ship he sank and 2,000 francs a gun for each unrated ship. Any prizes taken would be the property of his company. His only stipulation was that his sailors should be given naval rank to ensure their combatant status should they be captured. It was this demand to which the Directory objected and, in the words of a French historian, 'one can only be astonished that such scruples should trouble a government which had already launched Tate and his blackguards against England to raise a guerrilla war'. The Directory offered half the sinking money Fulton asked but the Minister of Marine commented:

The government cannot openly avow men who carry out this kind of operation. The English, who are ingenious with destructive machines, would soon be using similar devices and would, as a result be exempt from the code of war which justly inflicts punishment on those who are naturally inclined to behave in such an atrocious manner.

Fulton affected to be horrified by such scruples:

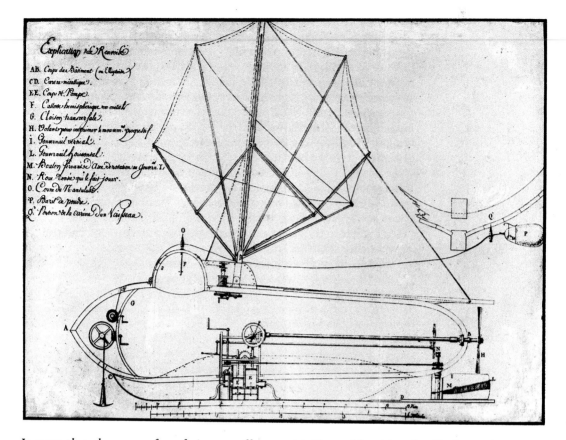

The longitudinal section of Fulton's *Nautilus*; showing the explosive *carcasse* (see text below) which was held in place under an enemy vessel by a grapnel

It seems that the reasons for refusing my offer are pitiable considerations of humanity, as if it were possible to protest against the use of a means of revenging oneself and of freeing onself of one's most implacable enemy, of annihilating the insolent despotism of the English navy and, in doing so, of ensuring the freedom of the seas for the commerce of all nations, of draining the spring which nourishes the new coalition and of giving peace to the world.

He was, nevertheless, prepared to build his submarine or, to be more exact, his semi-submersible and on 30 July 1800 *Nautilus* was launched at Rouen. She was 5.7 metres long and 1.8 metres in the beam with motive power provided by a hand-operated propellor while the machine was controlled by two rudders, one vertical and one horizontal. To dive, water was admitted to the hull and, when it was wished to surface, this was driven out by a hand-operated pump. A barometer was provided to measure the depth. On top of the hull was a dome, fitted with thick glass panels, which never submerged and through this the craft was directed. A collapsible mast and sail were provided to propel her when surfaced. There was a crew of three and 'with two lighted candles' they could stay almost under water for three hours. They were equipped with an explosive *carcasse* which could be attached to a hostile vessel with 'a barbed point' and fired, at the end of 100 metres of cable, by an electric battery.

Once the craft was complete, Fulton asked the government for a credit of 60,000 francs but by this time Bonaparte was First Consul and he was extremely conservative about all new weapons. He would supply nothing more than a small quantity of gunpowder. Fulton therefore gave a demonstration in which *Nautilus* blew up an empty hogshead moored off the quay at Le Hâvre on 31 October 1800. This persuaded the Ministry of Marine to make an inquiry which reported that this submarine was far from perfect but might repay research. This gained Fulton a credit of 10,000 francs and permission to continue his experiments at Brest where, in July 1801, he blew up an elderly sloop with a charge of 9 kilograms. According to the Maritime Prefect, 'The *chaloupe* leapt in the air and dissolved into a thousand pieces.'

Encouraged, Fulton sought permission to make an attempt on two British frigates anchored in the roadstead. All he asked was the support of six armed pinnaces to cover his withdrawal but these the admiral and the Maritime Prefect refused to supply on the grounds that anyone captured in such a venture would certainly be hanged. This, they said, was 'no death for a military man'.

As a last resort, Fulton appealed directly to Bonaparte:

With three of these devices England would be forced to submit. Each craft carries 20 or 30 carcasses and one has only to take them to the approaches to the naval bases of England and let them drift with the current or anchor them at the entrances to Portsmouth, Plymouth, Torbay or at the mouth of the Thames. I have two kinds of carcasses. The first has a mechanism, like that of a clock, which can be set to operate between 4 minutes and 4 hours later. The other can be fixed by grapnels to the bottom of a ship four or five feet below the waterline. No navigator could avoid these secret dangers and, at little cost, the enemy ports could be blocked.
The interruption of trade on the Thames would be enough to bring England down for it would stop the trade which is the nerve and soul of the government of St James.

Bonaparte's reaction to this appeal was to cut off all assistance to Fulton who, being a shrewd business man as well as a talented inventor, took his business across the Channel and offered it to 'the insolent despotism of the English navy'. Admiral Lord St Vincent, now First Lord of the Admiralty, was of the opinion that:

Such ways of waging war are useless to those who already possess command of the sea. If it is successful, they will deprive themselves of their supremacy.

This did not prevent him authorizing further experiments at government expense and Fulton developed an unmanned, fully submersible, explosive craft. One of these was used in a raid against the invasion flotilla at Boulogne on 2 October 1805 and succeeded in sinking a French pinnace but no information of its success reached England and, in the aftermath of Trafalgar, the Admiralty lost interest in submarines. Fulton returned to the United States and by 1807 had a steamboat running on the Hudson river between New York and Albany.

Algeciras, 6 and 12 July 1801

F RANCE'S WAR WITH AUSTRIA was ended, for the second time, by the Peace of Lunéville (9 February 1801) and, once again, France faced an isolated Britain. The First Consul realized that stalemate had been reached between the two countries and determined to make a temporary peace. He wished to go to the conference table with as many conquests in hand as possible and was above all anxious to secure two areas – Egypt and Portugal – which the British considered as vital to their safety. To consolidate his hold on the first he ordered Admiral Ganteaume to sail from Brest with seven of the line and two frigates carrying reinforcements for Alexandria. Simultaneously he made the Treaty of San Ildefonso with Spain under which, apart from retroceding Louisiana to France, Spain would invade Portugal and make over to France six battleships which would receive French crews at Cadiz. With these France undertook to make a seaborne attack on Lisbon.

Ganteaume, when he eventually escaped from Brest, had to put into Toulon for repairs and, before he could finally set sail for Egypt, had to leave three of his big ships at Leghorn. He failed to reach Alexandria and returned to Toulon on 25 July 1801 having captured SWIFTSURE(74) which made a stout defence against great odds.

The Spanish invasion of Portugal also failed to give Bonaparte satisfaction. Seeing themselves overmatched the Lisbon government, on British advice, made peace as quickly as possible, ceding to Spain the ramshackle fortress of Olivenza and to France a small strip of Portuguese Guinea. She also undertook to close her ports to British trade, an agreement she could not afford to honour. Bonaparte, who had expected a long campaign with British involvement, was angry at the early peace, the more so since his brother Lucien, his ambassador to Madrid, had approved the peace treaty without reference to Paris. To make the best of a bad job, he ordered the three ships which Ganteaume had left at Leghorn to sail to Cadiz, pick up the six vessels which the Spaniards had ceded to France and six more Spanish ships and, with the resultant squadron of fifteen of the line, make a fresh attempt to assist the army stranded in Egypt.

Rear-Admiral Charles Alexandre Leon de Linois was delayed at Leghorn by adverse winds and it was not until 1 July 1801 that he reached the Strait of Gibraltar with *Formidable*(80), *Indomptable*(80), *Desaix*(74) and the frigate *Muiron*(40). The wind was blowing strongly from the WNW and, two days later, the French squadron was still trying to make its way through the strait but meanwhile the captain of the only British man of war in Gibraltar, the polacre sloop CALPE(14), had managed to send a despatch boat to contact the fleet blockading Cadiz. This reached Rear-Admiral Sir James Saumarez at 2 am on 5 July and he decided to sail for Gibraltar at once with six of the line, detaching his only frigate, THAMES(32), to bring on the rest of his squadron, SUPERB(74) and the PASLEY brig, stationed some 30 kilometres north of Cadiz. It was unfortunate that as soon as THAMES was within signalling distance of SUPERB the wind failed completely, leaving all three ships becalmed.

Meanwhile Saumarez and the main force were carried south-east by a strong current and were not able to make progress towards their objective until the late afternoon when a light WNW breeze sprang up. This fell off again before nightfall and did not revive until 3 am on 6 July when the squadron crowded on all sail. At 7 am the leading ship cleared Calbrita point and signalled that she could see the four French ships in Algeciras Bay. Saumarez, who had already given his captains orders for the formation to be adopted, signalled to 'Engage the enemy in succession on arriving up with him'. He was third in the line in his flagship CAESAR(80). Ahead were VENERABLE(74) and POMPÉE(74), which had been taken at Toulon in 1793, while AUDACIOUS(74), SPENCER(74), and HANNIBAL(74) brought up the rear.

While working through the straits, Linois had captured a packet boat and Lord Cochrane's brig-sloop SPEEDY(14) and from them he learned that a strong squadron was blockading Cadiz. It was this news that decided him to put into Algeciras where he could get some support from shore batteries and gunboats and he anchored his ships of the line across the bay from Puente de San Garçia on the south to a swell in the coastline (now built over) to the north. His rearmost ship, *Indomptable* was moored near the 5 fathom line off the Isla Verde, on which was a battery of seven heavy guns. *Desaix* was 450 metres ahead of *Indomptable* and about the same distance from *Formidable* which also had her bows close to the 5 fathom line. *Muiron* was stationed inside the Isla Verde supported by three Spanish gunboats while eleven more of these craft, armed with 18- and 24-pounders, and a powerful shore battery supported the north end of the line. The position was a powerful one since the shoals left little room for manoeuvre and there were a number of shallows unmarked on the British charts. Nevertheless Linois, on seeing the strength coming against him, ordered his ships of the line to kedge themselves inshore until they grounded.

Saumarez's plan was disrupted by the 'partial and failing nature of the wind'. VENERABLE had to anchor at long range from *Desaix* and CAESAR became becalmed almost between VENERABLE and her target. AUDACIOUS came within moderate range of *Indomptable* but SPENCER was hard put to it to make her fire tell on any of the enemy ships. POMPÉE seems to have got most of the wind. She was fired at first from the southerly shore batteries and then moved up the French line

ABOVE: Rear-Admiral Sir James Saumarez (1757–1836)

PREVIOUS PAGE: Sir James Saumarez's squadron leaving Gibraltar in pursuit of the French squadron on 12 July

exchanging broadsides with each of the three ships. She then dropped her anchor so close to the starboard bow of *Formidable* that the latter's buoy was on POMPÉE's seaward side.

In the exchange of broadsides between these two ships the heavier-armed Frenchman had the advantage and POMPÉE was fortunate that her opponent was steadily kedging herself inshore so that the range continually opened. In fact, after thirty minutes firing, the current swung POMPÉE bows-on to the enemy and *Formidable* was unable to rake her effectively although POMPÉE could only reply with her bowchasers. Seeing the position at this end of his line Saumarez, fearing that POMPÉE might be overwhelmed, sent a boat to HANNIBAL, now at last coming on the scene, with orders to 'go and rake the French admiral', using boats to tow the ship if necessary.

Captain Solomon Ferris immediately ordered HANNIBAL's cable to be cut and, a slight breeze coming, tacked in shore, keeping a close luff, hoping to turn the head of the French line and to 'lay the French admiral on board on the side next the shore'. Unfortunately this manoeuvre took him into shallower water than his charts showed and, when she was directly between *Formidable* and the shore battery of Torre de Almirante, HANNIBAL struck a sandbank. Boats were sent from CAESAR and VENERABLE but the one from the flagship was sunk by a roundshot and no amount of towing by the other available boats would drag her off the bottom. Meanwhile a gun duel continued between the stranded ship, the French flagship, the Torre de Almirante, and the Spanish gunboats.

Ferris' attempt to turn the French line, the manoeuvre which had proved so disastrous to the French at the Nile, greatly alarmed Linois who signalled for his ships to cease kedging, cut their cables and let the current carry them ashore. At this moment a 'light and puffy breeze' sprang up from the NE which drove *Desaix* and *Indomptable* aground, but Linois, changing his mind, kept *Formidable* afloat. This breeze died before Saumarez could close the range and, becalmed once more, he turned his attention to POMPÉE which was now in serious trouble from gunboats and shore batteries. She had 'not a mast, yard, spar, shroud, rope, or sail but which was more or less injured by the enemy's shot' and the admiral decided that his first task must be to get her clear. All the undamaged boats in the squadron were sent to tow her and, realizing that nothing could be done for HANNIBAL, Saumarez ordered the remainder to make for Gibraltar. Ferris, whose ship had already lost her fore and mainmasts, continued firing for a further half hour but, seeing that to prolong his defence could only waste lives, he struck his colours. HANNIBAL became the only British ship of the line which, between 1793 and 1814, was taken by the enemy and not recaptured.

The battle of 6 July had been a bad day for the Royal Navy. The apparently simple operation of securing three of the line with six, had, thanks to the vagaries of the wind, turned out to be an expensive fiasco. HANNIBAL was lost and her crew, who had lost 75 killed and 66 wounded before firing ceased, were prisoners as were the crews of CALPÉ's boats which were sent, too late, to assist her. The rest of the squadron had suffered 232 casualties and POMPÉE was unfit for further service pending dockyard repairs. CAESAR was so damaged that Rear-

Admiral Saumarez shifted his flag into AUDACIOUS.

The admiral believed and reported that he had rendered the French squadron 'entirely unserviceable' but this was not the case. 586 Frenchmen had been killed or wounded and five Spanish gunboats sunk or driven ashore but the two grounded battleships were refloated without difficulty and the four French ships were soon ready for sea. Linois was determined to get them out of the bay as soon as possible since he knew that, given a fair wind, Saumarez would be back to complete his task. He sent a message overland to Cadiz asking for a force which could escort his ships into that harbour.

THE SECOND BATTLE

At Cadiz was Rear-Admiral Dumanoir de Pelley who had arrived there with the frigates *Liberté*(38) and *Indienne*(40) to take over the six Spanish ships of the line promised at the Treaty of Ildefonso. Only one of these ships, *St Antoine* (formerly *San Antonio*)(74) was ready for sea. However four Spanish battleships (2×112s, 1×94, 1×74) could sail under Vice-Admiral Don Juan Joaquin de Moreno and the combined squadron should have been enough to deal with Saumarez' damaged ships. They set sail on 9 July observed by SUPERB and THAMES which kept ahead of them, sending the PASLEY brig to warn Saumarez of their approach. By that afternoon the opposing squadrons were ranged in the harbours of Algeciras and Gibraltar respectively.

It had been a busy time in all the ships which had fought on 6 July except POMPÉE whose crew had been drafted into the other ships to assist with repairs. The busiest ship had been CAESAR. On hearing that Saumarez had decided that he must shift his flag, Captain Jahleel Brenton had called his crew and told them the news:

They answered, with three cheers, 'All hands to work day and night till she is ready'. The captain ordered them to work all day and watch and watch all night; by these means they accomplished what has, probably, never been exceeded. On the 8th they warped her into the mole and shipped the lower masts; on the 9th they got their new mainmast in. On the 11th the enemy showed symptoms of sailing which only increased, if possible, the energies of the seamen. On Saturday, at dawn of day, the enemy loosed sails; the CAESAR still refitting in the mole, receiving powder, shot and other stores and preparing to haul out. At noon the enemy began to move. At one o'clock the enemy's squadron was nearly all underway: the CAESAR was warping out of the mole. The whole population of the Rock came out to witness the scene; the line-wall, mole-head and batteries were crowded from the dockyard to the ragged staff; CAESAR's band playing Come cheer up my lads, 'tis to glory we steer, *the military bands of the garrison answering with* Britons strike home. *At 3 pm just as she passed under the stern of AUDACIOUS, CAESAR rehoisted the flag of Sir James Saumarez and made the signal to weigh and prepare for battle.*

With CAESAR leading the line, Saumarez could see the rearmost of the Franco–Spanish squadron at about 8 pm and, since he was anxious to engage before darkness fell, he hailed his next astern, SUPERB, to make sail and attack the enemy. SUPERB was the only undamaged ship in the

The battle of Algeciras on
6 July

squadron and was, in any case, the fastest sailer. With all the canvas that
could be set, she pulled ahead fast and by 11 pm she was 5 kilometres
clear of the flagship while the rest of the ships trailed far astern led by
VENERABLE. SUPERB, however, needed no assistance. At 11.20 pm she
sailed between two Spanish first rates. She opened fire on both and after
three broadsides at a range of 320 metres the ship to larboard, *Real
Carlos*(112), had lost her foretopmast and was on fire. SUPERB then
pressed on and, at 11.50 opened fire on the next ahead, *St Antoine*(74)
which struck after half an hour's fight.

   Before CAESAR could reach the scene of the fighting, a different
battle had broken out. The second Spanish ship, *Hermengildo*(112), into
which SUPERB had fired, failed to realize that SUPERB was no longer close
to her and began to pour broadsides into the burning *Real Carlos* which,
in the confusion of the darkness and the fire, shot back at her. Things
went from bad to worse until the two great ships collided just as the
magazine of *Real Carlos* exploded sending her to the bottom and setting
fire to *Hermengildo* which, twenty minutes later, also exploded and sank.

The crews of the two amounted to about 2,000 men but only 300 were picked up by SUPERB and the captured *St Antoine.*

There was then a lull in the battle until 4 am when *Formidable* was sighted by VENERABLE, CAESAR, and THAMES while approaching the shoals of Conil de la Frontera, only a few kilometres from the entrance to Cadiz harbour. By this time the wind, which had blown hard during the night, fell light and intermittent. CAESAR could not approach the enemy and a brisk exchange of fire began to take place between *Formidable* and VENERABLE with occasional interventions from the lightly-built THAMES. The two ships of the line were 'within musket shot' and, as at the battle on 6 July, the Frenchman's gunnery was excellent while CAESAR, 'at a distance of about a mile and a half was perfectly becalmed [but] the boats were sent ahead in the hopes of being able to tow her within gun-shot of the enemy'.

At 5.30 am VENERABLE's mizen topmast was shot away. An hour and a quarter later her mainmast was brought down and she fell away from her opponent who was still making her best possible speed towards Cadiz. She could soon only use her sternchasers but with these she felled VENERABLE's foremast at 7.50 am. A few minutes later the British ship struck the shoals of Sancti Petri, off the future battlefield of Barossa, and her mizen went over the side. *Formidable* made her way to Cadiz followed only by a few rounds, at extreme range, from CAESAR.

VENERABLE was towed off the shoal by THAMES and the boats of the squadron and, having raised three jury masts, sailed back to Gibraltar for repairs. She had lost 18 killed and 87 wounded, the rest of the squadron losing only 15 wounded, all of them in SUPERB.

The French claimed both battles of Algeciras as victories. Their success in the first cannot be disputed but their claim for the second was based on ignoring the loss of *St Antoine* and the two big Spaniards and believing the report of the captain of *Formidable.* With Linois, conforming to Spanish custom and embarking on a frigate, *Capitaine de Vaisseau* Amable Gilles Troude, was able to give his imagination full scope. By this account *Formidable* beat off attacks from four British battleships and a frigate and in the course of this epic struggle VENERABLE was wrecked and CAESAR disabled. He did not claim to have engaged SUPERB but merely asserted that she 'bore up, passed under the lee of *Formidable* and joined the rest, rather than face her fire'.

In fact the second battle, which they called the action in the Gut of Gibraltar, was an undoubted British victory. They deprived the enemy of three of the line, which more than compensated for the single ship they had lost in the first battle. The French and Spanish survivors were blockaded in Cadiz and did not re-emerge until the war ended. Bonaparte's last attempt to relieve the *Armée de l'Orient* failed and the French in Egypt surrendered on 2 September. Deprived of his bargaining counter, the First Consul agreed to the preliminaries of peace with Britain which were signed on 1 October.

OPPOSITE: Vice-Admiral Lord Nelson, Duke of Bronte

CHAPTER FIFTEEN

The Command of the Narrow Seas

IF BONAPARTE HAD LACKED bargaining counters in his negotiations with Britain, he obtained almost all that he wanted without them. Britain gave up all her colonial conquests except Ceylon and Trinidad and was almost persuaded to hand the vital naval base of Malta back to the effete and ineffective Knights of St John.

When peace was signed the French navy had, apart from 3 ex-Venetian and 3 ex-Spanish battleships, 43 ships of the line and 42 frigates of which all but 4 of the former and 3 of the latter were reported to be '*en état et propre à toutes missions*'. To show that he regarded the peace to be no more than a truce, the First Consul gave orders for 23 new ships of the line to be built at dockyards from the Scheldt to Genoa. The Royal Navy had ended the war with 104 of the line and 109 frigates in commission but, following normal British practice, this fleet was drastically reduced as soon as the ink was dry on the treaty. The estimates for 1803 called for only 32 of the line and 70 frigates and the establishment of seamen and marines was cut from 130,000 to 50,000.

The British declaration of renewed war on 16 May 1803 came sooner than Bonaparte had expected or wished. Twenty-two of his new ships of the line were incomplete and, for a war that was certain to be predominately maritime, he found himself, having sent 9 of the line to the West Indies and 1 to the east, with only 13 battleships in commission in Europe. By contrast the Royal Navy had taken early measures to increase its strength and 55 of the line had been authorized to be commissioned, the number of men being set at 100,000.

William Pitt, who was then out of office, declared on 23 May that, if the French:

indulge themselves in any expectation of success in the present contest, it is chiefly built on the supposition that they can either break the spirit and shake the determination of the country by harassing us with perpetual apprehension of descent upon our coasts, or that they can impair our resources and undermine our credit by the effects of an expensive and protracted contest.

As the Republic had done in the earlier war, the Consulate and, later, the Empire determined to pursue both these aims and achieved neither.

From the outset of the new war, the British blockade of Brest was greatly more effective than that practised by Howe and Bridport. The new style had, in fact, been started in the last few months of the old war when Lord St Vincent commanded the Channel Fleet. He was First Lord of the Admiralty in 1803 and it was under his orders that, on 17 May, Admiral the Hon. William Cornwallis sailed from Cawsand Bay with, initially, 10 of the line to pin the main French fleet to its base. Henceforward the main strength of the Royal Navy was not to lurk in Spithead but to be stationed within easy reach of Brest itself. St Vincent's advice was:

I recommend you in the strongest manner never to be farther than six or eight leagues from Ushant with the wind easterly [i.e. when the French could come out]; and, if westerly, to make the Saintes as often as the weather will permit.

In advance of this force, usually ten or twelve battleships, was the Inshore Squadron, some five ships of the line, which were:

always anchored during an easterly wind between the Black Rocks and the Parquette shoal. Inside, between them and the Goulet, cruise a squadron of frigates and cutters plying day and night in the opening of the Goulet, three sail of the line cruise to support the five anchored.

Each ship put to sea with provisions for six months and even after this time none returned to port, since a small fleet of victuallers and water-hoys regularly resupplied them. If a ship required repairs that could not be carried out at sea, she had to seek permission to put back to Cawsand or Plymouth and her captain would be told that the time spent there 'never ought to exceed six days unless a mast is to be shifted, and in that event not more than ten days'. No officer was permitted to sleep on shore or to go more than 5 kilometres from the beach. Only in a westerly gale, an occurrence which would make it impossible for the French to emerge, would the fleet leave their station off Ushant and find temporary shelter in Torbay or Cawsand.

Almost every day a frigate or a cutter would go in close to the mouth of the Goulet to count the masts of the ships in the inner roadstead, information greatly needed by the fleet as giving an indication of the number of French ready for sea. A typical report was that made by Captain the Hon. Michael de Courcy of SIRIUS(36) on 3 January 1804:

Eight ships of the line, among which he was certain there was not a three decker.
Four ships supposed to be store ships.
One ship, supposed to be a hospital ship.
Three smaller vessels.
Total number sixteen.
The yards and topmasts of those ships were struck.

How the blockade looked to the French is described in a letter from the Port Prefect on 25 July 1803:

PAGE 216: HMS VICTORY at the battle of Trafalgar

PREVIOUS PAGES: Trafalgar, Nelson's last battle

The English are always off the coast. Several sail of the line are off Ouessant (Ushant), four or five anchor during the day off the Black Rocks, a frigate and a corvette are off Douarnenez under sail, a corvette and a cutter come right up to the entrance to the Goulet and constantly cruise there. Their landing parties disembark on islands without garrisons; they also go to unfrequented parts of the coast and extract information from those they meet by means of threats or insinuations.

An inhabitant of Béniguet island made a report, of the 22nd, which has just reached me: 'the English, landed under arms on Béniguet; they asked if there was not at Conquet [an inlet in the mainland east of Béniguet], a convoy of 15 chasse-marées coming from the north and what they were loaded with. He replied that he knew nothing of the matter. The English said that they had found 10 more ships in Conquet, making 25 in all. An English officer wagered the man's wife that, within a few days, they would have seized several of them. The wager was ten louis *against one of their cows.*

This new style of blockade which was also applied, if less effectively, to all the other French ports, imposed a vast strain on the ships and crews of the Royal Navy. Officers and men alike never set foot on shore for years at a stretch, seldom even catching sight of the shore of England for more than a few hours or days, when storms or essential repairs drove them from their stations. The ships themselves suffered the strain as much and more than the men and had it not been for the introduction of copper sheathing for the hull below the waterline, a practice which had been introduced from 1758, the prolonged cruising which the blockade involved would have been impossible. There were ships which had nothing but a sheet of copper 'between them and eternity'. The

The port of Brest, showing the rocky coastline which made the blockade so hazardous

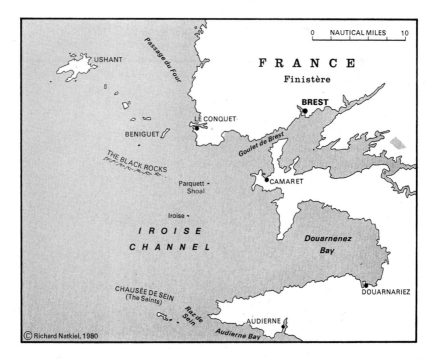

continuous watch on a dangerous coast, maintained from 1803–05 must be one of the most outstanding feats of seamanship and endurance in naval history. The blockade was, in fact, effective beyond the strength of the squadrons actually taking part. The numbers could not always be kept up since some ships had to go to effect repairs and others had to be detached for convoy duty and other tasks. What was important was that the French, and above all Bonaparte, believed that the Brest squadron was almost permanently in check. When the critical time came in 1805, 21 French ships of the line were ready to leave the port and their admiral believed that, if they emerged, 'Success is not doubtful' since only 15 British ships were off the port to oppose them. Napoleon would not take the risk and so missed the chance of getting them to join the great naval concentration he was planning.

THE INVASION OF BRITAIN

Between 1803 and 1805 Bonaparte believed that he could achieve temporary command of the Straits of Dover for long enough to land the *Armée d'Angleterre* in Kent and he went to enormous lengths to prepare for the crossing. From the earlier invasion flotilla only 28 gun-brigs (*chaloupes canonnières*) and 193 gunboats (*bateaux-canonniers*) were seaworthy, so he gave orders for 2,000 small craft to be constructed. By 8 August 1805 the flotilla consisted of 18 *prames* (3-masted ships, 34 metres long), 320 gun-brigs, 572 gunboats, 349 pinnaces, 10 *paquebots*, 3 bomb ketches, 19 caiques, 6 sloops of war, 81 troop transports, 405 horse transports, 80 artillery transports, and 580 other assorted vessels. These were assembled in the ports of Étaples, Boulogne, Wimereux, Ambleteuse, Calais, Dunkirk, and Ostend. This vast assemblage of craft could carry 167,590 men and 9,149 horses in a single lift but, despite the huge improvements made to the harbours, it would take six tides, three days, to get them all to sea. Thus, as Napoleon calculated, he must have command of the Straits for 'four or five days' to be able to invade.

The problem of securing this period of time was the most difficult that Napoleon ever had to face but there is no reason to suppose that it was insoluble. Admiral Lord Keith, whose squadron in the Downs had direct responsibility for the defence of the Kentish coast, was convinced that it was possible for:

a fleet or a squadron to get out of Brest unperceived and watch for an opportunity for running up the Downs or Margate Road, in which case it might be superior to our squadron long enough to cover the landing of any extent of force from the opposite coast.

Napoleon, as has been seen, had less confidence in the Brest fleet's ability to escape but he believed the British superiority in battleships could be dispersed by feints for long enough to get the army across the Straits. He knew, with reasonable accuracy, that the Royal Navy had just over 100 ships of the line in commission but that a dozen of these were in either the East or West Indies. Of the remainder, 11 were with Keith at the Downs, 24 were with Cornwallis in the Channel Fleet while 6 watched Rochefort, 8 were off Ferrol, and 6 off Cadiz. Nelson had 12 in the

PREVIOUS PAGES: The battle of Trafalgar

ABOVE: Napoleon contemplates the invasion of Britain

Mediterranean Fleet. His own naval force he reckoned at 77 of the line of which 11 were Batavian (Dutch) and 20 Spanish. These, apart from small detachments or single ships at Rochefort, Lorient, and Cartagena, were distributed between the Texel (11 ready for sea), Brest (21), Ferrol (15), Cadiz (7), and Toulon (11).

The essence of Napoleon's plan was to concentrate at least 40, preferably 60, of these ships in the Straits of Dover where they would be able to overwhelm Keith's squadron and give time for the great flotilla to cross. To do this the Channel and Mediterranean Fleets and the smaller detached squadrons would have to be misled into undertaking wild-goose chases. The fact that the plan, or rather series of plans, which the French adopted failed does not invalidate the whole concept. Any such scheme required at least its share of good luck, which was not forthcoming, and it was further weakened by errors of judgment, not least on the part of Napoleon himself when he refused to let the Brest squadron take its chance of getting to sea. Many historians have suggested that the plan was impracticable but none has put forward one that had a greater chance of success.

The schemes adopted relied on the disadvantages under which every British admiral in independent command inevitably laboured – the lack of information and the slowness of communications. If a French squadron left its harbour it had a fair chance of eluding the British force which was watching it. The British commander could not know its destination and could consult neither the Admiralty nor the commanders of other squadrons as to which way he should lead the pursuit. If, for example, the Rochefort squadron broke away it might be heading for the Mediterranean, for Cadiz, for the West Indies, for Ireland, or for Île de France (Mauritius). The admiral watching it would have to guess which way it was heading and would probably guess wrong. All he could do was to back his judgment and send a small vessel to inform London and his nearby colleagues of what was happening. It could be weeks before any co-ordinated counter moves could be devised and more weeks before it could be implemented. Napoleon's plans depended on a fair proportion

order for the *Armée d'Angleterre*, now retitled the *Grande Armée*, to take the road which led to Ulm, Austerlitz, Jena, Eylau, and Friedland.

The death of Nelson. The artist has considerably exaggerated the space between decks belowship

THE BATTLE OF TRAFALGAR AND AFTER

It is widely believed, and taught in many British schools, that the battle of Trafalgar frustrated Napoleon's attempt to invade England. The fact is that the troops who had been detailed to carry out the landing had been redirected deep into Germany and that when Villeneuve, with 33 of the line, 5 frigates and 2 brigs, sailed from Cadiz on 20 October he was steering not for England but for Naples. Nelson's achievement at Trafalgar was temporarily to destroy any chance Napoleon had of reviving his scheme for obtaining the mastery of the Channel, a scheme his other commitments would, in any case, have made impracticable until after the Treaty of Tilsit. The eventual total of the Combined Fleet's loss – eighteen of the line, nine of them French – meant that only a long building programme could make an invasion of England even a remote possibility.

Although in his last battle Nelson was pitting twenty-seven of the line against thirty-three, the result was never in doubt. Nelson knew that he was superior in everything but numbers and, with his captains, had planned the form of the battle in advance. He was therefore able to manage with a minimum of signalling in the six hours between the time that the two fleets sighted one another and the first shot was fired.

Soon after dawn, at 6.40 am, he made his first, No. 72, 'to chase and form the line of battle in two columns, each ship to engage her opponent'. This was soon followed by No. 13, 'Prepare for battle', and No. 76, 'to bear up [i.e. to change direction so that the ships ran before the wind] and steer east'. It was not until 11.30 am that apart from sending to some individual ships No. 88, 'Make more sail', he made another general signal. This was a precaution against over-enthusiastic captains pursuing too far and getting among the shoals of San Petri and Trafalgar, No. 63 preparative, 'Prepare to anchor at close of day'. Meanwhile, using a semaphore telegraph, he had made to his second in command, a mile away to starboard in ROYAL SOVEREIGN(100), 'I intend to pass through the enemy's line to prevent them getting to Cadiz'. Then, since there was no further tactical instruction to give, he declared, 'I'll now amuse the fleet with a signal', and at 11.40 am there soared to the masthead his most famous phrase:

253: 269: 863: 261: 471: 598: 220: 370: 4(D): 21(U): 19(T): 24(Y)

As soon as that had been acknowledged a final signal was hoisted and kept flying until it was shot away, No. 16, 'Engage the enemy more closely'.

As VICTORY's log recorded:

Partial firing continued until 4.30 when a victory having been reported to the Right Honourable Lord, Viscount Nelson, K.B. and Commander in Chief, he then died of his wounds. At 5, the mizen mast fell about 10 feet above the poop. The lower masts, yards and bowsprit all crippled.

The final end of the battle came two days later when the French Commodore Cosmao made a gallant but ineffective attempt to recapture some of the British prizes. He secured *Santa Ana*(112) and *Neptuno*(80) but the latter was wrecked before she could be brought into harbour and two of the ships he took with him, *Indomptable*(80), the flagship at Algeciras, and *San Francisco de Asis*(74) drove ashore and were lost while *Rayo*(100) lost her masts and was taken by a fresh British ship just arrived from Gibraltar only to sink later.

Even this was not the end of the Combined Fleet's losses. Four damaged French ships (1×80, 3×74s) under Dumanoir de Pelley escaped from Trafalgar and tried to make Rochefort. They were intercepted by four undamaged ships of the line supported by four frigates under Sir Richard Strachan and, despite a most gallant defence, all Pelley's ships were taken.

In 1805, twenty-four of the seventy-seven ships of the line available to Napoleon at the beginning of the year were lost to him in the actions against Calder, Nelson, and Strachan and the following year started badly when, on 6 February, Sir John Duckworth caught a French squadron lying unprepared off St Domingue. Three ships of the line were taken and two, one of them the magnificent *Impérial*(120), were driven on to the rocks and wrecked. Later in 1806 the *Impétueux*(74) was cornered by two of the line and a frigate. She ran herself on to the shore at Cape Henry, Virginia, but, with a flagrant disregard for American neutrality, the British sent boats to her, took her crew prisoner and burned the ship. Thus in two years the Franco–Spanish fleet lost thirty of the line apart from fifteen frigates which were taken while one was wrecked. The comparable British loss in 1805–06 was two ships of the line (one foundered, one wrecked), one 50-gun ship and two frigates captured, two frigates wrecked. In January 1807, with few Spanish ships fit for sea, Napoleon could only count on thirty French and Dutch ships of the line while the British sent 103 to sea, although twenty of these were 64-gun ships suitable only for duty in the North Sea and for colonial stations.

This disparity did nothing to discourage Napoleon from planning to invade the British Isles but it persuaded him to change his approach to the problem. Henceforward he abandoned his attempt to gain a temporary superiority over the Straits of Dover, where the completion of the Martello Towers in 1806 made an assault landing a less attractive proposition, and set out to achieve an overwhelming naval superiority sufficiently large to overwhelm the greater skill of the Royal Navy:

We shall be able to make peace with safety when we have 150 ships of the line.

This total he set out to achieve. Twenty-one battleships were laid down in 1806 and more were ordered as soon as slipways became vacant. At the height of the Eylau–Friedland campaign against Russia he never lost sight of his naval building programme. From Poland he bombarded the Minister of Marine with injunctions to speed up the construction of battleships. *'Tous les efforts doivent se jeter du côté de la marine.'*

The Treaty of Tilsit gave him a chance to achieve his target. His alliance with Russia, whose fleet contained 36 of the line, could give him numerical equality with the Royal Navy's 103 ships. By that time France had 36 battleships, Holland 6 (apart from 2 in the East Indies) and Spain 24, although it was doubtful how many of the last were seaworthy. The 50 further ships which were needed to give a 3:2 superiority could be obtained if three neutral navies could be coerced into co-operation. At Tilsit it was agreed that the Czar should obtain Swedish co-operation while France would acquire the use of the navies of Denmark and Portugal. On 2 August 1807 Marshal Bernadotte was given command of an army destined to invade Denmark and in the same month the Spanish government was informed that the *Corps d'Observation de la Gironde* was being formed near Bayonne. Its task was to be the subjugation of Portugal and Spanish co-operation was asked, and gladly given, for the operation.

Both plans misfired. The British heard of the Danish plan and, acting with uncharacteristic determination, sent sixteen of the line and 18,000 soldiers to Copenhagen to demand that the Danish fleet be given into British safekeeping until a general peace. The Danes refused and their capital was thereupon bombarded for three days after which they agreed to part with their ships (15 September). 13 battleships and 14 frigates were sailed to British ports, and 6 more sail of the line, which could not be made ready for sea, were burned. The only remaining Danish battleship, *Prinz Christian Frederic*(74), was destroyed by two British 64-gun ships off the coast of Jutland in the following year.

The attempt to seize the Portuguese fleet was no more successful. When, on 30 November 1807, the advance guard of the *Corps d'Observation de la Gironde* came in sight of Lisbon they saw eight Portuguese battleships leaving the Tagus under British escort. Three unserviceable ships were left behind but, before they could be made ready for sea, British troops occupied Lisbon taking possession also of a squadron of nine Russian battleships which had been sheltering in the estuary. This was not the whole of the naval loss incurred by Napoleon in his Peninsular venture. By his ill-advised attempt to seize the Spanish government by stealth (see pp. 118–19), he lost not only the 24 Spanish ships but 6 French, 5 survivors from Trafalgar which had never again ventured out of Cadiz and one which had subsequently taken refuge in Vigo. As the Russians failed to persuade the Swedish navy to take any part against Britain, the naval plans made at Tilsit resulted not in a gain of 50 ships but in the loss of 39 (6 French, 9 Russian, 24 Spanish) which were already available.

Napoleon was not discouraged by this setback. He merely concentrated his efforts on building ships in the dockyards under his own control. He had the resources and the seamen and he believed that, given time, he could make the French navy large enough to overwhelm the British. The British were in no doubt that his aim was not unattainable. The last wartime First Lord of the Admiralty, speaking when the danger was past, in August 1814, confessed that:

Had Bonaparte's empire existed a few years longer, he would have been enabled to compete with our naval power, and probably overcome us in the end from the great numerical superiority he would have obtained. At Antwerp the French built 19 sail of the line every year, which number they could increase to 25 sail. They had no difficulty in procuring timber, which was found (tho' not of the best sort) in great abundance all down the Rhine. Neither had they any great obstacles to encounter in manning their vessels, although some time must elapse before the crews became good seamen. With such facilities, in the course of a few years, he would have sent forth such powerful fleets that our navy must eventually have been destroyed, since we could never have kept pace with him in building ships, or have equipped sufficient numbers to cope with the tremendous power he would have brought against us.

Naval ports were also given close attention. The inadequacies of Brest had been very clearly shown and two more bases were developed for operations in the Channel. One of these was Cherbourg where, as early as July 1807, reports reaching London showed that more than 5,000 people were 'constantly employed at the basons and wet docks for large men-of-war, two thirds of them women, who work by moonlight'. The intention, not fulfilled before the war ended, was to construct a safe harbour at Cherbourg for 30 of the line but this was small compared with the works undertaken on the Scheldt. There anchorages were being prepared for 90 battleships, 30 at Antwerp, 40 at Terneuse, and 20 at Flushing. The Terneuse basin could never be completed since the soil was too wet to support the construction work but the remaining 50 berths were being filled at the rate of 19 a year and, together with the

CHAPTER SIXTEEN

Restraint of Trade

THE FRENCH EMPIRE was no more successful in crippling Britain's trade than the Republic had been. The prohibition on the import of British goods was restored on 20 June 1803. Between 1802, a year of peace, and 1806, British exports dropped only slightly, a fall more than compensated for by a series of good harvests which reduced the need to import corn. The needs of France made it essential to permit some trade and approved imports of British cotton yarn, 310,000 kilograms in 1804, soared to 1,368,000 two years later. This was only the tip of the iceberg. All over the French Empire and its satellites – France, Holland, Northern Italy, and Spain – smuggling became a national industry and few of Napoleon's most senior subordinates could be trusted not to connive at it. Some, notably Marshal Massena, profited greatly from the illicit trade. The French occupation of Hanover merely resulted in open trade moving east from Hamburg and Cuxhaven to the Baltic ports.

The campaigns of 1805–07 changed the picture. Italy, Dalmatia, and the entire German coastline came under French control. Denmark, which then included Norway, and Portugal were occupied. Russia became a French ally and Britain succeeded in embroiling herself in a war with Turkey. The Berlin Decrees (21 November 1806) and the supplementary decrees of Milan and Fontainebleau declared the British Isles to be in a state of blockade, all goods coming from Britain and her colonies became contraband and liable to seizure. As the Continental System developed even goods carried in ships which had touched at British ports were outlawed. Only Sweden and Sicily in all Europe could still legally trade with Britain and it seemed as if, as Napoleon prophesied, the day would come when British ships:

laden with useless wealth [would] wander round the high seas, which they claim to rule, seeking from the Sound to the Hellespont a port that will receive them.

The blockade of Britain was carried on with all the harshness that a new army of *douaniers* could devise. Europe was deprived of sugar, tea, coffee, and many more essential commodities. Vast stores of confiscated British goods were publicly burned and boom conditions developed in the smuggling industry. The blockade was not conspicuously successful. In

vacant post of Prince Royal, or heir apparent to the Swedish throne, he:

professed his firm intention, as far as depended on him, to maintain the relative situations between England and Sweden, and that his proposing himself was without the participation of Bonaparte.

The election of Bernadotte as Prince Royal led to a declaration of war but notice of the declaration was coupled with an intimation that 'it was by no means the intention of the Swedish government to follow up its declaration by any act of hostility'. In the event they continued to provide water, vegetables, and cattle to the Baltic Fleet, only stipulating that these should be transported to the ships in hired craft rather than in the boats of the fleet.

Vice Admiral Sir James Saumarez was appointed to command the Baltic Fleet early in 1808 and it was soon built up to a strength of 11 ships of the line (1×100, $8 \times 74s$, $2 \times 64s$), 5 frigates and a considerable number of smaller vessels. In his orders he was 'directed and required', among other things, to:

consider as one of the principal objects of the service on which you are employed the affording of every protection in your power to the trade of his Majesty's subjects by granting convoy from time to time (as far as the force under your command will admit of your doing so) to the said trade to and from the different ports of the Baltic, and also to ships and vessels under neutral colours which may be furnished with licences from one of his Majesty's principal Secretaries of State.

In practice British ships were only engaged in the Swedish trade since any port official at French, Russian, Danish, or Prussian harbours, however well-disposed or corrupt, would certainly impound any British vessel.

Even for neutral vessels an elaborate system of deceit had to be practised to convince the authorities, and more importantly, the captains of privateers, that they had nothing to do with Britain. Each one was provided with carefully forged documents, apparently issued by the French, establishing that she was trading between ports in countries not at war with France. At the same time her captain was issued with another official document, which he had to keep carefully hidden, recommending:

to the captains and commanders of his Majesty's ships to permit the said vessel to pass unmolested unless she be found deviating from her course without apparent necessity.

Such a *laissez-passer* was issued only on condition that the ship should move only under British convoy and that any ship found moving independently to a hostile port would be regarded as fair prize.

There were many hazards, quite apart from the difficulties of navigation, for trading vessels in the Baltic. The Danish and Prussian coastlines swarmed with privateers and French-occupied Danzig was the base for a large number of French-operated ships which preyed on the traffic.

The Danes, although they had lost their battle fleet in 1807, retained a large number of gunboats able to move in very shallow water and under oars so that they were able to manoeuvre when every sailing ship was at a standstill.

On 4 June 1808 the gun-brig TICKLER, becalmed in the Great Belt, was attacked by 4 gunboats each armed with two long 18-pounders. TICKLER was armed only with carronades and, after a four-hour battle in which her commander and 36 out of her 50-man crew were killed or wounded, she was forced to surrender. Five days later 25 gunboats attacked a homeward bound convoy of 70 merchant ships which were becalmed off the southern end of Saltholm. There was an escort of a bomb-ketch and 3 brigs but, since they were unable to move, the Danes, attacking from the rear, were opposed only by the brig TURBULENT and the THUNDER bomb. They concentrated on TURBULENT whose 18-pounder carronades were outranged by the Danish long guns and after twenty minutes she was disabled, boarded, and taken. The gunboats then turned their attention to the bomb but THUNDER's captain, Commander James Caulfield, had had time to move two 6-pounders so that they could fire out of the stern ports. These, and his 24-pounder carronades, were enough to keep the Danes at bay and they withdrew after four hours' firing taking a dozen merchant ships with them. Even ships of the line were vulnerable to oared gunboats. In October 1808, AFRICA(64) was attacked by twenty-five gun and mortar boats supported by seven armed launches off the island of Amager in the Sound. The Danes stationed themselves off her bows and quarters where, since AFRICA was becalmed, the broadsides could not be brought to bear. She was saved only by a slight breeze just before darkness which enabled her to drive the gunboats away and sink two of them but she had suffered sixty casualties and her hull and rigging were so damaged that she had to be withdrawn for a refit.

The answer to these gunboats was found chiefly in counter-attacking them with the armed boats of the larger men of war and soon a highly efficient convoy system was evolved throughout the months when ice-free navigation allowed shipping to move at all in the Baltic.

The British landing on Martinique in 1809 was part of their continuous effort to destroy France's overseas Empire

GUERRIÈRE(38)
surrendering to
Constitution(44)

the war. In 1810 the conquest of the French islands in the Indian Ocean, Île de France (Mauritius) and Île Bourbon (Réunion) was undertaken. Bourbon fell easily but, before the troops could be assembled to seize the larger island, a fire-eating captain jeopardized the whole operation. Five French 40-gun frigates were blockaded in Grand Port and the entrance was sealed by the occupation and arming of Île de Passe. There was no need to fight the French squadron but the senior officer present, Captain Samuel Pym, decided that he could capture it with his own force of four 36-gun ships. It was a 'wanton and unnecessary enterprise' and made more so when Captain Willoughby of the leading ship NÉRÉIDE signalled, on entering the harbour 'Enemy of Inferior Strength'. The result was that two British ships were captured and the other two ran aground and were burned by their crews to avoid capture.

Pym and the other captains were found not guilty of hazarding their ships, although the court martial found that Willoughby's signal about the enemy's strength had been 'injudicious' and the lesson of Grand Port was not learned. When war broke out between Britain and the United States in 1812 over-confidence was still the hallmark of British frigate captains and this was serious since the United States navy though small was extremely formidable. Four of their frigates were larger and more powerful than any other frigates in the world, two of them being built on keels laid down for 74-gun ships. Though rated as 44-gun ships each was armed with thirty long 24-pounders in the broadsides, twenty-four 42-pounder carronades and two additional 24-pounder long guns on the fo'c'sle. As a result each of these four ships could outshoot any frigate and outsail any ship of the line.

Their first victim was GUERRIÈRE, rated as a 38 and actually armed with 30 long 18-pounders and 16 32-pounder carronades. She was returning from Halifax to Britain for a much-needed refit since she was leaking badly and her mainmast and bowsprit had been struck by lightning. Nevertheless on 19 August 1812 Captain Dacres deliberately

242

SHANNON(38) captures the
Chesapeake(36) off Boston

courted a fight with *USS Constitution.* He surrendered after two hours
fighting by which time GUERRIÈRE was without masts and had
suffered seventy-eight casualties. She was so damaged that she
had to be burned by her captors on the following day. The
pattern was twice repeated. On 12 October MACEDONIAN(38) was
crippled and sustained 104 casualties after three hours engagement
with *United States* and on 29 December JAVA (formerly *Renommé*)(38)
hauled down her colours to *Constitution.* Seventeen of her guns had been
dismounted and 124 of her men were casualties.

This, however, was the last of the American victories at sea. 1813
saw SHANNON(38) beat *Chesapeake*(36) in an evenly matched duel off
Boston and in 1814 *Essex*(32) was forced to surrender by PHOEBE(36)
and an 18-gun sloop.

The final actions of the war were fought after peace had been agreed
at Ghent. *Constitution* succeeded in capturing two British corvettes
(1×22, 1×20) off Madeira but *President* was not so fortunate. On 15
January 1815 she fought a long action off New York with ENDYM-
ION(40) and ended by surrendering to other British ships coming on the
scene. It was an unsatisfactory end to a great ship but a suitable end to a
war which turned out to be thoroughly unsatisfactory to both Britain
and the United States.

EPILOGUE

T HE TWENTY-THREE YEARS OF WAR which followed the French revolution saw the science of war at a standstill while the art of war advanced at a gallop. Technology contributed a crude form of mass production for muskets, the shrapnel shell and the erratic Congreve rocket. Even the Marine Vocabulary, which so greatly simplified the problems of communications at sea, was only introduced shortly before the last fleet action was fought in 1805. The weapons employed on land and sea at the time of Waterloo were scarcely altered from those which had been used in the American War of Independence, most of them were unchanged since the Seven Years' War.

At sea the ships of 1815 were indistinguishable from those which had put to sea in 1793. Many of them, indeed, were the same ships and many had survived from earlier wars. HMS VICTORY had been launched in 1765 and was forty years old at Trafalgar and approaching her half-century when she was Saumarez' flagship in the Baltic. It was only towards the end of the war that substantial improvements in ship design began to be introduced. Sir Robert Sepping, surveyor to the Royal Navy, proposed that instead of building the hull out of rectangular frames it should be constructed of triangles of timber. This not only reduced 'hogging', the twisting of the keel under strain, but allowed the ship to be longer – thus extending the gundeck and increasing the possible size of the broadsides to be mounted on each deck. Practical tests on vessels of various sizes were carried out successfully but the first line of battle ship to be constructed entirely on Sepping's plan was HOWE, launched in May 1815.

During the war the Royal Navy had been tending towards smaller ships of the line. In 1794 there had been 14×3-deckers and 91×2-deckers in commission. By 1814 there were only 6×3-deckers at sea, mostly for use as flagships, and the third rates had increased to 94. This was partly due to the superior manoeuvrability of the smaller ships but another factor was the smaller drain they made on the navy's dwindling supply of manpower. The number of seamen and marines voted had reached its peak at 145,000 in 1810–12 and fallen to 117,000 by 1814 despite the calls of the American war. (The number of admirals, however, had increased from 132 in 1803 to 219 in 1815.) A first rate had a complement of about 840; a 74-gun ship needed less than 600. Frigates, conversely, grew in size. Between 1794 and 1814, the larger types (32–44 guns) increased from 66 to 121 while the 28-gun frigates dwindled from 22 to 2.

The French took an opposite course. Aiming at achieving maritime superiority through weight of numbers and firepower, they clung to the idea of huge battleships. In 1814 there were fifteen 3-deckers either afloat or building.

On land the changes in warfare appeared to be sweeping but the change was wholly due to a more efficient application of means that had been available for a century or more. Napoleon was no innovator. His genius lay in using the resources which were available to their maximum

Ezekiel Baker's rifle, accurate up to 275 metres was introduced into the British army in 1800 primarily for the use of the experimental Corps of Riflemen (later the Ninety-Fifth Rifles). In the butt can be seen the brass cover within which were kept greased patches on which the ball was forced down the grooves of the barrel

effect, while rejecting those which did not fit in with his ideas for speed and flexibility. As has been seen he rejected the rifle (see p. 172) because it was slow to load and thus left his army at a permanent disadvantage when fighting the British (who exploited the rifle's capability brilliantly) and his other enemies.

Napoleon's achievement was to greatly extend the limit of what was practicable in land warfare. Using essentially the same means which had been available to Marlborough and Frederick the Great, his campaigns were incomparably more sweeping, his victories decisive. His downfall came because he would not recognize what was practicable. Wielding armies of a size which his predecessors never imagined, his skill and power of decision brought him victory as long as he fought in fertile regions. Once he attempted to manoeuvre in country where the inhabitants lived, at best, little above subsistence level, where the French had to fight the peasantry for food, his losses became more than France and her satrapies could bear.

He always regarded Austerlitz as his supreme achievement and it would be hard to fault his tactical direction of the battle. But his proper pride at the victory must have been tempered with a sense of deliverance. If the Austro–Russian army had continued its retreat into Poland as Kutusov had advised, the French army must have fallen back and the campaign ended in anti-climax or worse. Napoleon might then have learned that an army could not fight unless it was fed. In 1807 he wrote contemptuously to Junot, 'An army of 20,000 men can feed themselves anywhere, even in a desert.' Bonaparte would not have been so ready with such a remark if Kutusov had managed to tempt him to a week's march east of Austerlitz.

In 1812 the Russians drew the French into increasingly inhospitable country so that, gallantly as the Russians fought, it was starvation that wrecked the *Grande Armée* even before the snow started to fall. The lesson should have been learned in Spain and Portugal; Marmont spelled it out for the Emperor (see p. 131) but he would not listen.

After Waterloo, Napoleon said of Wellington that 'in the management of an army [he] is fully the equal of myself, with the advantage of possessing more prudence'. Certainly Wellington possessed an ample supply of prudence but what he possessed in addition, and what Napoleon so conspicuously lacked in his later campaigns, was a sense of what was possible. In 1813 the Duke remarked, 'It is a very common error . . . to believe that there are no limits to military success.' Napoleon forgot this truth and embarked on campaigns which could only have been successful if he had had railways to move his supplies and electric telegraphs to carry his orders.

Appendix
Chronology of the Wars, 1792-1815

1792

20 April	France declares war on Hapsburg Empire.
15 May	France declares war on Sardinia.
13 August	French Royal Family imprisoned.
20 August	Prussian army invades France.
20 September	French defeat Prussians at Valmy.
21–28 September	French occupy Savoy and Nice.
22 September	Abolition of French monarchy. First day of *An I*.
20 October	French occupy Mainz and Frankfort.
22 October	Prussians evacuate France.
6 November	Austrians defeated at Jemappes, near Mons.
20 November	Navigation of the Scheldt declared open.
1–16 December	French driven from east Bank of Rhine.

1793

23 January	2nd Partition of Poland by Russia and Prussia.
24 January	Execution of Louis XVI.
1 February	France declares war on Britain and United Provinces (Holland).
20 February	France calls up 300,000 conscripts.
9 March	France declares war on Spain.
10 March	Outbreak of revolt in La Vendée.
18 March	French invasion of Holland halted by defeat at Neerwinden.
6 April	Committee of Public Safety established.
14 April	British take Tobago.
28 June	Allies take Valenciennes.
	Robespierre joins Committee of Public Safety.
22 August	Toulon occupied by British Mediterranean Fleet.
9 October	French embargo on British goods.
16 October	Execution of Marie Antoinette.
19 December	French re-occupy Toulon having lost 13 ships of the line.
23 December	1st Vendéan revolt ended by battle of Savernay.

1794

5 February – 23 March	British take Martinique.
7 February – 10 August	British take Corsica.
2 April	British take St Lucia.
11–21 April	British take Guadaloupe.
22–30 April	Allies take Landrécies.
17–18 May	*Battle of Tourcoing*. French defeat allies.
28 May – 1 June	Howe's actions against French fleet ('Glorious First of June') French lose 7 of the line.
26 June	French defeat Austrians at Fleurus: Austrians decide to evacuate Netherlands.
27–28 July	*Coup d'état* of 9 Thermidor: Execution of Robespierre.
29 August	French retake Valenciennes.
10 December	French retake Guadaloupe.

1795

3 January	3rd (final) Partition of Poland.
23 January	French cavalry capture Dutch Texel squadron (14 of the line).
14 March	Action off Genoa. French lose 3 of the line.
5 April	Treaty of Bâle; peace between France and Prussia.
14 April	British troops leave continent from Bremen.
16 May	Treaty of the Hague; alliance between France and Batavian republic (Holland).
18 June	British evacuate St Lucia.
23 June	Action off Lorient. French lose 3 of the line.
29 June – 19 July	Abortive *emigré* expedition to Quiberon Bay.
22 July–16 August	British take Cape of Good Hope.
1 August	British invade Ceylon.
1 October	Belgium annexed to France.
5 October	Attempted *coup d'état* of 13 Vendemaire ('whiff of grapeshot').
30 October	Directory takes over government of France.

1796

5 February	Ceylon surrenders to Britain.
1 March	Bonaparte appointed to command *Armée d'Italie*.
12 April	Bonaparte defeats Austrians at Montenotte.
13 April	Bonaparte defeats Sardinians at Millesimo.
14–15 April	Bonaparte defeats Austrians at Dego.
21 April	Bonaparte defeats Sardinians at Mondovi.
28 April	Armistice of Cherasco: Sardinians leave war.
10 May	Action at the bridge of Lodi.
15 May	Bonaparte enters Milan.
25 May	British re-occupy St Lucia.
3 June	British take St Vincent.
14–19 June	French occupy Bologna and Ferrara.
29 July	Austrian counterattack to relieve Mantua.
5 August	*Battle of Castiglione*. Bonaparte defeats Austrians.
17 August	3 Dutch ships of the line surrender to British at Cape of Good Hope.
1–12 September	Würmser breaks through to Mantua.
3 September	Austrians defeat French at Würzburg.
8 October	Treaty of San Ildefonso: Franco-Spanish alliance.

10 October	Peace between France and Naples.
1 November	3rd Austrian counterattack to relieve Mantua.
2 November	British evacuate Corsica.
8 November	Spain declares war on Britain.
15–17 November	Bonaparte defeats Austrians at Arcole.
16 November	Death of Catherine the Great.
1 December	Royal Navy leaves Mediterranean.
16–30 December	French squadron in Bantry Bay.

1797

14 January	Bonaparte defeats Austrians at Rivoli.
2 February	Mantua surrenders to the French.
14 February	Jervis defeats Spaniards off Cape St Vincent. Spaniards lose 4 of the line.
17 February	British take Trinidad. Spaniards lose 4 of the line.
22–24 February	Abortive French invasion of Wales.
28 March	Massena occupies Klagenfurt.
16–24 April	Mutiny at Spithead.
18 April	Preliminary Franco-Austrian peace.
12 May – 15 June	Mutiny at the Nore.
16 May	Bonaparte occupies Venice.
28 June	French occupy Corfu.
9 July	Cisalpine republic established.
11 October	Duncan defeats Dutch off Camperdown. Dutch lose 9 of the line.
17 October	Treaty of Campo Formio; peace between France and Austria.
16 November	Frederick William III succeeds to Prussian throne.

1798

5–15 February	French establish Roman republic and deport Pope Pius VI.
12 April	Bonaparte appointed to command *Armée de l'Orient*.
15–29 April	French invade Switzerland and establish Helvetic republic.
26 April	Genoa annexed to France.
8 May	Nelson, with 3 of the line, re-enters Mediterranean.
19 May	Bonaparte sails from Toulon.
23 May	Rebellion in Ireland.
6 June	Nelson reinforced to 13 of the line.
12 June	Malta surrenders to Bonaparte.
21 June	Irish rebels crushed at Vinegar Hill.
1 July	Bonaparte lands at Alexandria.
21 July	Bonaparte defeats Mamelukes at battle of the Pyramids.
25 July	Bonaparte occupies Cairo.
1 August	Nelson defeats French at the Nile. French lose 11 of the line.
22 August	French under Humbert land at Killala Bay, Co. Mayo.
25 August	Humbert defeats Lake at Castlebar
2 September	Turkey declares war on France
8 September	Humbert surrenders at Ballinamuck.
12 October	Warren captures 1 of the line and 2 frigates off Irish coast.
15 November	British take Minorca.
20 November	Naples declares war on France.
3 December	Income tax introduced in Britain.

1799

23–29 January	French occupy Naples and establish Parthenopian republic.
20 February	Bonaparte invades Palestine.
1 March	Russia declares war on France.
3 March	Russo–Turkish squadron captures Corfu.
7 March	Bonaparte storms Jaffa.
10 March	British troops garrison Sicily.
12 March	Austria declares war on France.
17 March	Bonaparte besieges Acre.
25 March	Archduke Charles defeats French at Stockach.
5 April	*Armée d'Italie* defeated at Magnano.
28 April	Suvarov occupies Milan.
7 May	French evacuate Naples.
17 May	Bonaparte raises siege of Acre.
20 May	French evacuate Rome.
5 June	Massena evacuates Zurich.
17–19 June	*Armée de Naples* defeated on the Trebia.
30 July	French garrison of Mantua surrenders.
15 August	*Armée d'Italie* defeated at Novi.
23 August	Bonaparte sails from Alexandria in frigate *Muiron*.
27 August	Anglo–Russian expedition lands in north Holland.
30 August	7 Dutch ships of the line surrender near the Texel.
25–30 September	Massena defeats Suvarov near Zurich.
9 October	Bonaparte lands at Fréjus.
18 October	Anglo–Russians agree to evacuate north Holland.
9–10 November	*Coup d'état* of 18 Brumaire; Consulate established.
25 December	Bonaparte First Consul.

1800

5 April	Melas attacks *Armée d'Italie* near Genoa.
8 April	Massena besieged in Genoa.
4 May	Moreau defeats Austrians at Stockach.
15–20 May	*Armée de Réserve* crosses Great St Bernard pass.
4 June	Massena surrenders Genoa.
9 June	Lannes defeats Austrians at Montebello.
14 June	*Battle of Marengo*. Bonaparte defeats Melas.
19 June	Moreau defeats Austrians at Höchstadt. Abortive British attempt against Belle Isle.
28 June	Moreau captures Munich.
26 August	Abortive British attack on Ferrol.
5 September	Malta surrenders to the British.
7 October	Treaty of San Ildefonso: Spain cedes Louisiana and 6 of the line to France. Abortive British attempt on Cadiz.
3 December	Moreau defeats Austrians at Höhenlinden.
16 December	Armed Neutrality of the North formed.

1801

1 January	Act of Union between Britain and Ireland.
9 February	Treaty of Lunéville: Peace between France and Austria.
14 February	Resignation of William Pitt as Prime

8 March	Minister. Henry Addington succeeds (4 March).
21 March	British land in Aboukir Bay.
23 March	British defeat *Armée de l'Orient* outside Alexandria.
2 April	Czar Paul murdered: Alexander I succeeds.
3 May	Nelson destroys sea defences of Copenhagen.
6 June	Spain invades Portugal.
17 June	Treaty of Badajoz. Peace between Spain and Portugal.
27 June	Anglo–Russian convention; end of Armed Neutrality.
6 July	British take Cairo.
12–13 July	*1st Battle of Algeciras.* British lose 1 ship of the line.
2 September	*2nd Battle of Algeciras* (or Battle of the Gut of Gibraltar). 3 Franco-Spanish ships of the line lost.
1 October	*Armée de l'Orient* capitulates. Preliminaries of peace signed between Britain and France.

1802

26 January	Italian republic established with Bonaparte as president.
25 March	Peace of Amiens concluded.
2 August	Bonaparte proclaimed Consul for life. Elba annexed to France.
11 September	Piedmont annexed to France.
15 October	Switzerland annexed to France.

1803

3 May	France sells Louisiana to USA.
16 May	Britain declares war on France.
31 May – 3 June	French seize Hanover.
22 June	British capture St Lucia.
30 June	British capture Tobago.
20 September	British capture Demerara and Essequibo (British Guiana).

1804

21 March	Murder of Duc d'Enghein.
5 May	British capture Surinam: 1st use of shrapnel shells.
7 May	William Pitt becomes Prime Minister again.
18 May	Napoleon proclaimed Emperor.
19 May	18 French generals promoted Marshals of the Empire.
5 October	Commodore Moore seizes Spanish treasure fleet.
2 December	Napoleon's coronation.
14 December	Spain declares war on Britain.

1805

30 March	Villeneuve sails from Toulon.
5 April	Alliance between Britain and Russia.
9 April	Villeneuve passes Strait of Gibraltar.
6 May	Nelson reaches Gibraltar.
14 May	Villeneuve reaches Martinique.
4 June	Nelson reaches Barbados. France annexes Genoa.
19 July	Nelson returns to Gibraltar.

22 July	Action off Ferrol. Villeneuve loses 2 of the line.
9 August	Austria joins Anglo–Russian alliance.
18 August	Villeneuve reaches Cadiz.
27 August	*Grande Armée* leaves Channel coast for Germany.
5 September	Austria invades Bavaria.
25 September	*Grande Armée* crosses the Rhine.
20 October	Mack and 30,000 Austrians surrender at Ulm.
21 October	Nelson defeats Villeneuve off Cape Trafalgar. 18 Franco-Spanish ships of the line lost.
4 November	Action off Rochefort. French lose 4 of the line.
14 November	Napoleon enters Vienna.
17 November–15 February	British expedition to Cuxhaven.
2 December	Napoleon defeats Austro–Russian army at Austerlitz.
26 December	Treaty of Pressburg. Peace between France and Austria.

1806

4–18 January	British take Cape of Good Hope.
23 January	Death of William Pitt.
6 February	Action off St Dominique. French lose 5 of the line.
11 February	Lord Grenville Prime Minister with 'All the Talents'.
1 April	Joseph Bonaparte declared King of Naples.
12 April	War declared between Britain and Prussia.
12 May	British capture Capri.
20 June	Louis Bonaparte declared King of Holland.
27 June	British capture Buenos Ayres.
9 July	Prussian army mobilized.
12 July	British surrender at Buenos Ayres.
1 October	Prussian ultimatum to France.
14 October	Napoleon and Davout defeat Prussians at Jena and Auerstadt.
25 October	Napoleon enters Berlin.
21 November	Berlin Decree proclaiming blockade of British Isles.
10 December	Treaty of Posen: Franco–Saxon alliance.
18 December	Napoleon enters Warsaw.
26 December	Inconclusive actions at Pultusk and Golymin.

1807

7 January	1st Order in Council replying to Berlin Decree.
28 January	French invade Swedish Pomerania.
3 February	British take Monte Video.
8 February	*Battle of Eylau* drawn between Napoleon and Bennigsen.
19 February – 3 March	Abortive British naval demonstration in Dardanelles.
17 March	British landing in Egypt.
18 March	Resignation of Grenville and the 'Talents'. Duke of Portland Prime Minister (19 March).

26 May	French take Danzig.
13 June	Napoleon defeats Bennigsen at Friedland.
25 June	Napoleon and Czar Alexander meet at Tilsit.
28 June	British land near Buenos Ayres.
5 July	British surrender at Buenos Ayres.
7 July	Treaty of Tilsit. Franco–Russian alliance.
16 August	British disembark near Copenhagen.
20 August	Stralsund (Swedish) surrenders to French.
2–5 September	British bombard Copenhagen.
7 September	Danes agree to surrender their fleet.
19 September	British evacuate Egypt by capitulation.
20 October	France declares war on Portugal.
2 November	Russia declares war on Britain.
29 November	Portuguese fleet and Royal Family sail for Brazil.
30 November	French occupy Lisbon.

1808

21 February	Russians invade (Swedish) Finland.
2 May	*Dos de Mayo.* Anti-French riot in Madrid.
6 June	Joseph Bonaparte declared King of Spain.
5 July	Peace between Britain and Spain proclaimed.
19 July	Spaniards defeat French at Bailen.
20 July	King Joseph enters Madrid.
1 August	Wellesley begins to disembark troops in Portugal.
21 August	Wellesley defeats French at Vimeiro. Royal Navy evacuates Spanish army from Funen Island.
30 August	Convention of 'Cintra'. French to evacuate Portugal.
16 October	French recapture Capri.
4 November	Napoleon enters Spain.
30 November	Storm of Somosierra pass.
4 December	Napoleon enters Madrid.

1809

5 January	Peace between Britain and Turkey.
16–17 January	British evacuate Spain after battle of Corunna.
24 January	Napoleon returns to Paris.
21 February	French capture Saragossa.
24 March	British capture Martinique.
9 April	Austrians invade Bavaria.
11–12 April	British attack French squadron in Aix roads. French lose 4 of the line.
16 April	Napoleon defeats Austrians at Eckmühl.
22 April	Wellesley assumes command of Anglo–Portuguese army at Lisbon.
23 April	French storm Regensberg.
24 April	Anglo–Austrian alliance concluded.
12 May	Wellesley forces the Douro at Oporto. French driven out of Portugal.
13 May	French enter Vienna.
20–23 May	Napoleon defeated at Aspern and Essling.

5–6 July	Napoleon defeats Austrians at Wagram.
11 July	Armistice between France and Austria.
27–28 July	Wellesley and Cuesta defeat French at Talavera de la Reina.
30 July	British land on Walcheren island.
16 August	British take Flushing.
29 August	Wellesley's army withdraws into Portugal.
17 September	Treaty of Frederikshamm; Sweden cedes Finland to Russia
1–4 October	Duke of Portland resigns as Prime Minister. Spencer Perceval succeeds
14 October	Treaty of Schönbrunn; peace between France and Austria.
20 October	Wellington (Wellesley) gives orders for building lines of Torres Vedras.
26 October	Action in Gulf of Lyons. French lose 2 of the line.
9 December	British evacuate Walcheren.
15 December	Napoleon divorces Josephine.

1810

6 January	Peace between France and Sweden: Swedish ports closed to British trade.
4 February	British take Guadaloupe.
5 February	French besiege Cadiz.
17 February	British take Amboina.
2 April	Napoleon marries Archduchess Maria Luisa.
17 April	Massena appointed to command *Armée de Portugal.*
1 July	Holland annexed to France. King Louis escapes to Austria.
7–10 July	British capture Île Bourbon.
21 July	*Armée de Portugal* begins invasion of Portugal.
21 August	Bernadotte elected Prince Royal of Sweden.
23–28 August	British defeated at Grand Port, Île de France, losing 4 frigates.
18 September	Abortive French invasion of Sicily.
27 September	Wellington defeats *Armée de Portugal* at Busaco.
10 October	*Armée de Portugal* halted by lines of Torres Vedras.
17 November	Sweden declares war on Britain.
29 November – 2 December	British take Île de France.

1811

5 March	*Armée de Portugal* starts to retreat.
13 March	Hoste defeats French and Italian frigates off Lissa.
20 March	Napoleon's son, King of Rome, born.
3 April	*Armée de Portugal* leaves Portugal.
4 August – 18 September	British capture Java.
24 December	3 British ships of the line lost in gale.

1812

10 January	French invade Swedish Pomerania.
19 January	Wellington storms Ciudad Rodrigo.
6 April	Wellington storms Badajoz.
24 April	Czar Alexander demands French evacuation of Prussia.

11 May	Spencer Perceval assassinated.
8 June	Lord Liverpool, Prime Minister.
18 June	United States declares war on Britain.
24 June	Napoleon invades Russia.
12 July – 8 August	1st abortive US invasion of Canada.
18 July	Treaty of Orebo. Peace between Britain, Russian, and Sweden.
22 July	*Battle of Salamanca.* Wellington defeats *Armée de Portugal.*
12 August	Wellington enters Madrid.
16 August	British capture Detroit.
17–18 August	Napoleon defeats Russians at Smolensk.
19 August	USS *Constitution* captures GUERRIÈRE.
24 August	French abandon siege of Cadiz.
7 September	Napoleon defeats Kutusov at Borodino.
14 September	Napoleon enters Moscow.
17 September	Wellington besieges Burgos.
9–13 October	2nd abortive US invasion of Canada.
12 October	USS *United States* captures MACEDONIAN.
19 October	Napoleon evacuates Moscow.
21 October	Wellington abandons siege of Burgos.
19 November	Wellington returns to Portuguese frontier.
26–28 November	*Grande Armée* recrosses Beresina river.
5 December	Napoleon leaves *Grande Armée.*
18 December	Napoleon returns to Paris.
29 December	USS *Constitution* captures JAVA.
30 December	Convention of Tauroggen between Russian and Prussian troops.

1813

4 March	Russians enter Berlin.
16 March	Prussia declares war on France.
27 April – 1 May	3rd abortive US invasion of Canada. US troops sack York (Toronto).
1–2 May	Napoleon defeats Russo–Prussian army at Lützen.
20–21 May	Napoleon defeats Russo–Prussian army at Bautzen.
23 May	Wellington advances into Spain.
1 June	SHANNON captures USS *Chesapeake.*
4 June – 17 August	Armistice of Pleischwitz between France, Prussia, and Russia.
21 June	Wellington defeats French armies at Vitoria.
12 August	Austria declares war on France.
23 August	Eastern allies defeat Oudinot at Gross Beeren.
26 August	Eastern allies defeat Macdonald on the Katzbach.
26–27 August	Napoleon defeats eastern allies at Dresden.
30 August	Eastern allies defeat Vandamme at Kulm.

31 August	Wellington storms San Sebastian.
6 September	Eastern allies defeat Ney at Dennewitz.
7 October	Wellington forces the Bidassoa and advances into France.
16–19 October	Eastern allies defeat Napoleon at Leipzig.
24 October–13 November	4th abortive US invasion of Canada.
10 November	Wellington defeats Soult on the Nivelle.
9–13 December	Wellington defeats Soult on the Nive.

1814

1 February	Blücher defeats Napoleon at La Rothière.
10 February	Napoleon defeats Russians at Champaubert.
11 February	Napoleon defeats Russians at Montmirail and Prussians at Château Thierry.
14 February	Napoleon defeats Blücher at Vauchamps.
7 March	Napoleon defeats Russians at Craonne.
9 March	Blücher defeats Marmont at Laon.
12 March	Anglo–Portuguese army enters Bordeaux.
25 March	Schwarzenberg defeats Marmont and Mortier at Fère-Champenoise.
31 March	Eastern allies enter Paris.
6 April	Napoleon abdicates.
10 April	Wellington defeats Soult at Toulouse.
4 May	Napoleon reaches Elba.
24 August	British occupy Washington DC, and burn White House.
14 September	British repulsed at Baltimore.
1 November	Congress of Vienna assembles.
24 December	Treaty of Ghent; peace between Britain and USA.

1815

8 January	British defeated at New Orleans.
1 March	Napoleon returns to France.
20 March	Napoleon returns to Paris.
15 June	Napoleon invades Netherlands.
16 June	Napoleon defeats Blücher at Ligny. Wellington defeats Ney at Quatre Bras.
18 June	*Battle of Waterloo.* Wellington and Blücher defeat Napoleon.
22 June	Napoleon abdicates.
7 July	Wellington and Blücher enter Paris.
15 July	Napoleon surrenders to BELLEROPHON off Rochefort.

Select Bibliography

John Adye, *Napoleon of the Snows* (1931)
R. G. Albion, *Forests and Sea Power* (1926)
A. Aspinall (Ed.), *The Later Correspondence of George III* (vol ii, 1963)
Eugène Beauharnais, *Memoire et Correspondance* (Ed. Du Casse) (3 vols, 1858)
E. P. Brenton, *Naval History of Great Britain 1783–1836* (2 vols, 1837)
Harry Calvert, *Journals & Correspondence* (Ed. H. Verney) (1853)
A. du Casse, *Le Général Vandamme et sa Correspondance* (2 vols, 1870)
David Chandler, *The Campaigns of Napoleon* (1966)
E. Chevalier, *Histoire de la Marine Francaise sous la 1er Republique* (1886)
W. L. Clowes, *The Royal Navy: A History* (vols iv & v, 1899, 1900)
J. Colin, *Études sur la Campagne de 1796–97 en Italie* (1898)
Julian S. Corbett, *Fighting Instructions 1530–1816* (Navy Records Soc., 1905)
H. Coutanceau & H. Leplus, *La Camapagne de 1794. Part II Tome 2me* (1908)
Capitaine de Cugnac, *Campagne de l'Armée de Réserve en 1800* (2 vols, 1901)
Marshal Davout, *Operations du 3me Corps 1806–07* (Ed. Gen. Davout) (1896)
Alex. Delavoye, *Life of Thomas Graham, Lord Lyndoch* (1880)
General Derrécagaix, *Le Maréchal Berthier* (2 vols, 1904)
Eduard Desbrière, *Projets et Tentatives de Débarquements aux Îles Britanniques 1793–1805* (93 vols, 1900)
Christopher Duffy, *Borodino & the War of 1812* (1973); *Austerlitz 1805* (1977); *The Army of Maria Theresa* (1977)
John Fortescue, *History of the British Army* (vols iv–x, 1915–20)
Michael Glover, *The Napoleonic Wars: An Illustrated History* (1979); *Wellington as Military Commander* (1968); *The Peninsular War 1807–14* (1974)
Richard Glover, *Peninsular Preparation* (1963); *Britain at Bay* (1973)
T. S. Jackson, *Logs of the Great Sea Fights* (2 vols, Navy Records Soc., 1899–1900)

William James, *Old Oak, The Life of John Jervis, Earl St. Vincent* (1950)
William James, *The Naval History of Great Britain* (6 vols) (7th Edn, 1902)
John Leyland (Ed), *Dispatches & Letters relating to the Blockade of Brest 1803–05* (2 vols, Navy Records Soc., 1899–1900)
J. E. J. A. Macdonald, *Souvenirs du Maréchal Macdonald* (Ed. C. Rousset) (2nd edn 1892)
A. T. Mahan, *The Influence of Sea Power upon the French Revolution and Empire 1793–1812* (2 vols, 1893)
A. F. L. V. Marmont, *Mémoires du Maréchal Duc de Raguse* (9 vols, 1858)
James Marshal Cornwall, *Napoleon as Military Commander* (1967); *Marshal Massena* (1965)
Napoleon, *Correspondance de Napoleon 1er* (32 vols, 1854–69); *Lettres Inédites de Napoleon 1er* (Ed. L. Lecestre) (2 vols, 1897)
Charles Oman, *History of the Peninsular War* (7 vols, 1902–30)
Edward Osler, *Life of Admiral Lord Exmouth* (1835)
F. Lorraine Petrie, *Napoleon's Campaign in Poland 1806–07* (1901)
R. W. Phipps, *The Armies of the First French Republic* (5 vols, 1926–39)
R. S. Quimby, *The Background of Napoleonic Warfare* (1957)
John Ross, *Memoirs & Correspondence of Admiral Lord Saumarez* (2 vols, 1838)
G. E. Rothenburg, *The Art of Warfare in the Age of Napoleon* (1977)
A. N. Ryan (Ed.), *The Saumarez Papers: Selections from the Baltic Correspondence of Vice-Admiral Sir James Saumarez* (Navy Records Soc., 1968)
A. A. R. de St Chamans, *Mémoires* (1898)
R. H. Thoumine, *Scientific Soldier: A Life of General Le Marchant* (1968)
Wellington, *The Despatches of Field Marshal the Duke of Wellington* (Ed. J. Gurwood, 12 vols, 1834–39); *Supplementary Despatches and Memoranda of Field Marshal the Duke of Wellington* (Ed. 2nd Duke) (14 vols, 1858–72)
Spenser Wilkinson, *The French Army before Napoleon* (1915)
Robert Wilson, *Brief Remarks on the Character and Composition of the Russian Army and a Sketch of the Campaigns in Poland in the years 1806 and 1807* (1810); *Life of Sir Robert Wilson from Autobiographical memoirs etc.* (Ed. H. Randolph) (2 vols, 1862)

Acknowledgments

Archiv fur kunst und Geschichte: Endpapers, p. 10.
BCA Picture Library: pp. 42–3, 45, 50.
Bildarchiv Preussischer Kulturbesitz: pp. 114, 150–1.
Bulloz: Frontispiece, pp. 22, 70, 74–5, 102, 116, 146, 147, 166–7.
Cooper-Bridgeman Library: p. 123 (top).
Foliot: pp. 14–15 (both).
Giraudon: pp. 48, 67.
Mansell Collection: p. 123 (bottom).
MARS: p. 244.
J. G. Moore: pp. 126–7, 186, 210, 242.
National Army Museum: pp. 68, 128, 131, 162–3, 225.
National Maritime Museum, London: pp. 174, 178 (all), 179 (both), 182, 191, 194, 196, 215, 216, 222–3, 228, 234, 239.

National Portrait Gallery/J. G. Moore: pp. 132, 177, 190, 210.
Picturepoint: pp. 218–19.
Radio Times Hulton Picture Library: pp. 6, 13, 17, 20, 24, 26, 33, 34, 35, 44 (top), 53, 58, 92, 112, 121, 124, 137, 140, 142, 152, 158–9, 165, 170, 188, 198, 204, 208, 213, 243.
Science Museum, London/J. G. Moore: p. 206.
Roger Viollet: pp. 30, 40, 44 (bottom), 56–7, 60, 66, 80–1, 82–3, 84, 86, 90–1, 100, 105, 109, 144–5, 169.

Line artwork: John Batchelor
Map artwork: Richard Natkiel
Figure artwork: Richard Scollins

Index

Entries in italics refer to illustrations